❯ *Ulysses in Black* ❮

Publication of this volume has been made possible in
large part through the generous support and enduring vision of
Warren G. Moon.

# ⫷• *Ulysses in Black* •⫸

## Ralph Ellison, Classicism, and
## African American Literature

PATRICE D. RANKINE

THE UNIVERSITY OF WISCONSIN PRESS

The University of Wisconsin Press
1930 Monroe Street, 3rd Floor
Madison, Wisconsin 53711-2059

www.wisc.edu/wisconsinpress/

3 Henrietta Street
London WC2E 8LU, England

5   4   3   2

Printed in the United States of America

Library of Congress Cataloging-in-Publication Data

Rankine, Patrice D.
Ulysses in Black: Ralph Ellison, classicism, and
African American literature / Patrice D. Rankine.
p. cm.—(Wisconsin studies in classics)
Includes bibliographical references and index.
ISBN 0-299-22000-1 (cloth: alk. paper)
1. American literature—African American authors—History and
criticism. 2. American literature—African American authors—
Greek influences. 3. American literature—African American authors—
Classical influences. 4. Ellison, Ralph—Criticism and interpretation.
5. Odysseus (Greek mythology) in literature. 6. Mythology, Classical,
in literature. 7. Classicism in literature. 8. Literature, Comparative—
Modern and classical. I. Title. II. Series.
PS153.N5R34       2006
818´.5409—dc22       2006008598
ISBN 978-0-299-22004-4 (pbk.: alk. paper)

FOR

*Donté Nesta Shaw,*
*Trevin D. Gibson,*

AND THE NEXT
GENERATION OF READERS

# Contents

# ❯❯ *Ulysses in Black* ❮❮

# Prologue

## *Preparing for the Journey of*
## *Ulysses in Black*

> Some of the classical people here [at the American Academy in Rome] are snobbish about this mess but it belongs to anyone who can dig it.
>
> —RALPH ELLISON, *Trading Twelves*

This is a book of parts. The whole advances our understanding of the relationship between black literature and the classics (the body of European texts and ideas that I define more clearly later). I argue that, as the recent boom in interest in black classicism within the academic fields of Classical Studies and outside of it attests, black writers have always been interested in the classics and have at times used them to master their own American experience. Rather than an alien (or alienating) body of texts, black authors like Ralph Ellison have discoursed with the classics to engage immediate concerns of racism and oppression. *Ulysses in Black* takes the next step in black classicism. Studies in black classicism have thus far focused on turning attention toward such black Americans as William Sanders Scarborough, who was a slave and, later, a classical scholar; *Ulysses in Black* explores the end to which black writers engaged the classics. By extending Ulysses (another name for the Greek hero Odysseus) beyond the actual, classical hero with whom Ralph Ellison was enamored, I have arrived at a trope, that of "Ulysses in Black," for the relationship between classical European myth and literature and African American literature. This is a relationship for which Ellison's work is emblematic.

Similar to the "man of parts" whom Ralph Ellison describes in his essay "The Little Man at Chehaw Station" as a thinker-tinker who puts a Rolls-Royce radiator in a "classic" blue Volkswagen Beetle, I have taken seemingly disparate academic disciplines and combined them into what I trust is an integral whole.[1] At first glance, the distance between African American literature and the classics might seem treacherous to traverse. More to the point, one might ask what concern an African American has with what appears on the surface to be a Eurocentric, hegemonic academic discipline—in fact the center of European cultural and artistic hegemony in the modern world. The quest for an identity-defining past, as Wilson Moses suggests in *Afrotopia,* might point to a more natural connection between Western classics and black thought than we would immediately assume. In this regard, I am a case (albeit atypical) in point. I have contained these parts within me from the time I decided to pursue graduate studies in Classical Languages and Literatures in the early 1990s. These parts, moreover, have warred for primacy since they entered my consciousness. I will return to some autobiographical observations in a moment.

Ideal readers of this book of parts should mirror the heterogeneity of its subject matter. Graduate students and professors in Classical Languages and Literatures, or in Comparative Literature, might read *Ulysses in Black* for background material on the relationship between the classics and African American literature. Conversely, graduate students and professors in African American Studies should be able to find in *Ulysses in Black* some sources and background material for reading the classical influence, and the problems inherent in this influence, on black literature. In addition to this primary audience, undergraduates and their teachers in the emerging classes on race and literature, ancient and modern, should find much here for discussion. All readers interested in Ralph Ellison, and particularly those returning to Ellison's work since the publication of *Juneteenth* in 1999, should find *Ulysses in Black* to be a good read, and even more, it should be an important resource for their intellectual endeavors.

Before sharing how I came to this project (or, how I came to reconcile what appears on the surface to be incongruent parts), something should be said on the subject of race because it is indeed a constructed category—some say it does not exist—with many difficulties. As is the case with the overview of classical literature contained in chapter 2, I anticipate that some readers will find the following paragraph or so superfluous. Race is an obvious part of the American experience, and as such it is in inescapable part of American letters. The difficulty is that while some readers have thought a great deal about race, others believe they experience it incidentally. (Such is the nature of race—and race relations—in America.)

In the same way, some readers have thought a great deal about the classics; others hardly at all. This book's audience includes both groups, just as it invites the classical scholar along with the novice. I trust that each group of readers will be patient with the other, and with me, and the result will be not only an assembly of parts but also an integration of knowledge.

Throughout this book, I use the terms "black," "white," "African American," "white American," and "Negro" to designate ethnic and cultural distinctions within the United States. While the idea of race begins outside of America, these rubrics hint at a genealogy of the construction of race within the United States: "Negro" as the apogee of segregation in the twentieth century, "black" as the post–Civil Rights reaction to politics, culture, and esthetics, and "African American" as a turn toward reintegration.[2] There is scholarly consensus that race is a modern (post–sixteenth century), pseudobiological, pseudoscience, but the classification of persons and groups based on their outward appearance can be traced to classical societies, as Frank Snowden (1970), Lloyd Thompson (1999), and Benjamin Isaac (2004) all argue, with disparate conclusions. Recent scholarship in classical studies challenges the argument that the ancients did not know color prejudice, but, even in the conclusions advanced in Snowden's *Before Color Prejudice*, it is clear that the ancients *did* know color. They named entire groups of people, such as the Ethiopians ("burnt-skin people"), by skin color and by their ideas regarding how skin color comes about. Unlike later Europeans, however, Greeks and Romans on the whole did not use skin color as the determining factor in the enslavement of these groups (as the Portuguese did beginning in 1444). Aristotle's theory of natural slavery, the idea that there were particular ethnicities inevitably marked for enslavement because of their lack of intellectual and cultural development, did not apply specifically to Africans.[3] (This is not to say, as Snowden's thesis suggests, that classical prejudice was any less insidious or less harmful than modern attitudes.)

In contrast to the approach of the ancients, modern Europeans, as a practice, designated black Africans specifically as an inferior group marked for enslavement, and they developed an entire ideology around this choice, which included such ideas as a dark continent in need of civilization and soulless people who could be the beasts of burden for the building of empire.[4] Race became arguably the most important feature of Europe's encounter with the New World, although the cultural outlooks underpinning this new concept were already in play by 1492.[5]

In *The Conquest of America*, Tzvetan Todorov demonstrates the extent to which otherness, and specifically blackness, marked Christopher Columbus's encounter with the New World. The dichotomy of self and other inevitably became a determining factor in Europe's interaction with the indigenous peoples of the Americas, as Scott Malcolmson indicates in his study, *One Drop of Blood*. Even before the first slave was brought to Virginia in 1619, the social category of whiteness was taking form in the parlance and literature of the time. The population of black slaves, the humanity of which was already being questioned and debated in Europe, further reified the category of whiteness; an ever-increasing system of laws throughout the colonies in the eighteenth century reinforced the distinction between black and white through prohibitions against intermarriage.[6] Although law and practice are often at odds, custom and taboo conspired with the legal system to drive a wedge between black slaves and white Americans. It is worth noting that, in contrast to whiteness, a black-consciousness in the form of literature, nationalism, and political and social ideology has been an ongoing aspect of the relationship between black and white in America.

A complete history of the relationship between black and white, African American and white American, would be both impractical and undesirable in this context. Suffice it to say that, despite Dinesh D'Souza's proclamation of the end of race in his 1996 book, the hue of one's skin continues to be a factor in identity, and individuals feel the impact of race in education, employment, and housing, to name only a handful of the most salient categories.[7] Although there is now (and perhaps to some extent always was) a privileged class of African Americans (Graham 2000), and although race is not always concomitant with economic and social disadvantage, even a privileged class of blacks, as Ellis Cose (1994) articulated, continues to have in certain ways a significantly different American experience from its white counterparts. Neither race nor racism has ended. New immigrants to the United States reify race and, in some cases, fuel the fires of racism.[8] Immigrants still to some extent assimilate to one pole—black or white—depending on the hue of their skin. (While this is historically true, I realize that recent Latino immigration is also transforming racial politics in America.) The racial dichotomy colors every aspect of American life and at times threatens to diffuse America into two distinct nations. These two nations, incidentally, also constitute two different readerships, and this is a nuance that *Ulysses in Black* appreciates.

Culturally and symbolically, there continues to be an implicit—and often explicit—dichotomy between white and black, which is also, at times, good and evil, the norm and the aberration. We see this, as one example, in the representation of black men throughout the mass media, which I discuss in more detail in chapter 6.[9] Malcolm X's comments about his first encounter with "black" and "white" in the dictionary are still relevant today.[10] He noted that bad things were overwhelmingly associated with black, and he wondered, like Addison Gayle, what effect this simple fact was having on his psyche, as a socially constructed "black," as well as on the national psyche. The racial dichotomy in America fueled the New Negro movement and then the Black Aesthetic movement, wherein artists and writers undertook a deconstruction of categories that, in their estimation, extended as far back as the writings of Plato and Aristotle.[11]

So we see and sense race as a reality in American life and letters, and in this book we will not go around it but through it. I accept "black" and "white" as ethnic, political, and, to some extent, economic markers. Equally important is the term "African American," which I read not so much as a diasporic identity stretching back to an imagined homeland, as John McWorter complains, but as an attempt to give social and cultural legitimacy to hue—that is, black or white—as a social category.[12] Although these categories are artificial constructs, they are very real, and they matter in the imagination and in the lived experiences of entire populations, past and contemporary. For example, I use the term Negro when speaking about pre-1960s, but I turn to black when I discuss Toni Morrison. These categories are, indeed, unscientific. Yet I see as superfluous, and hairsplitting, Orlando Patterson's attempt to do away with unscientific racial categories through his designation of Euro-American and Afro-American cultural groups. For this study, I have embraced black and white as useful cultural designations, evident in many aspects of American society, including literature and music. Although I appreciate the subtleties of McWhorter's article "Why I'm Black, Not African American," I use African American and white American as more-or-less synonyms for black and white throughout *Ulysses in Black*.

Now that I have established the parameters of this study vis-à-vis race, a brief word should be said on the issue of classicism. The major study of classicism in America is Meyer Reinhold's *Classica Americana: The Greek and Roman Heritage in the United States*. Michele Valerie Ronnick, in her resurrection of William Sanders Scarborough and other black classicists, creates *Classica Africana* as a subset of Reinhold's inquiry. In his book *The Founders and the Classics: Greece, Rome, and the American Enlightenment,* Carl J. Richard showed the extent to which "the classics," as the study of the literature, art, architecture, or ideas of the ancient Greeks and Romans, influenced the intellectual and social lives of the founding fathers.[13] Even a cursory knowledge of the classics had cachet. Classicism, as an esthetic in literature or art that looks to the ideals and ideas of ancient Greece and Rome, has been cyclical in America, so that the post-emancipation era brought arguments against it, while the culture wars of the post–Civil Rights era saw its revival. In academia, the study of the classics includes college curriculum majors and minors in Greek, Latin, and Classical Civilization. Ancillary disciplines range from philosophy and art history, to archaeology and anthropology. In *Ulysses in Black,* I use "the classics" as defined here (and not limited to academic disciplines), and "the Classics" or "Classical Languages and Literatures" to refer to the *academic* disciplines taught on university campuses across America. The book, as a whole, is interested in the phenomenon of black classicism.

I would like to turn for a moment to my experience as a black graduate student in Classical Languages and Literature beginning in 1992. In 1995, as I approached the office of one of my professors to discuss a special area examination in Pindar, the early fifth-century poet who celebrated victors in the Panhellenic games, I toted a copy of Martin Bernal's *Black Athena,* volume 1 (1987), under my arm. I had dabbled in *Black Athena*'s arguments for a deeper African influence on Greco-Roman civilization as an undergraduate at Brooklyn College out of the sheer pleasure of identification. Since I had recently completed coursework for my doctoral, passed a series of exams in Greek and Latin, and had a little more spare time and courage to read secondary material, I felt ready to revisit the book. I scarce expected the greeting I would receive. "You certainly aren't reading *that* nonsense, are you?" asked my professor. While the condemnation of the Black Athena idea might well have been warranted, I realized that the professor had dismissed the book without even visiting its central arguments. Nor was he to any extent aware of why the notion of a Black Athena might appeal to me as a strongly black-identified individual.

Mary Lefkowitz, Martin Bernal's central combatant in the Black Athena debates that carried over from the late 1980s into the 1990s—and that remain, despite many classicists' claims to the contrary, to some extent unresolved—was right about at least one thing.[14] We all seek to identify with an idealized past, one that reflects who we are, what we believe, and even how we look. The descendents of European stock are as guilty of this nostalgia as persons of African heritage. What we have each neglected to understand is the extent to which our contact with one another, as white and black Americans, has changed us irrevocably, or, indeed, the extent of our simultaneous sameness and difference. As a member of a minute group of African American classicists, I sought identification, perhaps naively, in Bernal because his arguments, though inflammatory, were, to my knowledge at the time, the only contemporary efforts to reconcile my inner conflict as black and a classicist. In those years at Yale, I learned that my academic discipline of choice was not yet equipped to contain the part of me that was African American. If I sought a personal integrity, I would have to find it elsewhere—I would have somehow to be *in* the academy but not *of* it.

Living in Harlem from 1995 to 1998, I continued to nurture my cultural awareness as an African American even while I was writing a doctoral dissertation on character and selfhood in Senecan drama. During that time, I read Ralph Ellison's *Invisible Man*. I immediately recognized certain apparent allusions to Homer's *Odyssey* throughout the narrative, and I was fairly convinced that Homer's *Iliad* and Virgil's *Aeneid* were also present in the text.[15] Here was an African American novelist who had used classical literature and myth for narrative structure and character construction. I would put these ideas to paper someday, I thought, as I jotted down notes excitedly—*after* I write my book on Seneca, *after* I gain some security in academia, *after* I prove myself to the establishment. As African Americans, we still sometimes bear the Sisyphean burden of proving our value and competency within a particular domain, especially those in which we are a rarity. The axiom "if at first you don't succeed, try, try again" seldom applies to us: we must succeed, or we prove certain unstated rules. What I thought was my need to remain within certain confines is emblematically Ellisonian; I was an automaton, and I sought to imitate my counterparts without any concern for whom or what I was.

As I began to emerge from my self-imposed confinement, Ellison, as himself a man of parts, a not-so-successful Latin student who went on to teach himself the deeper mysteries of classical myth and literature, provided me with an *imago*, an icon, and a *black* one, for sacred reflection.[16] Here again, examples of people who have excelled in our area of interest can sometimes lighten our individual loads. More importantly, these individuals contribute to the broader, unfinished project of American identity and diversity.

Since discovering Ralph Ellison's *Invisible Man,* my knowledge of the classical influence on black thought throughout the Americas, including, for example, Derek Walcott's *Omeros,* has only increased. While *Ulysses in Black* concentrates on a few African American authors in the United States and their works, it marks only the beginning of a broader project, for which there will be many laborers. Michele Ronnick, for one, has been a trailblazer in the study of black men and women who were professional classicists. These individuals taught Greek and Latin on the secondary and college level, and they also published in the area. A discussion of their lives and works, and, to some extent, what made them unique, is inevitable. For the moment, it is worthwhile to explore the emblematic work of Ralph Ellison in the context of the classics.

It should be noted that the classicism I found in Ralph Ellison's novel, and the classicism I would later find in the posthumous novel *Juneteenth,* are, in certain important regards, entirely different enterprises from the Egyptocentrism many find in Martin Bernal's *Black Athena.* Again, Ronnick has made the point that Bernal's inquiry into the past is to some extent a separate discussion from that of black classicism, but the Black Athena debate certainly provided an opening for discussing race in general as it pertains to the professional discipline of Classical Studies. At the same time, Bernal's inquiry is distinct from the wave of scholarship regarding black classicism. The former is concerned with questions of cultural origins and cultural authority. It situates the foundations of Western civilization *outside of* Europe, in Africa and the Near East. For modern students and scholars of classical mythology, there is nothing surreptitious about extra-European cultural influences. The cosmogony of Hesiod's *Theogony,* to name only one example, has older parallels in Mesopotamia and Egypt.[17] Yet within a society so consumed with the concept of race, the notion of a "black" Athena would certainly be devoured, and Bernal was well aware of this.[18]

As it pertains to black classicism, *Black Athena* served at least two key functions. First, the project alerted us to the undeniable role of race-thinking in the creation of the discipline of Classical Studies, errors and overstatements notwithstanding. (Bernal's sweeping overhaul of the discipline was an act of hubris that alienated his classicist audience and to some extent obscured his deeper message.) Secondly, *Black Athena* tapped into the issue of what the classics might represent to many African Americans.

Regarding Ellison's co-option of the classics, we find that, origins notwithstanding, black and white Americans alike share common cultural and literary models that can be called upon to shape and reform our understanding of ourselves and the world around us. Without *this* vernacular, there is no meeting of the minds, no shared meaning, no common culture.

The recent work of Michele Valerie Ronnick on black classicists, coupled with my own inability to let things go, provides the context for this study of classicism in Ellison's writings (prose and fiction), and more broadly, the relationship between the black idiom and classicism in American thought. While Ronnick has done painstaking archival work to recall from obscurity the lives and achievements of classicists who were black, this study turns to the broader but equally critical question of why the classics might have appealed to African American writers. This question is important for at least two reasons. First, the case of Ralph Ellison reveals the ambivalence with which African American classicism, historically, has been met. Ellison's reception among some African American critics is legendary. Although Ellison was born in 1914 in Oklahoma City during segregated times, and although he suffered the same discrimination as that of other black authors, from the moment *Invisible Man* was published in 1952 his status among his peers changed, in some cases for the worst. Indeed he had, even before 1952, rejected communism as an alternative to America's social and political problems, but his literary manifesto bespoke a new cultural orientation. The broader esthetic evident in *Invisible Man* had (and still has) a direct political implication, perhaps owing to Ellison's silence throughout the Civil Rights movement. Some critics, such as Jerry Gafio Watts, have suggested that Ellison became more elitist (read European-oriented) even as he, according to Watts, distanced himself from the "'black masses."[19] Ellison was not a professional classicist, but his example, which has implications for how we receive other intellectuals, reveals that black classicism is a conundrum that critics would sooner dismiss than resolve.

The question of what African American writers saw in the classics is important for a second reason. One of the unstated premises of this book is that human diversity, as a relatively new cultural value that we uphold—in many domains, in America, and throughout the modern world—should yield a diversity of perspectives. That is, not only should an African American pursue a discipline such as Classical Studies without the admonition of his or her peers but, if the idea of diversity is borne out to its logical conclusion, such a pursuit might also yield new perspectives and insights. These new insights should have implications both for African American culture and for Classical Studies. If this is not the case, then as a society we should wonder what diversity really is: Do we want our workplaces, schools, and universities to have a superficial appearance of racial hetero-geneity without underlying differences? Do we want persons of many hues to perform identical labor, with the same proficiencies, and with the same perspective? As an ideal, diversity might well cut deeper than this.

Within the professional field of Classical Studies, the burgeoning areas of gender and gay studies provide excellent examples of how scholars of different orientations have enriched our study of the past. Such scholars as Judith P. Hallett (1984), David Halperin (1989), or even Michel Foucault (1988) have transformed the questions we ask of the past. In this way they have added to our understanding of a number of Greek and Roman social institutions—and to our understanding of ourselves. This is not to say that all female, gay, or African American scholars must approach their disciples from the viewpoint of their respective identities. Rather, I am suggesting that when we honestly engage irrepressible concerns of identity in the main, everyone reaps the benefits. In the professional field of Classical Studies, a minority presence of 2.5 percent between 1997 and 2001 (*including* a number of other minorities along with blacks) has hampered diversity as defined here.[20]

As I have stated, the idea for this book originated with Ralph Ellison; the book began as an essay I wrote in 1998 on the Ulysses theme in *Invisible Man*. (The essay, reprinted by permission of *Amphora*, forms the core of chapter five.) With the publication of *Juneteenth* in 1999, I realized that the Ulysses theme—and by extension classical myth as a whole—had an even deeper place in Ellison's imagination than what he was able to convey in *Invisible Man*. Although many scholars have hinted at the relationship between the protagonist in *Invisible Man* and Ulysses, no one has provided the context for this relationship, nor has anyone considered its depth. One interpretation, moreover, of Ellison's classicism prevailed: The novelist had sold out from the black masses, the Civil Rights movement, and progressive causes in general. I move against this grain. Ellison's interest in the classics indeed increased after the publication of his watershed novel. His stint at the American Academy at Rome from 1955 to 1957 brought him into further contact with professors of Classical Studies, tangible remains from the ancient world, and mythology, through such works as W. B. Stanford's

*The Ulysses Theme,* whose early edition he read.[21] At the same time, a pre-occupation with such themes as lynching, as we see in *Juneteenth,* continued to manifest itself in his writing.

Originally conceived as an exploration of the classicism of Ralph Ellison, *Ulysses in Black* found a broader context in the burgeoning study of black classicism, a field Ronnick refers to as *Classica Africana.* She has been at the forefront of *Classica Africana,* and her archival work on African American classicists will eventually yield necessary and eye-opening studies of their lives, works, and ideas. It is already clear, for example, that William Sanders Scarborough, a freed slave and one of the earliest black members of the American Philological Association, as well as the first African American member of the Modern Language Association, had a great deal to say on the subject of race.[22] Ronnick's edition of Scarborough's autobiography (2005), along with her work on other black classicists, will allow readers to journey through the mind, life, and times of African American classicists.

Meanwhile, a significant tradition of classicism in African American thought already exists.[23] The few authors who frame this book's central inquiry into Ralph Ellison's simultaneously classical and Afrocentrist imagination are by no means comprehensive. Rather, I have chosen them because their works either prefigure or reiterate three central points that I raise throughout *Ulysses in Black* regarding Ralph Ellison's vision of the Western heritage and American culture.

First, we find that a serious engagement with craft was prerequisite for black classicism. That is, each author was interested, first and foremost, with mastering languages (Greek and Latin), and/or their chosen literary genres (lyric poetry, the novel, and the like). This mastery of craft was vital for blacks, such as Phillis Wheatley, whose very humanity was in question. A letter to the reader from her master verifying her ability to read Latin accompanied Wheatley's 1773 collection of poems. In his essay "Little Man at Chehaw Station," Ellison, borrowing from his early training in music (he played the trumpet), advanced the idea that craft *completes* the person.[24] For Ellison, the individual is not fully alive, not fully human, without a skill. While Ellison's notion of craft is somewhat radical, the idea that an African American is no different from anyone else in mastering a range of crafts, from languages and poetry to music and the plastic arts, should seem banal. Yet this banal premise, as Wheatley's case shows, is allowed only after a long and costly historical and cultural struggle in

America. Countee Cullen, a celebrated poet and champion of black culture during the Harlem Renaissance, traded in his cache for his 1935 rendition of *Medea*. As I argue here, Cullen's *Medea*, which was dismissed out-of-turn both by critics of his time and later readers, takes on a different appearance when viewed in light of the poet's early training in the classics. Cullen's superb education aside, critics and the American audience at large wanted Negroes to address the race problem; any divergence from it could portend the wreckage of one's literary career.

The reception of authors such as Phillis Wheatley and, later, Countee Cullen provides a different context for how critics have read Ralph Ellison's work. Ellison returned throughout his essays and interviews to the theme of the novelist's craft. By emphasizing his commitment to writing he helped to carve an unprecedented place for the black intellectual, namely, a place for the imagination and the free play of ideas. This site, moreover, was not a place of escape or evasion, although Watts, among others, saw it as such. Ellison's engagement with craft gave him an objective correlative for his experiences as a black American. The second overarching point of this book, therefore, is that craft, in this case the craft of reading in Greek, Latin, or of engaging myth in translation, allowed African American writers a different vantage point on their own journey. In Phillis Wheatley's case, the writer discovered the Roman comedian Terence from Africa. Countee Cullen's black heroine gains from his understanding of *Medea*. For Toni Morrison, Ulysses, and classicism in general, raised penetrating questions about manhood, womanhood, and adventure vis-à-vis black men and women, and her perspective on the classical hero is profoundly unique. Nor is this a case of black authors abandoning African models for European ones. Particularly in the cases of Toni Morrison and Ralph Ellison, Western myth works in tandem with African and African American folklore to form the writer's broader imagination. That is, classicism enriches—and is enriched by—these correlatives.

The third major point raised in this book is, to my mind, the most important for reshaping how we see black classicism, and it brings us back to the idea of diversity. In many cases, and particularly in the case of Ralph Ellison, the objective correlative of classicism in African American literature merged with local idiom to form unprecedented perspectives on American identity. I argue that Ellison's classicism performed just the opposite function of what his critics claim. Rather than a symptom of his escapism or his literary and political conservatism, Ellison's mastery of myth and ritual brought him to uncommon positions on such pressing concerns for blacks living in the twentieth century as lynching. There was an *annual* average of a little over fifty reported cases of the lynching of black men between 1859 and 1962, making the ritual something of a ritualized, American pastime.[25] In the case of Wheatley or Cullen, some critics have argued, against the grain, that their classical orientation was actually a guise for a more subversive subtext. Lillian Corti (1998), for example, sees Cullen's Medea as a figure for Black Nationalism.[26] In contrast to this, I argue that what we find in these works is not a superficial cover for a more radical message but rather a serious engagement with craft that yielded new perspectives. The authors were as preoccupied with their art as they were with their plight as black Americans, in some cases in segregated environments, and as such classicism was part of a broader esthetic imagination.

Ellison addresses the problem of violence against blacks in the battle royal scene in *Invisible Man* (and again through the theme of lynching in *Juneteenth*) because such violence was a problem that African Americans faced daily. Yet Ellison's conception of myth and ritual allowed him what Orlando Patterson sees as a unique perspective on lynching. By honestly accounting for the disparate parts of which he was comprised as an African American, Ellison offered his experience as an integral whole.

In sum, Ralph Ellison, along with the other authors touched upon in this book, supports the hypothesis that the classics might resonate on a different frequency in the hands of a black writer concerned with his or her personal and cultural integrity. Ellison put the case succinctly in a letter he wrote to Albert Murray, author of *The Hero and the Blues,* from Rome. He noted, somewhat comically, that "some of the classical people here are snobbish about this mess but it belongs to anyone who can dig it." The classics, for Ellison, along with African American folklore, held "one of the keys" to understanding myth and ritual. Regarding the degree to which African American thought (in folklore or orality, for example) might influence our understanding of the classics, a fuller diversity would have to be achieved within the field of classics to test Ellison's hypothesis. For the time being, readers might return to the lives and works of black classicists of an earlier generation, such as Daniel B. Williams, to prepare for the intellectual journey.[27]

Finally, it is necessary to say a bit about the figure of Ulysses. As I have already stated, I am using Ulysses as a metaphor for black classicism. Despite the vexing notions of "black Athena" or "black Socrates" or "black

Cleopatra" in the public domain, I deploy the symbol of Ulysses in part because of Ellison's own draw to it. Ulysses is a predominant figure in the novelist's classicism, as the reader will discover in chapter 5, the title of which quotes from *Juneteenth*. Because of this, the symbol of Ulysses, for Ellison and throughout this book, becomes quite real: Ellison's heroes in *Invisible Man* and *Juneteenth* are, in a manner of speaking, black Ulysses, as is Toni Morrison's Milkman. I ground my reading of the classics in Homer's character Odysseus, who is later known to the Romans as Ulysses. This is not to say that *Ulysses in Black* is at all a *study* of the Ulysses theme. I am also concerned, for example, with Countee Cullen's *Medea*. Ulysses is a uniting motif and trope for my study of black classicism.

If *Ulysses in Black* represents black classicism, similar to its namesake who traveled far from home and even to the Underworld, the book takes a *journey* through classical and American thought toward an emergence. In other words, the journey of Ulysses in black is an exploration of the hero's (or America's) travels through a classical past, into the abyss of race, and to a potential triumph, namely our realization of a broader cultural integrity. I use the structure of the mythological hero's journey—Joseph Campbell's monomyth—to organize my exploration of black classicism: here, the hero travels through a frontier and across an abyss to emerge with some unprecedented truth for his society. In America, this heroic journey is across the abyss of race. In mythology, the journey through the abyss, or the *katabasis,*

> is the heroic quest par excellence in that it represents the triumph of the vital principle over the forces of death as a successful descent into and return from the underworld. (Cook 1995, 161)

The hero who is interested in a broader cultural understanding in America encounters race-thinking as the abyss, the quintessential challenge to the nation's founding principles. While the notion of *blackness* throughout European and American thought (outside of the influence of the Black Aesthetic) has negative connotations, I am able to invert blackness, or at least play on its signification, through the notion of the abyss. Death is a *black* and final experience, yet in the notion of the monomyth (or the quest) the hero travels through the abyss as a "vital principle," and he returns from it. In a similar fashion, American culture and literature find their integrity in part through an encounter with race.[28]

Ulysses and his heroic journey are the tropes to which I return through-out the book because of their conceptual force. *Ulysses in Black,* in its very structure, comprises two heroic journeys: the first, a journey from clas-sical texts to black classicism, and the second, a journey through Ralph Ellison's classicism. The first examines the merits of classical literature for a modern readership and attempts to move some of the roadblocks to an African American engagement with the classics. The second is a case study of one African American, Ralph Ellison, who engaged classical myth as a way to understand his own culture.

After an overview of the recent development in Classical Studies of *Classica Africana* in chapter 1, I turn in the second chapter, "Birth of a Hero," to a reading of works of classical literature from three distinct peri-ods. My reading of Homer here is aimed at giving the reader an idea of what authors like Ellison saw in Homeric epic in general and Odysseus in particular. In mythology, the birth of a hero or god is the first stage of any heroic journey. (The savvy reader might note a play on the 1915 film "Birth of a Nation," which began in America the twentieth-century approach to race on film, and beyond.) In mythology, birth comes with its own chal-lenges, such as attempts on the hero's life. Classical texts form an inevitable starting point in my reading of classicism. In this chapter I am concerned with a resuscitated birth—laying a *different* foundation for the use of the classics in counterhegemonic discourse. While the classics have come to represent Eurocentric ideals, I read such authors as Homer, Euripides, and Seneca to show what might have appealed to certain black authors in these works. These authors do not need to *be* black, any more than Socrates needs to be, in order to resonate with black authors concerned with hege-mony, oppression, and struggles against power. (It might, for argument's sake, be worth positing the classics as part of a distinct *Afrocentrism,* as opposed to Eurocentrism.)

In chapter 3, "Ulysses Lost on Racial Frontiers," I continue the journey motif, to the abyss of race. I examine the roadblocks to black classicism and construct a genealogy of classical reception aimed at demonstrating that race-discourse in the modern world is the abyss that separates African Americans from the classics. In other words, race, racism, and the attempt of early twentieth-century black scholars to counter the effects of slavery kept blacks away from *claiming* classical influence. Yet I continue my re-evaluation of the classics by demonstrating that "the Classics" were not always synonymous with Eurocentrism but that there were often shifting perspectives, what I call ruptures and breaks in the Western narrative. One such rupture was that between Greek and Latin. Roman culture did not necessarily receive the emblem of classical esthetics (or "Ulysses") without hesitation. I explore what I call the Europeanization of the classics, and then I turn to a presentation of twentieth-century African American poetics. In particular, the call for what Alain Locke in *The New Negro* named a "forced radicalism" increasingly made the classics troublesome for Negroes, who, prior to this period, had accepted the classics rather naturally (even with the consistent strand of a black-centeredness from the very beginning of African American letters).

Within the context of twentieth-century esthetics in African American influence, any claim of classical influence on black authors is noteworthy. At the same time, appropriation of the classics by African American writers, despite opposing cultural forces, is a natural result of a personal culture that includes a broader literacy as well as an idiomatic, local experience (what Houston A. Baker called a vernacular). Toni Morrison, for example, is clearly steeped in the Ulysses theme throughout *Song of Solomon*, but in her discussion of that novel, and of the Ulysses theme, she actively aims to distance herself from the classics. Self-construction and posture, in other words, are important considerations to any study of African American classicism.

If we return to the trope of a journey, one critical stage in the journey out of a racial abyss in American letters is the open acknowledgment of mutual influence. I find Houston Baker's notion of the black (w)hole of African American literature useful in my discussion of emergence (or reintegration). In chapter 4, "The New Negro Ulysses," I examine Baker's vernacular theory, particularly through his idea of the black (w)hole of African American literature, vis-à-vis the classical strand in Countee Cullen's *Medea* and Toni Morrison's *Song of Solomon*. For Baker, the black (w)hole is a way of talking about a particular gravitational pull in black literature, one toward a blues esthetic and a forced radicalism in the form of what Baker calls a zero-sum game. (Bigger Thomas in *Native Son* is Baker's primary example of the latter.) Yet the very real, very present blues esthetic in some regards obfuscates the bigger lens—the broader context—within which black literature is performed. I look at the problem of the reception of black literature as it pertains to black classicism, and I wonder about the possibility of returns from black (w)holes.

Return from the black (w)hole (or the abyss) is an inevitable point in the journey toward a wholly American culture and literature. Rather than rejecting black esthetics and identity, the black author who engages in the classics acknowledges that the black (w)hole is but a portion of the journey. Black esthetics exist *not* within an either/or identity but rather within a both/and, hyphenated identity. The first journey, or the book's first half, concludes with the reading of classical motifs in Cullen's *Medea* and Morrison's *Song of Solomon*. These works represent a heroic attempt to reintegrate the disparate parts of the American journey.

The second journey of *Ulysses in Black* is an exploration of Ralph Ellison's classicism. Ellison can be credited with being one of the few Americans to articulate a cultural integrity over seeming disparate parts. His classicism is clear throughout his writing, from the first pages of *Invisible Man*, itself structured as a *katabasis*, a heroic journey underground.

Ralph Ellison's Ulysses, therefore, is the starting point of a case study in black classicism. In chapter 5, "'Ulysses alone in Polly-what's-his-name's-cave': Ralph Ellison and the Uses of Myth," I explore Ellison's discussion of classical myth in his essays and travel around his deployment of black Ulysses in *Invisible Man* and *Juneteenth*. Through a close reading of the novels, I show how Ellison *dis*integrates the tale of Odysseus and the Cyclops throughout his narrative. The tale, particularly the issue of identity that Odysseus's self-naming as "Nobody" in Homer's *Odyssey* 9 raises, provides Ellison with a metaphor for the racialized individual's challenges within American society. Although a few articles have noted a classical current in *Invisible Man*, the extent to which the Ulysses theme permeates Ellison's prose and fiction has not been previously shown. To a great extent, previous scholarship, though sparse, reinforces my thesis that classicism negatively affects the reception of the works of black authors. In contrast to this, I argue that through the figure of Ulysses, Ellison casts America's homeward journey as a coming-to-terms with materialism, violence, and race.

With chapter 6, "Ulysses in Black: Lynching, Dismemberment, Dionysiac Rites," we return to an abyss, in this case the violence against blacks that has been, at least through the twentieth century, concomitant with coming-of-age for Americans. While some saw Ellison's classicism as an escape from contemporary realities to the pristine world of ideas, Ellison's understanding of classical myth actually helped him to come to his own understanding of a dark, American topic, namely lynching. Ellison's treatment of lynching, real and metaphorical, is based on his ritual approach to myth.

With lynching, we reenter an abysmal cultural reality, namely that of violence against blacks in America, and we grapple with one of America's
worst moments historically. The extent to which Ellison's reading of
lynching was visionary has only recently been argued. Ellison's classicism
brought him to the "vital principle" present in his own African American
abyss, the experience of violence against blacks evident in the lynching ritual. From an exploration of Ellison's use of classical myth, we journey into
his use of these themes and narratives to represent an experience that he
felt was part and parcel of a broader American one.

The second abyss, therefore, is represented through Ellison's black
Dionysus, the dismembered (or lynched) persona whom the rest of the
culture tries to forget. I move in this chapter to Dionysus as a primary
symbol because for Ellison ritual dismemberment (Greek *sparagmos,* a
theme found in Euripides' *Bacchae*) was symbolic of a real-life, American
problem that affected blacks disproportionately. Dionysus is a god who
stands in for a chthonic, underworld struggle (especially through his link
to Persephone) that even Ulysses has to experience.

The journey out of the second abyss comes in chapter 7, "Ulysses
(Re)Journeying Home." In this second and final case, emergence out of
the abysmal realities of race discourse in America is broached as a long-
overdue dialogue between the Classics and Black Studies. In this chapter,
I discuss Ellison in broader context of the classics and black literary theory. I question, along with Harold Cruse, whether forced radicalism for
blacks in America can be anything but symbolic. At the same time I see,
through a reading of Ellison's "The Little Man at Chehaw Station," that
even symbolism can help to radically reconstitute the world around us.
While black literature does itself a disservice by rejecting a (possibly radical) Ulysses in black, Classical Studies is equally hampered when it ignores
what Baker sees as the most important feature of the American vernacular, namely the battered and brutalized black body of slavery, made flesh
in the first black literature in America. This is a body—a physical body,
a body of texts, ideas, and events—that Bernard Knox entirely ignores
in *The Oldest Dead White European Males* when he cites the fifteenth-
century classical revival in Italy without any notice of the beginning of
the African slave trade in Europe during that same century, as one example of his incredible oversights. The current phenomenon of the study of
black classicism represents a yearning toward the discourse of race within
Classical Studies.

It is impossible to complete any journey without some help along the way. For the journey of *Ulysses in Black,* I have several colleagues and travel companions to acknowledge. In the beginning, George Cunningham at Brooklyn College read my initial essay on the Ulysses theme in *Invisible Man.* He can be credited with realizing that the exploration was, in his words, "tropically possible." During these early stages, my conversations with Ana María Gómez Laguna were indispensable. As a highly culturally- and self-conscious Spaniard, she was able to share her insights into such authors as Frederico García Lorca and Miguel de Unamuno, writers who impacted Ellison's imagination profoundly. This book owes a great deal to the Iberian influence, particularly Unamuno's existential approach to Spanish culture in *Tragic Sense of Life,* which seems to me to be structured as a heroic journey reminiscent of Vergil's *Aeneid.* (And I wonder if this is what Ellison saw in the work.) A release from teaching provided by Purdue University and a Woodrow Wilson Foundation Career Enhancement Fellowship allowed me the time necessary to expand my knowledge beyond the Classics and to learn Ellison's prose and fiction. Nancy Sultan's generous invitation to Illinois Wesleyan University to do a Humanities Series Lecture gave me a platform to explore my ideas. I thank Orlando Patterson for sharing his thoughts with me on the importance of the Classics to his own sociological work. At Purdue, Paul Dixon, Howard Mancing, James Saunders, Renae Shackleford, and Vernon Williams intervened at critical moments, and it is not extreme to say that the project would not have come to fruition without their support. Cary Newman at Baylor University Press was also a source of encouragement.

As important as intellectual support was emotional support. From a distance, Michele Valerie Ronnick's irrepressible spirit and her belief in the significance of her study of black classicists gave me a beacon of light on which to focus. John Kirby's friendship and encouragement have been unwavering, as has been the support of Erica Turnipseed and Alexander Ulanov. The intellectual and emotional support of Verónica María Pimentel was unmatched. She read her fair share of drafts, and her ideas and constructive criticism improved *Ulysses in Black* in the middle stages of the project. I also thank Patricia Rosenmeyer for her belief in this project and her continued, valiant support. Any shortcomings in this book or the ideas contained in it are entirely my own.

PATRICE D. RANKINE, *Lafayette, Indiana*

# ❖ 1 ❖

# *Classica Africana*

## The *Nascent* Study of *Black* Classicism

> The happier *Terence* all the choir inspired,
> His soul replenished, and his bosom sir'd;
> But say, ye *Muses*, why this partial grace,
> To one alone of *Afric's* fable race;
> From age to age transmitting thus his name
> With the first glory in the rolls of fame?
>
> —PHILLIS WHEATLEY, "To Maecenas"

African American literature is as obscure to some as the classics are to others. Apart from their common remoteness, the one might seem to have little to do with the other. The latter is an emblem of a European heritage extending back to at least the third century BCE with little real interruption.[1] The former, although born before America itself, is a field that entered American educational institutions only after the Civil Rights movement of the late twentieth century.[2] Yet despite the relative obscurity of each, the classics and African American literature are indelible features of an integral American historical, cultural, and political reality.[3] They are also more organically related than might be immediately apparent. Just as Africa's contact with Greece precedes the cultural order of Western civilization, so the African American mind encounters archetypal myths and classical wisdom clandestinely, in unseen, invisible places.[4] The paucity of African Americans in the academic field of Classical Studies belies the influence of the ancients on black life and thought, beginning with the clergy and congregation on any given Sunday. On a more academic level, Homer, Cicero, and Plato seep through the oratory and writings of Frederick Douglass, Martin Luther King Jr., Ralph Ellison, and Toni Morrison in profound and unexpected ways.[5]

The cataloging of the African American intellectual's contact with the classics—important if for no other reason than that it lifts the artificial veil of race that designates American culture as either integrated or segregated— is a practice that has recently come into vogue.[6] Race officially became an explicit point of contention in the academic field of Classical Studies in 1987 with Martin Bernal's publication of *Black Athena*, which, among other heretical assertions, claimed that Greece had African origins repressed in the Eurocentric study of antiquity.[7] More recently, Michele Valerie Ronnick has been a pioneer in a new area of scholarship, named (perhaps a bit misleadingly) *Classica Africana*. Ronnick characterized the study as follows:

> It is time for scholars and educators to look beyond the Martin Bernal– Mary Lefkowitz debate, and turn toward other types of research. One of these new approaches is *Classica Africana*, a name patterned upon Meyer Reinhold's pioneering book *Classica Americana* (Detroit: Wayne State University Press, 1984), which examined the impact of classics upon eighteenth- and nineteenth-century America. The new subfield sharpens the wide view taken by Reinhold concerning the influence of the Graeco-Roman heritage in America, and looks at the undeniable impact, both positive and negative, that this heritage has had upon people of African descent, not only in America but also in the Western World.[8]

With "the Martin Bernal–Mary Lefkowitz debate," Ronnick of course refers to the controversy over *Black Athena*. Reaction from classical scholars to Bernal's book crystallized in the 1990s with Mary Lefkowitz's work, which, as Stephen Howe sees, was aimed at protecting the linguistic, cultural, and moral integrity of the Western heritage.[9] I will discuss the Black Athena debate in chapter 3, but for present purposes it should suffice to note that *Classica Africana*, as Ronnick frames it, does not address the issues and concerns raised in the Black Athena debate. Ronnick clearly felt that, after over a decade of circular arguments, it was time for a new direction.[10] What she essentially called for was a change in the subject of inquiry, a shift from how we construct the past to how the past influences present thought. (In the end, we cannot answer one without the other.) Given the conceptual difference between these two investigations, it is noteworthy that Ronnick takes the Black Athena controversy as a springboard for the emerging area of *Classica Africana*. Indeed *Black Athena* was a watershed moment in the relationship between the classics and race discourse.

The obvious—though otherwise counterintuitive—connection between the Black Athena controversy and the new *Classica Africana* is, of course, race. Race is real,[11] and the abysmal representation of African Americans in Classical Studies is as real as the group's invisibility in other areas of American life, particularly on the higher frequencies.[12] What has not been seen is that previous forays into the subject of race, though undoubtedly well intentioned, sabotaged the field of Classical Studies and primed it for the Black Athena controversy. Frank Snowden's studies, *Blacks in Antiquity* (1970) and *Before Color Prejudice* (1983), were among the first to transfer modern racial questions to classical antiquity.[13] Although in some respects timely, these books emerged out of the search for an idyllic past that often accompanies classicism. The longing, in this case, was for a time when race, although real, was not as deterministic a factor in politics and culture. These works sabotaged the discussion because Snowden's posture put each party on the defense, with classicists, on the one hand, eager to maintain the "difference" of their classical subjects vis-à-vis prejudice, and outsiders (such as Addison Gayle), on the other, insistent on the classical roots of contemporary race discourse.

Tellingly, Snowden would become one of the opponents of the Afrocentric strain in *Black Athena*, despite the common search in both Eurocentric and Afrocentric camps for moral emblems from idealized times.[14] With this backdrop, *Classica Africana* becomes a somewhat unconscious attempt to undo the harm that the previous three decades of scholarship had done (bracketed, I maintain, by Snowden from 1970 and the Black Athena debate into the 1990s). It also allows us to reexamine the veil of race vis-à-vis Classical Studies and to take the discipline to task on its commitment to human and intellectual diversity.

"Cataloging" best characterizes the data-gathering stage of the nascent *Classica Africana*. Archival research has led to the unearthing of the names and publications of African American classicists, and biographical sketches of these men and women have appeared in a number of scholarly journals. Ronnick surveyed this work in the introduction to her 2001 pamphlet, published by the American Philological Association (APA). There she presents Richard T. Greener as the first black member of the APA, along with Edward Wilmot Blyden, a West Indian who joined the APA in 1880, and William Sanders Scarborough, whom Ronnick characterizes as the first professional classicist of African American descent.[15] Ronnick also began touring a photographic exhibit, funded by Harvard University's Loeb Foundation, titled "Twelve Black Classicists," on September 13, 2003, at the Detroit Public Library. The impact of *Classica Africana* is clear in the rewarding of Ronnick, who has spoken and taken part in symposia on a number of university campuses throughout the country, with a second Loeb Grant.

In addition to Ronnick's work, Trudy Harrington Becker (1999) published a biographical sketch of Daniel B. Williams, Virginia's "first black university classicist" (94). Nor were men alone in the pursuit of classical training. Ruth Cave Flowers, as Joy King (2001) writes, was "the first black female graduate of the University of Colorado" (59); Flowers was, in addition to this, a teacher of Latin (and one-time head of the Languages Department at Fairview High School in Boulder).[16] It is also significant that creative writers such as the slaves Jupiter Hammon and Phillis Wheatley prefaced the black ascent into the professional ranks of academicians.[17] In America, then, black classicism antedates and transcends the academic discipline of Classical Studies. Black classicism touches upon broader political and cultural issues throughout American society, as Ronnick's forays outside of biographical data and into the realm of imaginative speculation reveal.[18]

Of the proponents of *Classica Africana*, Ronnick has done the most to situate the inquiry in its broader social context. This includes considerations of classicism in America in general, i.e., the historical (and to some extent ongoing) tension in the country between the proponents of college education and those of technical training, and the relationship of these concerns to race.[19] Ronnick rightly casts *Classica Africana* as a subset of the well-researched area of the role that the classics have played in American life. Writers such as Carl J. Richard (1994) broaden our understanding of the extent to which Greek and Roman authors, both in translation and in their original languages, influenced the founding fathers. Leaders of the eighteenth and nineteenth centuries returned to classical models from Demosthenes to Tacitus for their sense of citizenship, style (both personal and literary), and nobility.[20] What often goes unstated in the inquiry into American classicism, however, is the extent to which these values, particularly the idea of nobility, culminated in a new social construct, that of whiteness.[21] Furthermore, white male citizenship, which a classical education reified and further refined, rested on the backs of black slaves and, later, emancipated workers.[22]

The story did not end with a stable "whiteness," juxtaposed to black identity and Negro segregation. With the liberation of slaves, the increasingly

industrialized nation would reexamine the purpose of education for blacks
and whites respectively.[23] The emerging agricultural institutions entered a
debate in the mid- to late-nineteenth century about whether a classical
education needed to be an aspect of the nation's technical training.[24] The
presence of a new mass of educable citizens, the former slaves, ensured
that race would continue to be an aspect of this debate for generations
to come. American history has shown the extent to which broader social
changes affect the parameters of such seemingly esoteric questions as the
role of a classical education in the lives of African Americans.

In Negro circles, Booker T. Washington and W. E. B. Du Bois were the
most prominent combatants on the issue of the proper education of African
American society at large, as Ronnick (2000a) rightly notes. Washington,
as founder of Tuskegee Institute, where Ralph Ellison attended college and
studied music for three years, advocated technical training as the means
by which the former slaves and their offspring could be productive and
gain affluence. He compared an institution that he attended between 1878
and 1879, where "there was no industrial training given to the students,"
to technical schools like Hampton Institute.[25] At schools "that empha-
sized the industries" he found that "the students, in most cases, had more
money, were better dressed, wore the latest style of all manner of cloth-
ing, and in some cases were more brilliant mentally."[26] Basing his philosophy of education on this technical model, he opened Tuskegee on July 4,
1881. In Washington's view, time was of the essence for African Americans.
Within this context, classical training could be little more than an afterthought, unnecessary dilettantism in a world of mass media and the emerging industries.

For Du Bois, who taught Cicero and was Harvard-trained, education
in general, and classical training specifically, was a necessary process in the
creation of black citizens. (Although Washington also touches on the issue
of citizenship in *Up from Slavery,* he of course takes a more practical
stance.) At least in his early years, Du Bois conceived of citizenship in
terms of the cultivation of humanity, a notion consistent with classicism.
He felt that teachers should "be broad-minded, cultured men and women,
to scatter civilization among a people whose ignorance was not simply
of letters, but of life itself."[27] This approach was, ostensibly, at odds with
that of Booker T. Washington. At the same time, Du Bois was not entirely
inclusive in his ideas. He subscribed to the idea of the "talented tenth,"
the concept that exemplary men determine the fate of their race.[28] Thus,

Washington and Du Bois represent a broader, far-reaching conflict within African American circles about our relationship to American society at large in general, and issues of education specifically.[29]

Although I am rehearsing the facts about Du Bois and Washington for the sake of context, it is without doubt trite to conceive of the early twentieth century debate about education, segregation, and the relationship between these as a Du Bois/Washington dichotomy. Future inquiries into the issue of education, as Trudy Harrington Becker sees, should first consider the broader context of the Du Bois/Washington conversation. In her work, Becker spends a significant amount of time discussing the 1862 Morrill Land Act, and the later reformulation of it in 1890. In this historical milieu, we might also consider J. A. Rogers, whose history of significant contributions by African Americans did, tellingly, include Cleopatra. That is, while we consider the broader context for the Du Bois/Washington conversation, it is also necessary to be aware of the rhetoric at the time among some blacks, which includes sometimes-curious strategies for racial uplift.

Although Washington and Du Bois played significant roles in educational policy, it is important to remember that the political positions of black leadership sometimes belie their lived experience. As Ronnick asserts, black classicists such as William Sanders Scarborough articulated positions that at times fell outside of the proscribed, segregated lines.[30] As we will come to see, in nonacademic, literary circles, the classics continued to have an impact on the life and thought of African Americans. Time, moreover, has added a much-needed perspective on the education debate of the early twentieth century as it pertains to race. Scholars have, for example, documented the extent to which Washington's public stance was at odds with his private ideas and ideal. Put otherwise, Washington's public positions were part of a strategy for Negro uplift, and, as we know, politics and political expediency are sometimes separate issues from one's deeper ideals and beliefs.[31] Washington clearly valued his own education, which he speaks about at length in his autobiography, *Up from Slavery*.[32] Both Washington and Du Bois were interested in the uplift of Negroes. What differed were their strategies vis-à-vis white audiences, a consideration that has not been a salient feature of discussions within *Classica Africana*.[33]

As we will see throughout *Ulysses in Black*, audience is an important determinant in the black artist's or writer's self-presentation as classicist or otherwise. In recent years, the rise of reception-theory has prompted us to consider the dynamic of rhetoric, which includes speaker (or writer) and context, in our analyses of texts and media. When we consider the "rhetorical paths of thought" (quoting rhetoric scholar Steven Mailloux), which are the recurrent themes that emerge in presentations and performances such as speeches, books, and other print media, we realize the significance of Washington's and Du Bois' primarily white American audience. Southern and Northern audiences alike were resistant to including Negroes at their schools, places of business, or country clubs. While the South and the North had radically different stances on social integration, the deep-seeded taboos against miscegenation influenced the entire culture. The black intellectual who spoke on behalf of his race would have to consider the context for his positions.

Nor was the white American audience the only rhetorical consideration with respect to the issue of the education of Negroes. Washington and Du Bois also had to appeal to a spectrum of blacks across class and, to some extent, gender. (Classical scholar Shelley Haley has contributed a great deal, more broadly, in the consideration of gender.) Put otherwise, the social integrity of both men, themselves part of an African American community, would inevitably remain a factor in their political positions. More specifically, for many African Americans, there are important personal and political considerations related to such ideas as black classicism. As we have seen, the public stance of blacks on many cultural and political issues is contingent upon particular rhetorical and social allegiances. The politics of black identity is similar to that of other communities, and particularly those that have suffered oppression. Mary Lefkowitz handled the issue of African American identity callously when she claimed that a connection to the classical past was somehow critical to issues of self-esteem. What she misrepresented was the broader phenomenon of identity construction, which extends to particular intellectual, social, and political alignments—and which is not at all limited to "Afrocentric" scholars.

When we view the Du Bois/Washington conversation in light of identity, rhetoric, and audience, we see that since at least the eighteenth century, black intellectuals have been embroiled in a wider cultural battle regarding the role of Africa and Europe—as ideals and as a tangible and historical part of their own legacy—in their American lives. Martin Delany's real and metaphorical return to Africa has a genealogy leading to Malcolm X's ideas of African American self-determination in the late twentieth century. It is also important to remember that even ideas of repatriation, which are a mainstay in Afrocentrist ideology, have roots in mainstream American politics. Leaders from Thomas Jefferson to Abraham Lincoln considered the return of blacks to Africa as a solution to what they saw as a deep-seated American problem. For many blacks, these concerns are as significant as the integrationist policies of Martin Luther King Jr. For others, the surrender suggested in a black classicism is unpalatable.

As Du Bois' metaphors of double-consciousness and the veil make clear, life in America is lived on both sides of an identity-defining hyphen.[34] Given Du Bois' ideal of the humanizing influence of classical education, it is symbolically significant that, in an ironically revealing twist of fate, the classically trained Du Bois himself would come to abandon America's promise of social integration. He transformed himself later in life into a Pan-Africanist and moved to Ghana.[35] The black intellectual's coming-to-terms with his or her selfhood therefore includes considerations of identity politics, the political viability of certain positions (including the problem of true cultural integration), and strategies—rhetorical and otherwise—for affirming a particular historical and cultural legacy. As we will see, black identity politics affect many aspects of African American cultural experience, from the problems implicit in classicism in black literature to the at-times deceptively black-conscious posture of hip-hop. Within this context, a black Socrates, though fictive, is as significant as any historical figure.

What has not been fully realized with either the idea of a Black Athena or in *Classica Africana* is that each is part of a broader politics of identity, and as such each self-consciously invites a different audience. Since classicism (which some might see as Eurocentric) and a black-conscious political or literary agenda (which others might want to be exclusively Afrocentric) each gives its proponent a sense of origins, models of citizenship, and godlike icons to which to aspire, one crosses the invisible veil between the two with profound intellectual and political consequences. Neither classicism nor Afrocentrism imagines an already integrated American audience. Albeit implicitly, *Classica Africana* is in part aimed at appealing to a young black audience while assuaging an older white one (with further diversity within the classics as an unstated goal). The question of how to attract and retain young black students was certainly a consideration in the rise of *Classica Africana*. This consideration is present in Ronnick's work, where the author cites Toni Morrison, who states that "the first gesture of contempt for working-class students is to trivialize and devalue their need for an interest in art, languages and culture" (2000a, 7). Yet, within the broader American society, the reality of miscegenation destabilizes a culture constructed around racial categories. Even within an ostensibly integrated American society, a black classicist is a curious and suspicious paradox (similar to the paradox that, for example, a white rapper might represent).

Although Lefkowitz assailed the Afrocentric position, she failed to account for the yearning for cultural origins—and for cultural authenticity— present even on the other side of the equation. The extreme Afrocentrist position of wholly rejecting the Western heritage, while an artificial and ultimately unviable one (which is not to say that black identity is unviable), is not far removed from Eurocentrism.[36] Because of the legacy of race in America, the black intellectual's advocacy of the classics, although noteworthy for some within classical circles, might smack to others of Uncle Tomism.

Given its broader cultural implications, black classicism might imply to some a conciliatory, integrationist stance, which is advocated with a degree of condescension. The rhetoric of *Classica Africana,* for example, calls for whites to accept blacks as their intellectual equals, while blacks gain reasons to take pride in the Western heritage. Each black classicist surveyed within *Classica Africana* is characterized as a highly intelligent, long-suffering individual who, despite being overlooked within the broader discipline, deserves consideration. Each is implicitly cast as having given up self-determination in terms of Afrocentrism for a Greek intellectual ancestry. A recurrent and subtly vexing theme throughout the surveys in *Classica Africana* is that of universal humanity. Black classicists like Ruth Cave Flowers ask "just to be considered as another human being," and her intellectual achievements were to earn her this right.[37]

Certainly the humanistic rhetoric has a historical context, the understanding of which is critical to any discussion of race. That is, if the idea of race is predicated upon the Negro's lack of humanity (the absence in the black body of a soul), then black intellectualism of any kind defies one of the key premises of race. (Who has ever heard of a "white" intellectual? There are, unfortunately, intellectuals, *Jewish* intellectuals, *black* intellectuals, and so forth.) Within this context, "an inclination for the Latin tongue," as the slave Phillis Wheatley's master characterized her interest, would affirm the educability of the Negro. Proponents of integration (white and black alike) used classicism to affirm that African Americans could take their place alongside the American elite—as human and refined.[38] The rhetoric, however, is a curious anachronism at the beginning of the twenty-first century. The rhetorical symbolism of black classicism at times comes across as just a slight step removed from Rodney King's desperate plea, after his brutal beating at the hands of white police officers: "Can't we all just get along?"

It is no wonder, within such a historical and cultural context, that classicism in African American literature has often been met with disapproval, particularly in black circles. While gaining access in elite circles, the black classicist risks alienation from his or her African American intellectual counterparts. The issue of reception gives us some perspective regarding the responses to Ralph Ellison's *Invisible Man* immediately after its publication in 1952. Although the deeper reaches of classical myth in the novel have not been fully explored until now, Ellison in other ways set himself squarely within the Western heritage.[39] His self-construction was that of a novelist—and expressly not a *Negro* novelist—who was not writing exclusively about race but about American identity (even if race is an indelible feature of it). As such, he was unduly assailed for distancing himself from black concerns during a time when he—ironically—lived in Harlem and was married to a Negro woman.[40] In other words, Ellison was unreasonably criticized for rejecting the politics of progressive blacks, a rejection concomitant with his distinctly Western esthetics, and classicism. Because of nothing more than *posture,* Ellison alienated a portion of his black audience.

Once we consider the audience (mainly white) for the claims that come with a black writer's acceptance of the Western heritage, we gain a better understanding of the countercurrent against such a position. Why should my humanity have to be proved? Why should my mental capacity have to be proved? And why should I accept a heritage that questioned these things? At the same time, if I, as an African American, allow myself to be influenced by certain strains of art, why should my authenticity be questioned by my black peers? The negative reception of black classicism, and of the black artist who engages seriously with classical forms, helps us to understand some of the historical factors that shape radical reactions within a black esthetic mode against identification with Western cultural forms.

Ellison framed the problem differently; he reconstitutes the discussion and the audience. He argued, for example, that although the slave was in origin African, it had become impossible, impractical, to conceive of America without blacks. Any Afrocentrist esthetic or political agenda would have to be homegrown. As a social agent, the African American had as much of a role to play in local problems as he or she did in a broader African selfhood. While others ostensibly looked exclusively to Africa for their identity construction, Ellison questioned the historicity of this position. This is not to say that he rejected the unique features of an African American selfhood, or its contribution to American identity as a whole. On the contrary, he was one of the few of his time to articulate in the main an African American selfhood, and, furthermore, to imagine an integral America. (As we will see, Jerry Gafio Watts accused Ellison of a sort of fetishism for this.) In *The Crisis of the Negro Intellectual,* Harold Cruse suggested that the conflict between segregation and integration result in part from "the great fiction of the assimilated America" (1984, 6), which is revealed as fantasy every four years when politicians appeal to particular ethnic groups for votes. Cruse's counterintuitive position, which helps our understanding of Ellison, was that a dis-integration in the form of pluralism, as opposed to social integration, was part of America's identity. As Cruse saw, the antithesis between separation and integration is misconceived, since the Negro, like the white citizen, was already a wholly American being. At the same time, the imposed enslavement and later segregation of blacks obscured their role within a pluralistic society. Nevertheless, despite the historical contingency of slavery and social death, the African American, Ellison asserted, was never less than human, never less than a contributor to the larger society—spiritually and artistically as well as intellectually.[41]

If American society, as Ellison asserts, is of a whole, then black classicism is a natural and inevitable result of the African American's engagement with his or her social condition, classicism being an element of the intellectual material from which the American draws.[42] Certainly, for some, a strongly African-conscious, black esthetics was a necessary redress for centuries of degradation. If classicism to any extent represented whiteness and a Eurocentric esthetic, its opposite would be a natural and necessary position for the social and political survival of blacks.[43] Yet a black esthetics was concomitant not only with a Pan-African movement but also with local, cultural phenomena in American, such as the Civil Rights movement. African Americans, although constituting a unique social group with a distinct history, are part of the panoply of Americans of diverse background, testing their rights in the main and by doing so expanding the limits of freedom and democracy.

Ellison provides a case study of a different use of black classicism. He offers a shift in the discussion. The idea of universalism, or universal humanism, has been at the center of former discussions of race and the classics (i.e., "can't we all just get along," "I want just to be considered as a human being."). In other words, the classics have been viewed as a standard of cultural and intellectual achievement. In this context, a black classicist rises to a certain standard and is used as a drawing card for other blacks to the inner sanctum of the Western heritage. The polarizing effects of this framework cannot be overstated. In contrast to this, we might ask, as Ellison did, what unique perspective on the human condition and, more immediately, American cultural reality, African Americans bring to the bargaining table. The shift in framework might not be immediately discernable, and when Ellison called for Negro humanity, his comments were often taken out of context. Yet Ellison was right that no one questioned Dostoyevsky's humanity, as one compelling parallel. Rather, it is clear that the Russian novelist deepened our understanding of the human condition in general, and more specifically he offered a unique perspective on what it meant to be Russian. As Ellison proffered, each ethnic group brought something different to bear on the Western tradition and, within the United States, on American identity. Put more directly, African Americans had as much to offer the classical heritage as the classics could contribute to a black person's understanding of the world.

From this it might be argued that cultural diversity should yield a diversity of perspectives. A black classicist who does exactly what his or her white counterparts do has positive cultural implications, from role models for young African Americans in the professional field, to the increase in integration for white students and colleagues. Yet, if we take the argument for diversity to its logical conclusion, an African American who engages in Classical Studies might emerge from the experience—which, given the social isolation he or she will experience, amounts to a heroic journey underground—with something unique.

An unexplored model for comparison to *Classica Africana,* one that demonstrates the impact of diversity on the classics, is the boom industry of the study of gender and sexuality within the field. The subdiscipline was met with a great deal of disparagement among some classicists (Hanson and Heath 2001). Nevertheless, the study of gender and sexuality has added to our understanding of the past, more specifically, of varying constructions of sexuality and approaches to gender. By doing so, these scholars

*Classica Africana*

have given perspective and empowerment to their audience. As it pertains to race, Ralph Ellison offers a vision of what black classicism could bring. Given the dearth of black classicists, the esthetic and social imagination of nonspecialists is a necessary consideration. The lack of educational opportunities across America for blacks and whites alike has limited the diversity of perspective within Classical Studies. If we are to understand how Ulysses in black moves, thinks, and breathes, we must turn to authors such as Countee Cullen, Toni Morrison, and Ralph Ellison. True diversity of ideas begins with the opening of the imagination.

JOURNEY 1

# ⊁ From Eurocentrism to Black Classicism ⊰

# ✤ 2 ✦

# Birth of a Hero

### The Poetics and Politics of
### Ulysses in Classical Literature

The archetypal Ulysses . . . offered a wider foundation for later
development than any other figure of Greek mythology, thanks to
Homer's far-reaching conception of his character and exploits.

— W. B. STANFORD, *The Ulysses Theme*

I knew the trickster Ulysses just as early as I knew the wily rabbit of
Negro American lore, and I could easily imagine myself a pint-sized
Ulysses but hardly a rabbit, no matter how human and resourceful
or Negro.

— RALPH ELLISON, "Change the Joke and Slip the Yoke,"
*Shadow and Act*

Ulysses, who marks Western literature from Homer's *Odyssey* to James
Joyce's novels, is emblematic of an endlessly adaptable heroic identity. For
the classical scholar W. B. Stanford, Ulysses was perhaps the single most
influential literary hero born in ancient times. In *The Ulysses Theme*, Stanford traces Ulysses from his pre-Homeric possibilities (as a folkloric trickster figure) to his visitation in the twentieth-century works of James Joyce
and Nikos Kazantzakis.[1] *The Ulysses Theme* offers some insight into why
Western authors have time and again returned to the character whose
name varies from Odysseus to Ulysses, another clue to his sociocultural
range.[2] It is perhaps natural (and not at all counterintuitive) that black
authors in America have also been in a long-standing dialog with Ulysses,
and not only the character per se but also the classicism of which he is a
part. The discourse of black classicism touches on the nature of heroism
and the cultural context in which the hero acts.

The aim of this chapter is to unearth some of the root qualities of classical literature that might have timeless appeal to writers—and, in this context, black writers specifically. In the first place, Homer initiates an autopsy of the emotions fundamental to subsequent representations of the self. While I do not discuss one of Homer's finest psychological profiles here, namely that of Achilles, even in Odysseus we find a character of significant human scope, a range present in his longing for home, his acquisitiveness, and his adaptability—his own ability to learn from his experiences. (As we see in ancient Egyptian writings on justice, humanistic values certainly existed prior to the arrival of the Greeks, so we must see an important contribution in Homer's ability to encapsulate these qualities in transportable, literary characters.) As I show later, black authors (such as Morrison and Ellison), who write particularly in an increasingly capitalistic setting, a homeland that often denied their citizenship—denied that they belonged—made correlations in Odysseus. In addition, later writers encountered models for social and political discussion. The classical authors who adapted Homer's characters were writing under one regime or other: a religious order in which man is subject to capricious gods; an autocratic regime; or even an ostensibly egalitarian, democratic rule that denies the humanity of a foreign woman. The counter-hegemonic discourse of the fifth-century tragedians included resistance to power on multiple fronts: resistance to the authoritative power of the gods that we find, to some extent, in Aeschylus or Sophocles, or an opposition to a political hegemony that we find in Euripides.

While I use Ulysses as a metaphor throughout *Ulysses in Black*, in this chapter I present works in which Ulysses is an actual character, beginning with Homer. The Homeric conversation on the nature of the hero and how she or he acts within a particular social context constitutes a literary conspiracy, a tacit agreement between readers and writers that renders the classics eternally relevant. As we will see in chapter 4, even where black authors reject aspects of classical heroism, such as is the case with the black Ulysses that is Toni Morrison's Milkman, we concede a necessary encounter (even by way of rejection) with a broader Western esthetic. Moving from Homer's *Odyssey* to Euripides' *Hecuba*, I offer the counter-hegemonic—rather than Eurocentric or European-supremacist—strand in Greek thought as a foundation for later writers. (Later, I explore the political implications of the seemingly esoteric, seemingly apolitical literary process by which the Roman author Lucius Annaeus Seneca, in his

*Trojan Women,* presents variations of Ulysses' heroic, or antiheroic, core.) It should become apparent by the end of this chapter that, despite the degree to which European cultural hegemony might incite radical reactions against the classics, Greco-Roman literature is not a monolith but the result of authors' ongoing engagement with their past in order to address the problems of their society. Ulysses, and by extensions classical literature, can be a component in a black-conscious, literary and cultural identity.

## Ulysses, Literature, and Influence

The beginning of Western literature, and thus the beginning of this inquiry, is Homer. The oral poet is the first to present Odysseus (Roman: Ulysses) to the world stage as, in Stanford's estimation, an integrated persona.[3] Homer is also the *terminus a quo* of literature and literary influence. Critical readers might wonder why this is the case—why the "European" Homer gains primacy over older Mediterranean or Indic traditions. [4] One reason for this dominance is the inevitably vexing claim of Homeric genius, over and above other epic poets.[5] Certainly the Hindu epic, which marks a tradition perhaps extending back four millennia, raises similar questions to those of Homeric works, such as the issue of the mythmaking process in cultures, or the relationship between oral and written composition.[6] (The Rāmāyana was not written down until at least the fourth century BCE.) The Sanskrit epic, as all literature, would tell us much about the role of the individual in society, and how literature serves to communicate that role.[7] The epic of *Gilgamesh* was written down by 2000 BCE, and this early date would make it a superior candidate in any discussion about the origins of literature. (Homer dates to no earlier than the eighth century BCE.) This is to say nothing of the Egyptian Book of the Dead, which was written as early as 4500 BCE, or of biblical texts. An important issue worth touching on here regarding the dominance of Homer is that of the shifting definitions of literature as opposed to, most notably, oral traditions.

The broader notion of literature and literary influence should show the inevitability of a black reader's contact with the classics, whether that contact leads to a certain degree of acquiescence or to more radical resistance against Western cultural modes. Literature as an institution wherein reading and rereading, reflection and moral development, and finally, influence, takes place—that is, literature as a tradition—should not be taken

for granted. In *The Invention of Literature,* Florence Dupont (1999) makes
a useful distinction between writing for the preservation of information
and writing as a dynamic, literary process. In the former case, writing happens in culture primarily for storage, such as inscriptions on tombstones
or monuments, and for memory.[8] The beginnings of many literary traditions, including the Rāmāyana, *Gilgamesh,* and Homer's epics, happen
through the use of writing for storage/cataloging. The written forms of
these ancient epics are primarily recordings of cultural events, a ritual
whose richer context and meaning cannot be fully known to readers. This
is not to say that, similar to inscriptions on tombstones or monuments,
the epic performances became inflexible after being written down, or that
henceforth they would be performed in the same way every time. This was
decidedly not the case.[9] At the same time, the scribes who transcribe the
works of oral poets do not *self-consciously* step into a tradition of reception, reflection, and personal interpretation, a process that is the defini-
tive mark of literature. (I say self-consciously because scribes *do* insert
their ideas in the margins of texts, through scholia, and thereby create a
dialog or discourse of interpretation. But this is another subject.[10])

As Dupont sees it, literature is an invention that happens later than
writing for memory or storage.[11] Literature is present in every written
text. That is, literature points to a conspiracy between readers and writers wherein each party receives and re-creates material. The "contract"
between readers and writers is similar to a speech act, such as that which
the common question of "how do you do?" triggers. The question has a
semantic meaning, but what is important is each party's experience of this
greeting as a convention. That is, we understand the question not primarily through its literal meaning but though our cultural norms. In a similar fashion, Dupont sees literature as a speech act, but in this case the
relationship between parties is rather more tenuous. Readers and writers
have a slippery sense of one another's intent.[12] It could well be the case,
for example, that Sappho, writing in the sixth century BCE, had a greater
understanding of Homer than the Roman author Vergil (who wrote the
*Aeneid* between 29 and 19 BCE). Sappho, to a greater extent than Vergil,
shares a common culture with Homer, and she is closer in time to the
"event" of Homeric epic. Nevertheless, each author receives a version of
Homer, one that the recipient refashions and reforms, and thus the importance of literature as an institution lies in the tradition present in each text:
"The existence of literature presupposes a sequence begun by a specific

reading of it. In other words, there can only be literature where there is an expectation of a literary institution" (Dupont, 7).

We turn to Homer because he marks the beginning of a literary tradition that is tangibly different from other epic or ritual traditions. Given the significance that writing seems to have held in early Europe, it is worth noting that Dupont, in keeping with an ongoing revision of our understanding of orality in the ancient and modern world, does not privilege writing over oral traditions.[13] Greece, as Dupont concurs, continued to have significant oral traditions simultaneous to writing. Literature is a different, which is not to say better, tradition.[14] As the beginning of literature by Dupont's definition, that is, literature as a tradition contained in each text, writers have been in dialog with Homer from early on. When Sappho asserts that "the most beautiful thing on the surface of the black earth" is not the army of horsemen or the infantry but "what the person loves," she is rewriting a heroic, epic tradition that Homer expresses (whether or not she is referring directly to Homer). To her, Helen *willingly* abandoned home, husband, and family for love, contrary to the Homeric perspective, and as such her actions justify the poet's own love(s). As the examples from the Greek stage and Roman tragedy will show, the way in which authors have received Homer might be compared to biblical hermeneutics. On the one hand, authors of lyric, tragedy, and even later epic, cite Homer or play with Homeric verse as an authority or standard. On the other hand, unlike fundamentalist biblical interpretation, authors are audacious in their adaptation of Homeric theme and character for their own cultural and individual purposes.

It is understandable that many modern readers might object to Homer's primacy in the "canon of Western literature."[15] Readers traditionally inscribed in the margins of Western literature, such as women or African Americans, might at times choose an activist stance of resistance against European cultural hegemony.[16] Certainly thematic objection to the male-centered, Greek-centered worldview expressed in the Homeric poems is valid. These poems are reflections of their surrounding society and culture, and they become, in some circles, emblematic of Eurocentric cultural arrogance, what Samir Amin (1989) calls "the eternal West." Dupont's thesis should serve as a mild remedy to this way of thinking. Toni Morrison, as an example of a figure who in 1977 stood outside of the tradition as an African American woman, recognized the inevitability of *reading* and coming to terms with Homer. As a writer entering a speech act and an implicit contract that transcended her race and time, Morrison clearly wanted to understand what Homer's role was, even if only to reject him and stand against his hegemony—and she certainly did more than that. By writing, Morrison was inscribing herself in a heritage not only of African American literature but also of literature per se. Given the place she holds in American culture as radical and yet at the same time canonical, she might help to correct a perception of black classicism as concomitant with literary and sociopolitical conservatism.

Ulysses is important as an emblem of literature (albeit, in the first analysis, *European* literature), but he is also a marker for a more transcendent anthropological, sociocultural issue. Outside of the notion of literature, it might be argued, as Ralph Ellison did throughout his writings, that European characters such as Ulysses are simply local manifestations of folkloric motifs that transcend time and cultures.[17] In this light, to study Ulysses, or Greek and Roman myth and folklore more broadly, is not to privilege him but to understand him in relation to other folklore, even if viewed from a structuralist perspective.[18] If Homer's Achilles grieves the loss in battle of his dearest companion, Patroclus, he is on some level echoing the loss Gilgamesh experiences of his alter ego, Enkidu. When Homer's Odysseus outsmarts the Cyclops Polyphemus, he is, on one level, reenacting the conflict of Rama and other folkloric personas with the at-large ogre of mythology. Even though critics such as Houston Baker suggest an esthetic choice on the part of Ralph Ellison that could alienate the black reader, adapting Ulysses is not tantamount to privileging him over African or African American trickster figures.[19] Certainly the unnamed protagonist of Ralph Ellison's novel *Invisible Man* has particular struggles within his society having to do with racism and segregation. Nevertheless, the phenomenon of literature, although it is carried on in cultures and has political implications, is not ethnically or culturally contained; literature is created within a limited space, is a particular speech act, but it resonates through space and time, with a potential for local and global impact. A black author's use of the classics is not necessarily an esthetic concession, and black classicism can in fact be part of a radical cultural identity.

Beginning with Homer, for the remainder of this chapter I will highlight a few works of classical literature with a dual aim. In the first place, I want to lay a foundation for a reading of classical characters and motifs in African American works. Second, I want to show how classical authors received Homeric themes and characters. By doing so, I hope to convey a sense of the multivalence and adaptability of the classics, particularly to the reader wary of Western influence. The classicist reader might consider seriously the counterhegemonic nature of classical literature: its ability not only to construct identity but also to challenge and reshape it. The role of classics as a counterhegemonic discourse is evident not only in Euripides but even in Aeschylus and Sophocles, Lucan and Seneca.

After the reading of Homer, I offer some problems in the post-Homeric, post–Trojan War play, Euripides' *Hecuba*. Euripides, as a playwright living in war-riddled city of Athens in the fifth century BCE, clearly did not see himself as a *European* author writing in the grand tradition of Western literature. Rather, he appreciated the themes and characters of Homer and used them to reconcile social and political concerns in his own time; *Hecuba*, as so many of Euripides' plays, might be read in part as a scathing critique of Greek power, and as such the play would be as counterhegemonic as any work, of any time, written from a marginal perspective. Toward the end of this chapter, Seneca's *Troades*, or *The Trojan Women*, provides another interpretation of the same themes and characters, and as a broader critique of power and regime generally, it is as counter-hegemonic as Euripides' work.

## Homer, *Odyssey* 9: Odysseus and the Cyclops

As the recent filmic interpretation of Homer's *Iliad* reiterates, Achilles, despite—or perhaps because of—his self-indulgent egoism, is the single most remarkable hero from the epic tradition in the Western world. His reach extends beyond this.[20] Homer creates a war-weary hero whose psychological transparency and the emotion it elicits from audiences, whether or not we agree with his actions, rival any modern hero. Yet modern authors returned, time and again, not to Achilles but to Odysseus/Ulysses, for a fuller scope of what it means to be a hero. Stanford rightly characterizes Ulysses as "by far the most complex in character and exploits" (1963, 6). In the *Iliad*, Achilles is placed in one circumstance: war. Certainly that war is nuanced and brings many opportunities for character and action, from disease to personal offence, loss and grief, vengeance, and reconciliation. Although he is a complex character, Achilles relies on a single (and simple), heroic code of action. He fights for honor, *timē*, and glory, *kleos*, and even when he rages outside of human bounds, he does so because of his sense of shame at the possibility of losing these.[21]

Homer's Odysseus, who lives on a postwar, postheroic frontier, no longer belongs within the social nexus in which Achilles breathes and thrives. Odysseus is unable to rely on any heroic code of war in his dealings with foreigners such as the Lotus-eaters, whose privileging of ecstasy over disciplined activity is not something to which a Greek war hero is accustomed. When Odysseus returns home after a twenty-year absence (ten of war and ten more of wandering), he turns to guile over brawny heroism to defeat the suitors of his wife, Penelope. To do so, he disguises himself as a beggar and becomes a quick study of life and times in Ithaca since his absence. Such is the hero to whom so many authors have returned for building blocks to their adaptations. And as Stanford puts it, "most significant of all for the possibility of later adaptations of [Ulysses'] myth, one of his chief qualities, as Homer portrayed him, was adaptability" (7).

In book 9 of the *Odyssey*, Odysseus begins to tell the story of his wandering after the Trojan War—or at least his version of it—to the Phaeacians, a people with no historical existence outside of the epic.[22] Odysseus was shipwrecked with the Phaeacians after traveling from the island of Calypso on a raft. For the reader of the epic, Odysseus's story, which extends through four books (books 9–12), is the first opportunity to hear the hero tell his own tale. The epic opened not with Odysseus but with the adventures of his son, Telemachus. Telemachus' outrage at the suitors' behavior prompts a journey through Greece (which Athena, disguised, suggests) in search of his absent, perhaps dead, father. The storyteller spends the first four books of the *Odyssey* on Telemachus' travels. The reader does not encounter Odysseus until book 5, when the gods decide to help him travel home. In our first impression, we find that seven years of sensual pleasure with a real-life goddess is not enough to soothe nostalgia. Odysseus rejects Calypso's offer of immortality, and he is sent along on a doomed raft (perhaps as punishment for his audacity).

Odysseus, by his own account, longs for homecoming, a seemingly simple desire but one that scholars have interpreted in a range of ways, including the reading of homecoming as redemption (with all of the ideological and spiritual connotations of the term).[23] In addition to his nostalgia—a word that is actually a compound of Greek *nostos*, "homecoming," and *algos*, "pain," at least three characteristics convey Odysseus's appeal: his acquisitiveness (stemming from a spirit of adventure), his learning from experiences, and his relationship to antagonists. By citing these three traits, I do not want to limit the epic or its hero but rather to suggest some features that are evident later in such works of African American literature as Ralph Ellison's *Juneteenth.* These traits are apparent in Odysseus's encounter with the Cyclops in Homer, *Odyssey* 9. The episode caught Ralph Ellison's attention, and the Ulysses theme is the single mythological idea cited most in his discussions of classical influences.[24]

Acquisitiveness, which I take not as greed but as an inevitable, materialistic drive, is a heroic trait that shapes Odysseus's relationship to the world around him.[25] The Muse's injunction at the beginning of the epic to sing of the man who "saw the cities of many people and knew their mindset" (*Odyssey* 1.3) suggests that Odysseus's subtlety, his quality of *polytropos* (the "intricate turnings" of his mind), might in part result from his tangible experiences.[26] The hero begins his report to the Phaeacians with the tale of his raid of the mythical Cicones, where his men linger too long and are nearly killed, and their subsequent encounter with the Lotus-eaters. After his difficult time with his men in the latter situation, Odysseus and company travel to the island of the Cyclopes. Odysseus, who tells his story with the wisdom of hindsight, reports that this was a land of "arrogant and wild men, not even just men, or kind to strangers, who fear gods in their minds" (9.175–76). Despite the clear and present danger of encountering a frontierlike mentality, Odysseus's curiosity and his hope to gain *xenia,* a "guest-gift," from the hands of the stranger compel him to meet the Cyclops.[27]

The reader sees Odyssean desire in the brief encounter with the Cicones leading up to the elaborate Cyclops episode. Why, for example, should Odysseus and his men raid the Cicones, almost immediately after sacking Troy, to gain more goods? Certainly such acquisitiveness borders on greed.[28] From the beginning of the epic, the narrator tells the reader that Odysseus's men lost their *nostos* because of their recklessness, evident in such acts as their consumption of the oxen of the Sun. In the episode with the Cicones, Odysseus reports that he divided all of the goods, the women, and the treasures as fairly as he could, yet "the senseless men were not persuaded. They drank much wine there, and they ate a lot of sheep and fat, winding-[horned] cattle along the shore" (9.45–46). In this incident, greed almost costs Odysseus's men their lives, and it eventually does. Nevertheless, there is a subtle distinction throughout the *Odyssey* between greed on the one hand, and the importance of the intellectual, material, and even moral gains that come from having a broad range of experiences on the other. Odyssean desire might to some extent be read as an early, capitalistic impulse, what Michael Clark calls bourgeoisie materialism.[29] Here as always in Greek literature, balance is the key to success. The Greek axiom, *mēden adēn*, "nothing to the fill" (nothing too much), suggests that acquisitiveness might be a good quality, so long as it is balanced with a reverence for cultural and moral taboos. Ralph Ellison's interpretation of Odysseus's encounter with the Cyclops in the novel *Juneteenth* will show the extent to which acquisitiveness—or at least intellectual curiosity and ingenuity—would continue to be an important quality for the modern (in this case American) hero. In the case of Ellison's novel, the hero is called upon to balance capitalistic desire on an American frontier with a black-inflected sense of home.

In the Cyclops episode in the *Odyssey*, Odysseus wants to meet the Cyclops for all the gains, despite the dangers that might come with this experience. As he tells the story, he is aware of the possibility of an adverse outcome. This awareness is evident in the fact that he brings a strong wine with him to the cave.[30] On one level, the wine might serve in an exchange of *xenia* with the stranger. In Odysseus's telling of it, he brought the wine because he had "a strong premonition we had a rendezvous with a man of great might, a savage with no notion of right and wrong" (9.215). The fact that this wine was a guest-gift to Odysseus from Maron, a priest of Apollo, might serve further to reinforce the sense of cultural and moral taboo.[31] Odysseus tells his audience, for example, that "whenever he [Maron] drank this sweet, dark red wine, he would fill one goblet and pour it into twenty parts of water." Polyphemus, the one-eyed, cannibalistic ogre, will drink this wine unmixed, leading to his complete intoxication. While Odysseus gains this unique bouquet from Maron the priest, what he gains from the savage Polyphemus will be more intellectual than material.

Odyssean desire, acted upon appropriately, results in a wealth of experiences from which the hero can draw, a cosmopolitanism that Seneca saw as essential to wisdom. In *Odyssey* 9, Maron's wine signifies the extent to which Odysseus implements past experiences in new encounters. That is to say, the second Odyssean characteristic is his learning from experience.[32]

In *Mimesis* Erich Auerbach (1953) makes a compelling claim in the opposite direction. Auerbach argues that Homeric characters do not in fact learn as the epic unfolds. Because the poet of the *Iliad* and the *Odyssey* foregrounds events and characters throughout the epics (so that narrative digressions are as immediate as the issues at hand), there is little space for psychological development, reflection, or growth. To Auerbach, Homeric characters "have no development, and their life-histories are clearly set forth once and for all" (17). While Auerbach makes a strong case for his thesis, comparing scenes from the *Odyssey* to the less impressionistic biblical narratives, his broad strokes might obscure some of the subtler developments of character and plot in the epic.[33] In addition to this, how readers and critics have received and understood the *Odyssey* is to some extent a separate issue from its immediate sociopolitical context, or its authorial esthetics. Here again, the reader, and the reading, makes the literature. While Auerbach argues against the representation of character growth in Homer, I see Odysseus's development in the *Odyssey* as a precursor to the Greek axiom of *mathos/pathos,* learning from suffering.[34] The idea of learning from suffering is traceable in the *Odyssey* and becomes a compelling feature of Homeric reception and criticism.

The Cyclops episode of Homer, *Odyssey* 9 is, once again, emblematic of how the hero learns from past experiences, as we have already seen in Odysseus's use of Maron's wine. In Odysseus's telling of the Cyclops episode, the reader might sense a certain degree of revision, what Frederick Ahl (1996) sees as Odysseus's own elusiveness. As with epic poetry itself, we cannot disentangle the truth from lies in Odysseus's story. The story is crafted, moreover, to make Odysseus look good. Thus in the tales of the Cicones and the Lotus-eaters, Odysseus continuously emphasizes that he warns his men away from danger. Yet in the encounter with Polyphemus, Odysseus is unable to repress the fact—or perhaps it is a fact strategically told—that his men *warned him* against going into the Cyclops's cave. Odysseus's eagerness to meet the Cyclopes is curious given his own insistence on their insolence. Many scholars have pointed to a heroic imperative of *kleos,* or fame, in Odysseus's stubbornness.[35] That is, similar to Achilles, Odysseus wants to be celebrated for his feat, and the guest-gifts he should receive from the Cyclops would help to validate the stories that he would later tell—and that would be told about him. Yet despite his desire for *kleos,* Odysseus learns the importance of denying himself the highest honor of Homeric man, namely that honor, in his encounter with Polyphemus.

In the Cyclops episode, Odysseus inevitably harms himself because of his inability to sustain a consistent, self-narrated identity—even if it is an identity of erasure ("I am nobody"). The issue of identity per se is perhaps beyond the scope of interpretation here, but it might be argued that the degree of psychological integrity a person can sustain is a determining factor of that personality's success in society. Even in Ralph Ellison's *Invisible Man*, it is important for the protagonist to come to a consistent, self-emanating narrative regarding what he is, one separate from what others say about him. Put another way, a trickster figure or even a minstrel in the Ellisonian context is successful because of his consistency (even, for the trickster, in being inconsistent), no matter how we view the issue of lying, or the erasure—of intelligence, of will—that comes with playing the clown.[36] I do not argue that this notion of psychological integrity is at all well articulated in Homeric epic.[37] Nevertheless, throughout the epic, the reader finds Odysseus toggling between a posture of self-preservation on the one hand, and his desire—to a great extent socially determined—for an external *kleos* on the other.

When Polyphemus asks Odysseus his name during their exchange, the hero replies, "Nobody." This answer is the Homeric variation of the standard folkloric reply in such situations: "Myself."[38] Odysseus's reply forestalls a cataclysmic turn of events because the Cyclops, as we later discover, would certainly have recognized the name Odysseus, such being the hero's fame (again, *kleos*). (Polyphemus later reveals that long ago he had been told a prophecy that he would lose his sight at Odysseus's hands.) Odysseus, as Nobody, endears himself to Polyphemus, who offers the hero a particular *xenia* for more wine: "Nobody I will eat last after his friends. Friends first, him last. That's my gift to you." Later in the episode, however, after blinding the drunk and slumbering one-eyed ogre and escaping from the cave, Odysseus proves ultimately uncomfortable with obscurity:

> Cyclops, if anyone among mortal men
> Asks you about the unwelcome blinding of your eye,
> Tell him that Odysseus the sacker of cities ruined your sight,
> Son of Laertes, with his home in Ithaca. (502–5)

The result of Odysseus's irrepressible desire for *kleos* is a curse, one that requires a named object for its effectiveness.[39] When the blinded Cyclops called out for help, he could only utter that "nobody" had harmed him; now Polyphemus is able to identify his antagonist and call for supernatural aid:

> Hear me, Poseidon, dark-haired Earth-Holder,
> If I am truly your son, and you vow that you are my father.

Grant that Odysseus, the sacker of cities, never arrives home—
Odysseus, the son of Laertes, whose home is in Ithaca.
But if his fate is to see his loved ones and to arrive
At his well-built house and his fatherland,
May he after a long time wretchedly, having lost his companions
In another man's ship, find woes at home. (528–35)

The fact that the Cyclops's prayer is heard is explicit in the subsequent lines and evident throughout the remainder of the epic. Odysseus does arrive home, ten years later, under the circumstances that Polyphemus requests.

The extent to which Odysseus learns from his mistake, which in this case is his lack of self-control, his inability to conceal his true identity for a sustained period of time despite his opposing desire for *kleos,* can be gauged by his behavior toward the close of the epic. Odysseus in fact must become a "nobody" in his own home. He disguises himself as a beggar, revealing his true identity not even to his wife, while he plots the murder of men who are themselves violating codes of *xenia* and dishonoring the absent hero's memory. Odysseus is unable to keep his identity as Nobody for the short encounter with the Cyclops; Odysseus remains as a nobody in the guise of a beggar, with all the injury and insult that comes with the status, for almost ten books in the last episodes of the *Odyssey.* The difference is narrated in perhaps as impressionistic a way as the foregrounding of events in the epic, but subtle changes in Odysseus's behavior render Auerbach's assertion about Homeric character suspect.

Odyssean acquisitiveness, along with his ability to revise his actions and his relationship to others, form the basis of a complex literary character. It would not be extreme to assert that Homeric character, evident in Odysseus's subtle but measurable psychological perspective, is the beginning of the representation of selfhood in Western literature (along with the *Iliad* and Achilles). There is no bildungsroman without Homer. Yet as we see in Ellison's bildungsroman *Invisible Man,* the hero ultimately comes to his identity through opposition, or what Albert Murray, in *The Hero and the Blues,* calls "antagonistic cooperation":

The fire in the forging process, like the dragon which the hero must always
encounter, is of its very nature antagonistic, but it is also cooperative at the
same time. For all its violence, it does not destroy the metal which becomes
the sword. It functions precisely to strengthen and prepare it to hold its

battle edge, even as the all but withering firedrake prepares the questing hero
for subsequent trials and adventures. (Murray, 38)

Put otherwise, "heroism, which like the sword is nothing if not steadfast,
is measured in terms of the stress and strain it can endure and the magnitude and complexity of the obstacles it overcomes" (38). The African
American hero is a different person entirely without the experiences of
slavery, segregation, and the struggle for civil rights, just as Dostoevsky's
hero comes to terms with local, immediate concerns in Russia before he
is able to have universal appeal. This is not to paint the suffering entailed
in the historical processes, rendered heroic in fiction, in bright, colorful
strokes. Rather, antagonism is a reality of human existence as inevitable
as the violent and chaotic "big bang" out of which our current state arises.

As we have seen, two characteristics that distinguish Odysseus are his
acquisitiveness and his learning from experiences. Murray's observations
about heroic antagonism are fitting as the third Odyssean characteristic.
The hero struggles against everything that is not he, against his antiself,
as it were, in his process of becoming. Thus if the hero is male, the dragon,
the antiself, is female; if he is controlled, she is violent and chaotic. More
daringly, if the hero is black, then the antiself is white. Odysseus's emphasis on the Cyclopes's inability to observe divine law, or *themis,* makes
sense in the context of antagonistic cooperation. In fact, for this antagonism Homer is forced, through Odysseus, to recast the Cyclopes, formerly
helpers of Zeus in mythology, as villains.[40] If the hero is an observer of
*xenia*—which is, ironically, not entirely the case with Odysseus—Polyphemus eats men as his guest-gift. Odysseus is small and unassuming; the
Cyclops is a giant. It has even been suggested that Polyphemus represents
the underside of Odyssean selfhood: the Cyclops's cave is Odysseus's own
mind.[41] The antiself here is within. By encountering an antagonist, or an
Other, the hero is in essence becoming more himself, learning who he is
and is *not* through trial and error.

## Can the Greek and the Barbarian Be Friends?:
## Odysseus in Euripides' *Hecuba*

As Stanford argues in *The Ulysses Theme,* in the Odysseus of Greek tragedy
we begin to detect, at times, a moral judgment against the Homeric character.[42] Perhaps this is because tragedy is a genre of nonreturn. If the hero

of epic has his homecoming, the tragic hero, such as Agamemnon, loses his return to death and destruction. The epic hero, on the one hand, learns a natural, moral balance of things and controls his acquisitiveness; the tragic hero, on the other hand, takes the path of deeper suffering. Despite Oedipus's learning, his tragedy ends with a self-blinding representative of the pain he has caused and must endure. Epic antagonism leads the hero to a victorious resolution; tragic antagonism leads to a painful but necessary outcome. In sum, if the epic Odysseus learns from his mistakes and finds his way home, then his tragic counterpart is a perpetual wanderer, fragmented from his ethics and from what Stanford calls his integrated self.

From this we might argue that Odysseus in Euripides' *Hecuba* is symbolic of a Greek ethical crisis, one stemming from the historical realities of internecine war, an unstable political identity, and the moral demands of imperialism.[43] *Hecuba* is a post–Trojan War play, set at the interval between the Greek conquest of Troy and the return of the heroes to their homes. In the myths of the fall of Troy, Greek heroes desecrate holy sites with such acts as rape and murder during their sack of the city, and this breakdown of ethical standards in some ways provides a prism through which the fifth-century Athenian audience might view its own political circumstances.[44] At the time of the first performance of *Hecuba* in 424 BCE, Athens itself was embroiled in a bitter war against Sparta, namely the Peloponnesian War. Complaints of Athenian abuse of power, in such instances as the takeover of Melos, echo in certain regards the political crisis of Troy's fall.

In Euripides' play, the ethical crisis is not war itself, since the Greeks have already conquered Troy, but rather the postwar hubris expressed in the demand for human sacrifice and the violation of the sacred institutions, such as *xenia*, the guest–host friendship that was central to Homer's *Odyssey*. In the context of a counterhegemonic poetics, *Hecuba* is noteworthy because of the way in which it privileges the marginal voices of slaves, foreign (called barbarian) women, over those of the Greek males.[45] *Hecuba*, moreover, is not the only play of Euripides to give voice to the oppressed; his *Bacchae* in part speaks for a group of women who are "foreign" in their abandonment of traditional, female roles for Bacchic frenzy.

*Hecuba* opens with the ghost of Polydorus, the last surviving prince of Troy, who tells the audience that Polymester, the guest-friend (*xenos*) of the royal family, has killed him for gold.[46] Hecuba, Polydorus's mother and the protagonist, will discover this murder only after enduring the sacrifice of her daughter, Polyxena, over Achilles' grave. The play foregrounds the moral development—or degeneration—of Hecuba, who finds herself incapable of stopping her daughter's sacrifice. Later in the play, she takes vengeance on Polymester after discovering her son's body. While Hecuba is Euripides' focal point, the playwright is also concerned with the behavior of the Greeks on this occasion, and in particular that of Odysseus (and, perhaps to an equal degree, Agamemnon).

While *Hecuba* is set in the mythological past, it clearly adapts for the playwright's own Athenian sociopolitical context certain Homeric themes, such as the relationship between individual and collective desire, which we might read as checks on acquisitiveness, the theme of hospitality, and notions of honor.[47] The play inverts the roles of protagonist and antagonist, so that Euripides' Cyclops, the ogre who fails to observe natural law (*themis*), is, at least by Hecuba's sophistic argument, Odysseus. Euripides in fact seems to play on the Cyclops theme throughout the drama. Early on, Hecuba accuses Odysseus of violations of *xenia,* and later, Hecuba becomes a heroic Odysseus in the Cyclops's cave: She traps her opponent in a tent before killing his sons and *blinding* him. Euripides inverts the hero and antagonist to draw attention to the *foreign female slave.* In the end, Euripides provides his audience with reflections on Athenian hegemony through the world of myth. Greek tragedy was no mere fantastical escape from daily realities. Rather, Euripides is a poet in the mode of the earlier epic and lyric bards that Bruno Gentili describes in *Poetry and its Public in Ancient Greece:*

> Poetic performance, whether epic or lyric, was conceived as more than a means for allowing audiences to see themselves in the mirror of mythical or contemporary events; it could also serve to arouse in them a new perception of reality and broaden their awareness to include the new modes of social and political activity which new needs and goals demanded. (Gentili, 55)

*Hecuba*'s relationship to contemporary reality is clear in subtle and not-so-subtle ways. For example, Euripides at one point uses the adjective *democharistes,* "flatterer of the people," to describe Odysseus. (This is a coinage that is not attested in Homeric works.) In the context of his role in convincing the Greeks that the sacrifice of Polyxena is honorable, the adjective calls to mind Thucydides' (the historian of the Peloponnesian

War) description of a contemporary Athenian leader, Cleon. In his account, Thucydides describes Cleon as a *demagogos* (or "popular leader," Thucydides 4.21) in keeping with his disparagement of post-Periclean leadership (Pericles died of symptoms associated with the recurrence of a plague he suffered after the first year of the war.):[48]

> Those who came later [i.e., after Pericles], in contrast, since they were more on an equal level with one another and each was striving to become first, even resorted to handing over affairs to the people's pleasure. As a result, many mistakes were made, since a great city ruling an empire was involved. (Thucydides 2.65, Steven Lattimore translation)

Although many scholars of Euripides' play have focused on Hecuba's moral decay (and opposition to this reading is already present in my valorization of Hecuba's actions as heroic), Odysseus is no hero here.[49] Odysseus's demand for sacrifice could not be seen in a positive light by the audience, and the consideration of human sacrifice as a natural occurrence in the ancient world will not suffice. (The latter claim is simply false.) In the criticism it contains of Odysseus and the Greeks, *Hecuba* is in every regard counterhegemonic and demonstrates the possibilities of classical literature for voicing the concerns of the marginalized.

The valorization of the foreign women, as Charles Segal and others have noted, begins with Polyxena, the sacrificial victim, who is represented as noble/beautiful. Nobility of character (*moral* beauty, a theme reiterated throughout the play) is the virtue of the slave girl, not of Odysseus or his Greek troops. In the case of Hecuba, the apparent ambivalence has to do with a breakdown of the (Greek) social context for moral action, or *beauty* in action, including speech and thought. In its inversion of Greek and barbarian somewhat typical in later classical tragedy (Hall 1989), the play suggests that the female slaves can be beautiful (ethically and esthetically), while Greeks are capable of barbaric acts (acquisitiveness without the appropriate checks and balances).[50] In the play, Polyxena's naked, limp, sacrificial body becomes the focal point of a bemused Greek army. Before her death, Polyxena proves to be nobler than the Greeks in her actions and her words: "I go with you because I must, but most because I wish to die. If I refuse, I prove myself a coward, in love with life" (*Hecuba*, lines 349–50). The Greek troops seem somehow quickened because of the heroic resolve of a slave they treated as less than human:

The execution finished, the soldiers set to work. Some scattered leaves upon her corpse, while others brought branches of pine and heaped her pyre. Those who shirked found themselves abused by the rest. (572–76)

In contrast to the representation of her daughter, Euripides' final presentation of Hecuba is indeed ambivalent.[51] Scholars have focused on Hecuba's act of vengeance, in direct juxtaposition to Polyxena's noble death.[52] After luring her son's murderer into the slaves' tents, a plot that the Greek leader Agamemnon aids, Hecuba and her attendants kill Polymester's sons and blind him. The semicircular (180°) reversal of Greek and barbarian might be complete (360°) in what appears to be Hecuba's return to a barbaric act, and yet her representation is not without complexity. Any condemnation of Hecuba in the play might be read as equivocal, to some extent, because it comes from Polymester. Polymester does prophesy Hecuba's later transformation into a dog, a symbol that is often read as, at the very least, subhuman, if even noble. Scholars have noted, however, the difficulty in interpreting this symbol.[53]

In modern readings of Euripides' *Hecuba,* scholars have tended to focus on the problem of Hecuba's actions; her violence has met a critique on par with that of Medea, whose lust for vengeance causes her to kill her own children. Some treatments have come close to suggesting what I read as the root causes of Hecuba's actions, namely her sense of betrayal at the hands of her captors. In 1985, Kenneth Reckford argued that

Hecuba collapses into savagery, and into spiritual slavery, not just because she is mistreated by men but because her mistreatment opens her eyes to the brutal, chancy, and godless world in which they are living, oppressors and oppressed alike. (125)

Reckford still seemed unable to elaborate on Hecuba's "mistreatment by men"; rather, he shifts blame to a "brutal, chancy, and godless world," a world that might be the ultimate cause not only of Hecuba's actions, but also of the less-than-noble Greeks ("oppressors and oppressed alike"). Ra'anana Meridor (1984) turned his critical gaze from Hecuba's act to the Greeks', particularly Agamemnon's, reaction to her vengeful acts. Meridor sees that Agamemnon "supplies Hecuba with both the social framework and the responsible authority" for her retaliation. More recent critics as diverse as Orlando Patterson (1991) and Judith Mossman (1995) see that

Hecuba's vengeance could just as easily have been interpreted as a justified, albeit primal, act.

Through her focus on *nomos,* or the social conventions for individual agency (under which rubric we are justified to include *xenia*), Martha Nussbaum (1986) raises important points about heroism and nobility in *Hecuba*.[54] What happens, for example, if the individual's society—the very place he or she should call "home"—is antagonistic? Certainly such an antagonism, as has been discussed, can be for the potential hero either a refining fire or a point of defeat. How do we interpret Hecuba's response to antagonism?

(This question is especially important to a black esthetic of heroism in the modern American context. The black American hero of the twentieth century, such as Ralph Ellison's unnamed protagonist, lives in a "home" or "homeland" that would seek to limit his heroic possibilities—his or her moral beauty—at every turn. America's antagonism to black agency can be found in everything from slavery to segregation, lynching to police brutality—the list is exhaustive.)

In the Greek as much as in the American context, antagonism is the backdrop against which the marginalized individual must act. In Hecuba's case, Nussbaum sees that antagonism in her new "soil" of Greece has everything to do with the directions she takes; circumstances, not an innate, female weakness and barbarian character, lead to Hecuba's final state. In her transformation into a dog, Hecuba becomes a talisman that might guide even more heroic—nobler and more beautiful—behavior, even from the Greek male/citizen (normative) observer.

A brief reading of one or two scenes from *Hecuba* should show the extent to which the Greeks in particular have failed Hecuba. We should be careful not to read Hecuba's plight as victimization; rather, she chooses her actions from any number of (albeit limited) possibilities. Early in the play, Hecuba tries to persuade Odysseus against sacrificing Polyxena. Polyxena's sacrifice, as should be clear, is thematically related to Hecuba's later vengeance on Polymestor, who killed her last remaining child. (I believe this is the case even though the immediate cause—the proverbial straw that breaks the camel's back—is Hecuba's discovery of *Polydorus's* body.) Hecuba is given a covered corpse after Polyxena's death, and she believes this is the body of her daughter. The shock of another loss is clearly too much for Hecuba to manage. In the earlier scene, Hecuba calls upon *xenia* (as well as the Greek notion of justice as helping friends and harming enemies) to prevent the chain of events that will lead to her demise.[55] In that earlier scene, she reminds Odysseus that, during the war, she hosted him and kept him safe from harm. Odysseus concedes *xenia* but refuses to reciprocate, and as a result Hecuba accuses him of rejecting his own ethical norms for the expediency of the moment:

> Are you not behaving badly in these plans,
> Since from me you experienced all you say,
> Yet you do nothing good for me
> And hurt me as much as you can?
> You thankless breed that seeks honors
> From popularity with the masses!
> I wish I never knew you—
> You that think nothing of harming friends,
> As long as you gain favor with the masses. (*Hecuba*, lines 251–57)

Hecuba accuses the Greek Odysseus of harming friends, the same judgment that comes to the barbarian Polymester later in the play.

While it might be argued that Hecuba's words are sophistic (or that ethics in war are different from ethics in times of peace), Odysseus would be equally guilty of sophistry when he aligns Polyxena's murder with heroic honor.[56] Polydorus tells the audience at the beginning of the play that the ghost of Achilles demands the sacrifice, but Odysseus makes the argument for the sacrifice based on an esthetics of citizenship. Achilles, Odysseus claimed, "died nobly," (or beautifully) *thanōn kallista* (*Hecuba*, 310), for Greece, and as a result he deserves honor.[57] The chorus reports this claim early in the play in the context of a seemingly democratic process:

> The debate was intense
> And there was no letting up
> Until the crafty-minded smooth-talker,
> A flatterer of the people [*democharistes*]—
> The son of Laertes—persuaded the army
> Not to begrudge the best of the Danaans
> For the sake of slave sacrifices,
> And that none of the dead
> Standing alongside Persephone

Should say that Danaans prove thankless to Danaans
That died on the plains of Troy
On behalf of Greece. (*Hecuba*, 130–40)

It is of course no mistake that the messenger who reports Polyxena's death later in the play uses similar language to that of Odysseus's description of Achilles. The messenger reports that the dying girl exposes her body and shows her "most beautiful breasts as of a statue" (*sterna agalmatos kallista; Hecuba*, 560–61). The playwright leaves the audience the task of reconciling the discrepancy of whose death was nobler (and thus more beautiful), or of which claims amount to sophistry.[58]

In the end, even if the play and the audience return to the status quo, we cannot escape the counterhegemonic voice in Euripides' *Hecuba*. Although I could not survey many of the sociocultural concerns of the Greek author here—such as the relationship between the human realm and the divine, or the cultural debate between *nomos* and inborn nature, *physis*, evident throughout the play—the adaptation of Homer for contemporary use in the fifth century should be clear.[59] Euripides' adaptation takes Homeric character and, to some extent, the Homeric context for action, to raise concerns that are at once local and universal, specifically cultural while at the same time extending beyond the given society. Much of this adaptation remains for the reader's further understanding. In the argument for Polyxena's sacrifice, for example, the victim becomes a *geras*, a "war-prize," which in the Homeric context is a mark of the hero's *timē*, his honor. In *Hecuba* we also find the inversion of the Homeric features that would come to be representative of the hero throughout literature. Odysseus's acquisitiveness, a mark of the hero's intellectual and material curiosity in the epic, knows no bounds in the tragic framework. He uses his knowledge, his ability to deploy language skillfully, to questionable ends. His sophistic argument in favor of Polyxena's sacrifice does not lead to learning but rather to the continued suffering of another.

In this reading of *Hecuba*, Odysseus is clearly not the hero; rather, the protagonist is the subaltern, foreign, barbarian slave woman. Nobility of character, beauty, is in the hands of the slave. It is no wonder, given the complexity of Euripides' *Hecuba*, that Orlando Patterson sees the play as an important moment in the making of freedom—as a sustainable human value that makes slavery ultimately immoral—in Western civilization.

## Ulysses at Nero's Court: Seneca's *Troades*[60]

As we have seen, classical literature is at times concerned with the critique of power. In the context of the possibility of a black Ulysses, I have been concerned first with the heroic characteristics of Ulysses, and secondly with the way in which a couple of emblematic classical works explore antiheroic behavior as resistance to hegemony. In some cases, such as in Homer's *Odyssey* (or in such works outside of our purview as Sophocles' *Oedipus the King* or Vergil's *Aeneid*), the author represents hegemony as the power of the gods, concretely, as with Oedipus's Apollo, or abstractly, the role of fortune or fate in Vergil's epic. Even where regimes aggressively advance one program, as in the case of the Augustan regime of Vergil's *Aeneid,* the poet contains alternative impressions within his or her work. Writing is, among other things, a form of resistance, or antagonism, the way in which an author inserts his or her will on history. As Shadi Bartsch and others have more recently explored vis-à-vis the literature of the early Roman Empire, the written word immediately lends itself to interpretation. (It is a sign of what is absent, namely the speaker or writer and his or her intent. Meaning is latent.) In the Roman context, those in power could also take the authoritative role of interpretation.

As we will see, this concern of the individual's relationship to power runs throughout Ralph Ellison's *Invisible Man,* as it does the other works of African American literature with which we will be concerned. Ellison distilled this binary opposition—of self to society, the individual to institutions—to the point of an artistic elegance, even if Ellison's take on individualism would cause some critics to question his dedication to the black masses.[61] In classical literature, one of the more vociferous pronouncements of selfhood in the face of antagonistic power is that of Senecan drama. Seneca wrote his tragedies, likely in Rome, presumably in the waning years of his political career.[62] The plays take the Stoic philosophy of Seneca's prose as their point of departure, and critics have at times interpreted them in light of their creator's relationship to the politics of his time.[63] More importantly for our purposes, the plays adapt the topics of Greek myth and drama to Latin stylistics and Roman ideas. At the core of Seneca's articulation of power and selfhood is, once again, the character Ulysses. Once again, Ulysses is a symbol for classicism, as he had already become by Roman times.

In one of his epistles, Seneca uses the mythological character Ulysses to urge his reader to attend to the care of the self. He warns his audience to treat vices as though they are Scylla and Charybdis, the monster and the whirlwind of which the hero is advised to navigate around cautiously if he is to arrive home safely. Seneca's deployment of the Ulysses theme is pedagogical and, as Stanford sees, ultimately anagogical. Seneca's examples are set within a particular approach to selfhood and power:

> These are the voices you must steer clear of like those which Ulysses refused to sail past until he was lashed to the mast. They have the same power: they lure men away from country, parents, friends and moral values, creating expectations in them only to make sport out of the wretchedness of lives of degradation. (*Letters* 123.12)

Elsewhere in Seneca's prose, Ulysses is an example—or counterexample—of the individual's encounter with his surrounding (Stoic) world. In another epistle, Seneca attributes Ulysses' long absence from home to seasickness: one should find a cure to such (in this case physical) sickness (*Letters* 53). In yet another letter, Ulysses teaches quietude in that he stopped-up his ears to avoid the song of the Sirens (*Letters* 56).[64] Certainly Seneca approaches Ulysses from an extremely self-conscious perspective and is not always to be taken at face value.

In the examples of Ulysses from Seneca's prose, the hero figures for the struggle of a self—an integral, inner, psychological life—against what we might call, simply, power. Here again is an antagonistic cooperation because, as we will see, the individual becomes heroic through the refinement of self: acquisitiveness, learning, and opposition to power. Ulysses' power struggle is against monsters, such as Scylla and Charybdis, and, ironically, against the overwhelming power of emotions and the body (seasickness, perpetual wandering), which might at times be alien to the *animus*, the inner-being and core of Seneca's self. In Senecan tragedy, the at-large "power" to which I am referring is often called *regnum*, or "royal power, authority," which might be read as a poetic counterpart to *imperium*, "power, command."[65] *Imperium* is already a feature of the relationship between gods and men in Vergil's *Aeneid*, and it bears a particular significance in the Roman social and political context. Literature is always part of a material environment, and *imperium* is as indelible to the idea of Rome as is race to the idea of America. This *imperium*—whether a political regime, emotions gone wild and out of control, or the gods and fellow man—stands opposed to the self in Senecan drama, and even in his prose. By writing, Seneca raises his voice against *imperium* in all of its forms.

Seneca's adaptation of the themes and characters that we have already seen in Homeric epic and in Euripides' *Hecuba* seems to rely on his understanding of an inner-being, an *animus*, as opposed to *external* power, that consists of reason, body, and emotions. While this tripartite division is consistent with a Stoic worldview, Senecan tragedy is not necessarily Stoic drama, as more recent scholars of Seneca realize.[66] What I show here is not only the extent to which the classics are fundamental to later literary discourses in the West, but also, again, that the classics provide us with the very notion of the self, as we have already seen in the case of Homer. Seneca further refines this self.

Characters throughout the plays often fail to heed reason, the "ruler" in a healthy self.[67] In *Phoeniciae*, for example, Jocasta appeals to her feuding sons, in somewhat Freudian language, to put away their swords in their sheaths (*vaginā; Phoeniciae,* line 467), and heed an ancestral wisdom. These are the sons of Oedipus, Eteocles and Polynices, who agreed to share power in Thebes after their father's self-blinding and exile. Jocasta argues that while Oedipus's patricide was inadvertent, the brothers' mutual fratricide would be a premeditated crime. The power of their own arguments wins the day, and as the myth has it, these would-be rulers kill each other at the last of the seven gates of Thebes.

In her reasoning in *Agamemnon*, Clytemnestra is equally concerned with guilt and premeditation, but the draw—the power—of her life since Agamemnon's departure (her adultery with Aegisthus and plot to murder her husband) wins out. Senecan characters seem to have a distinct sense of what they should do, but the tragedy is in their inability to act virtuously.

For Seneca, the body and the emotions are the two antagonists against the self, and a few examples will suffice to demonstrate how Seneca represents these in his tragedies. Profoundly, characters in Senecan drama are conscious of an essential self—the *animus*—separate from external matter. Where this body begins and ends is a matter of debate and dissolution throughout the plays. The representation of the power of the self throughout Seneca's plays is an important counter to the imposing, imperial power of kingdoms, and at times fate, within the play. Seneca, throughout his works, lauds the power of selfhood (or self-management, self-control, self-governance) within his social and political context.

Critics of Seneca notice, for example, the self-conscious statement of his Medea, who is not content with being, but wants to *become* Medea— *fiam Medea* (*Medea*, line 171).[68] Whether Medea becomes black or white, Roman or barbarian, her identity is somehow in what she does. Yet there is a body—marked somehow by pigment, gender, and the like—that carries out the character's will, within a context of social and political power(s).

In Seneca's treatment of Hercules' madness, the character that rages insanely and kills his wife, Megara, and their sons, awakens to find the Herculean bow and arrow beside his naked body. He sees the destruction that he alone could cause: "Is this my crime? You are quiet; it is my crime." Hercules recognizes (*agnoscere*) himself, although in his insanity he failed to recognize his own wife earlier in the play. Hercules' new perspective is suggestive of Aristotelian *peripeteia* ("reversal"), where a dramatic change of fortunes results in what might be seen as a new state of affairs. Hercules' murders and his disorientation are alienating. While in *Hercules Furens* Hercules is the audience (or the observer) of the surrounding events, a similar alienation might take place in the audience that hears (or reads) Hippolytus's dismemberment at the end of Seneca's *Phaedra*.

From *Medea*, *Hercules Furens*, and *Phaedra*, we see that Seneca calls our attention to bodies and their extensions. The bow and arrow are extensions of Hercules, and his separation from these causes the character to question what he has done and, ultimately, who he is. The reader (or observer) of these plays must experience a similar questioning, given the consistently self-conscious character construction throughout the tragedies. This is not the place to explore Senecan drama, but these brief observations should give the reader an impression of their power. Meanwhile, the relationship between Seneca's Roman drama and counterhegemony is the more pressing issue.

Any one of Seneca's individual plays lends itself to diverse and at times contradictory readings, but I will turn to *Troades* because the play returns us to the issues of resistance, adaptation, and also an antiheroic Ulysses. The play is also easily read alongside Euripides' *Hecuba* because it is centered on the same themes (the fall of Troy and Polyxena's sacrifice) and was likely one of Seneca's models for his play.

I have been discussing Seneca's plays in the context of the antagonism between self and society. To call these plays explicitly counterhegemonic, however, would be to set aside the acute difficulties of reading Senecan drama as social and political commentaries.[69] Certainly all literature grows out of a sociopolitical context, and despite earlier scholarship that argued for the artist's seclusion from politics during the early Roman Empire,[70] the pendulum has now swung in the opposite direction.[71] Recent scholarship on Senecan drama recognizes the potential for literature during this time to be read as critiques of the political regime, whatever the writer's intent might or might not have been.[72] Nevertheless, little should be taken for granted regarding the intent (political or otherwise), context (performance or otherwise), or impact of Senecan drama.[73] At the same time, the concerns about power, self-management, and revolt found in Seneca's prose are certainly present in the plays.

Regarding *Troades*, little can be said about its date of composition, although I play with the notion that it was written toward the end of Seneca's life and during Nero's reign, ca. 54–65 CE. Readers have long noted the connection between Seneca's essay *De clementia* ("On Mercy"), which implores the young emperor Nero to use his power in a merciful way, with the knowledge that his position is ultimately a precarious one, and arguments throughout the play.[74] In *Troades'* opening lines, Hecuba announces the theme of fickle fortune and the ruler's disposition to his subjects:

> Whoever trusts in power and, being strong,
> Rules the great palaces nor fears the easy gods
> And abandons his gullible mind to happy affairs,
> Let him take a look at me—and you Troy. (*Troades*, lines 1–4)

Hecuba once ruled with Priam in Troy, yet she is now at the mercy of the Greeks as their slave. Throughout *Troades*, Seneca adapts the themes and characters that we saw in *Hecuba*, but the focus on the ideas and actions of those in power is further distilled. Faced with the demand for Polyxena's sacrifice, Agamemnon argues for clemency:

> Why are you besprinkling the noble
> Grave of the distinguished leader with dire murder?
> You should know this thing above all:
> Whatever the victor wishes to do, the victim ought to suffer.
> And yet no one continues a violent regime for long:
> Moderate power endures. (*Troades*, lines 255–59)

In Greek mythology, Agamemnon sacrificed his daughter Iphigeneia at the behest of the goddess Artemis.[75] Iphigeneia's sacrifice takes place in the beginning of the Trojan War, and in Seneca's play the postwar Agamemnon claims that he has learned (*didici*, 264) a lesson from what he has endured.[76] The powerful can do as they please, and sometimes external forces—what the Greeks called *anagkē*, "necessity"—call for extreme actions. But moderation, Agamemnon argues, prevails.

The themes of power, mercy, and self-management (in this case as protest) run throughout the play. The playwright seems to ask the question of whether the lesson of fallen rulers—Hecuba, Agamemnon—can teach an audience, both within the play and outside of it. Hecuba goes as far as to call her experience a *documentum*, a philosophical proof, of the instability of power. Savage rulers such as Pyrrhus, the son of Achilles who killed Priam on an altar, somehow forget (*ignoscit*) their philosophical and moral training. In the play, Pyrrhus is the immediate audience for Agamemnon's lesson. Although the inevitability of the sacrifice is apparent in the response of the prophet, Calchas, the mouthpiece of fate, the possibility of learning the lesson of mercy is also present. In the play's final scene, the young ruler who had been warned about cruelty pauses before slaying his victim: "A spirit so bold strikes the heart of all and—strange prodigy—Pyrrhus is slow to kill" (*Troades*, lines 1153–54). Pyrrhus's hesitancy, which Seneca borrows from Euripides and Ovid, is framed within at least three audiences: Pyrrhus himself, who might be seen as recalling Agamemnon's lesson; the audience within the play that watches the sacrifice; and the play's reader or observer, who recalls the images of Hecuba and Agamemnon earlier in the play. (This third audience could well include Nero.)

Through checks on acquisitiveness, learning from his experience and that of others, and a moral dilemma (antagonism in the form of his father's request), the play requires heroism from Pyrrhus. Agamemnon, who apparently has learned from his experiences, provides a stoic model for the young ruler. Within the context of self-management and the teaching of mercy, Ulysses is a countermodel to Pyrrhus. In Seneca's play, Ulysses is the leader who must seize Troy's last prince, Astyanax, the son of Andromache and Hector, and slay him. (The single human sacrifice in *Hecuba* is doubled in *Troades* as the "audience" witnesses the sacrifice of Polyxena *and* Astyanax, both at the end of the play.) He is a villainous counter to the contrite Agamemnon.

In the play's third act, Andromache has hidden Astyanax, and Ulysses threatens to exhume Hector's grave in hopes of finding the boy there.

Ulysses goes as far as to suggest torturing Andromache, now a slave, to gain information about Astyanax, whose murder the Greeks feel will prevent later vengeance. An earlier critic dismissed the Ulysses scene, along with the entire second half of the play (subsequent to the final decision regarding Polyxena), for its length, excess of characters, and lack of direction.[78] Those later scenes of the play include Helen, and Seneca, as a pedant, might have felt that a play on Troy's fall would be incomplete without a representation of its first cause. The Ulysses scene, specifically, certainly raises the issue of spectatorship, with which (as we find in his prose) Seneca himself was deeply preoccupied. Similar to the Roman audience that watches cruel murders at the gladiatorial contests, Seneca's audience observes, even if just through recitation, Andromache's potential torture in this scene. Later in the play, the audience watches Polyxena's sacrifice and Astyanax's murder. Alternately, Ulysses is a foil to Agamemnon. While the Agamemnon learns from his errors to be merciful, Ulysses increases cruelty to gain his ends because he perceives his power as stable.

A recent critic, Jo-Ann Shelton, argues the opposite, namely that Ulysses actually follows in line with Agamemnon's call for temperance, and that the character "is unexpectedly honest and straightforward" (Shelton 2000, 105). I reject this reading, however, given the implications against the victors throughout the play. The very context that Shelton gives the spectatorship makes Ulysses' actions questionable. Although it is worth comparing the Roman crowd that Seneca describes in one of his letters (*Epistles* 7), as observers of gladiatorial contests, to the crowd in *Troades*, which watches with "sorrow, joy, admiration, relief, and an appreciation for the gravity of their deed" (Shelton 2000, 111), we cannot miss the protest of the victims. Similar to the Senecan hero whom Thomas Rosenmeyer describes as "controlling, prolonging, hastening, enjoying, protesting" death (1989, 59), Astyanax and Polyxena are defiant. Astyanax's death looks more like suicide than murder. The messenger reports that Astyanax "jumped down of his own volition into the midst of Priam's kingdom" (*sponte desiluit sua in media Priami regna*, 1102–3). For parallels to these suicides, we might turn not to merciful rulers who are "unexpectedly honest and straightforward" but to Seneca's own forced suicide under Nero in 65 CE.

In Polyxena's death scene, the fierce girl thrusts herself into the knife's blow (*conversa ad ictum stat truci vultu ferox*, 1152), and she strikes the ground with "an angry thud" (*irato impeto*). The messenger reports her bravery (*animus fortis*) and her readiness for death (*leto obvius*). In her death, Polyxena becomes the victor (*clarius victor gemit*). The messenger scene that describes these murder-suicides is compelling in the way that it synthesizes concerns found throughout Senecan drama about the body, emotions, and protest against *regnum*—power as physical and emotional force, or as the regimes that stand opposed to the individual. Within this context, Astyanax and Polyxena use their bodies and emotions in radical, revolutionary ways. Where arguments for clemency fail, individuals wield an unruly power, even if that power is only a symbolic one: *self*-control or *self*-determination. Within this context, Ulysses is no more powerful than the slaves he seeks to manage. Ultimately both ruler and oppressed answer to fortune (or fate), and perhaps to nobody but themselves.

At the very least, it should be clear that the classics are not monolithic. Greek and Roman literature are part of a broad nexus of images and icons that served the artists who handled them as material for esthetic, political, and social expression. The classics are as diverse as any literature, and some of the ideas and icons that come out of Greco-Roman culture are among the most persistent known to any society. I trust that I have shown how, within the context of classical literature, Ulysses, as a symbol of the classics, is as much the voice of the oppressed as he is the oppressor. More than a symbol, Ulysses is part of the lived experience of the society that handles him. Yet, as Stanford sees, once Greco-Roman antiquity comes to symbolize Western hegemony, Ulysses would do the same. In the American context, the notion of Western hegemony becomes a lens through which black authors view their esthetic, social, and political agendas, and through which others would examine the merit of black authors. We will explore this conundrum later. But first, let us look at the entry of Ulysses, and the classical tradition, into the abyss of race.

# ❧ 3 ❧

# Ulysses Lost on Racial Frontiers

## *The Limits of Classicism in the Modern World*

The notion that black people are human beings is a relatively new discovery in the modern West.

—CORNEL WEST, *The Cornel West Reader*

"If you're white, you're right," I said.

—*Invisible Man* (Protagonist riffing on the well known signification: "If you're white, you're right, if you're brown, stick around, if you're black, stay back.")

Race complicates the issue of classical reception more than any other ideological prism, including class, nationalism, or gender and sexuality. Given this hypothesis, the silence within the academic field of classical studies on questions of race and racism (excepting Frank Snowden) until relatively recent years (post–Black Athena) is curious and more than deafening.[1] Snowden raised the topic of race and the classics in the 1970s,[2] and his works are reflective of efforts in education and the broader culture to implement the political, social, and legal gains of the Civil Rights movement.[3] In this chapter, I am concerned with a genealogy of classical reception as it pertains to race. My genealogy is not exhaustive but rather indicative of the diversity of approaches to antiquity throughout the two millennia or so of the reception of the classical age, and Hellenism, in the West.

A genealogy of classical reception might seem misguided because no one chapter, no one book, can cover the topic.[4] My aim here, however, is narrower and simpler than a *history* of classical reception. I would like, simply, to complicate the idea of a monolith of "the classics" by pointing to the diversity of approaches to the classicism, and here philhellenism in particular, since antiquity. (Here again, Ulysses is emblematic.) Throughout the chapter, I highlight "ruptures and breaks" in the Western narrative of the classics. I hope to invite readers accustomed to viewing the classics in terms of canon, hegemony, and resistance to these to consider alternative takes. As it pertains to the black reception of the classics in the late nineteenth and early twentieth century, I raise questions about the social framework and the literary esthetics that caused African American writers to resist classical influence. Finally, I want to make troublesome the easy dismissal of "black classicism" as conservatism or as a rejection of black esthetics.

It might be necessary, before continuing, to emphasize here that I am *not* suggesting that race-thinking and hegemony did *not* exist both in antiquity and in later European society, or that the classics were *not* used to promote Eurocentrism and racism. The use of the classics to promote "the West," in opposition to the "Orient" and the "dark continent," is irrefutable, and history did not need Martin Bernal to prove the thesis.[5] Yet the sweeping indictment of the classics by Bernal, to whom I shall return later, does not tell the whole story any more than does the race-infused response of his main combatant, Mary Lefkowitz. European classicists of the eighteenth and nineteenth centuries *were* oftentimes racist, as Bernal suggests, and the classics *did* at times become a way of promoting a Eurocentric worldview.[6] Yet rejecting the classics as an intrinsically racist monolith is an evasion that misreads Western history by ignoring the ruptures and breaks in the narrative. Martin Bernal's idea of "models" of viewing the reception of the classics in the *Black Athena* volumes obscured alternative takes, as Jacques Berlinerblau's (1999) arguments suggest. Bernal in essence defined the classics as a Eurocentric and racist ideology. Ideologies, however, are not fixed but grow and change as they interact with new environments, cultures, and values. As an ideology that might at once be modern *and,* on a certain level, racist, the classics did not spring up fully formed, but the discourse *became* racialized as Europe developed. Rather than a conservative acceptance of the status quo, the black reception of the classics might be seen as a co-optation that forces the discourse to expand beyond its role in racism at certain junctures in Western history.

A brief genealogy of the classics shows the extent to which views of classical antiquity have changed from the Hellenistic period to the present. The narrative in this chapter begins with antiquity, moves briefly through the Europeanization of the classics, and ends in the world of modern race discourse. Ulysses guides the reader through the issue of reception, and we see that Ulysses was received differently from period to period, context to context. It should become apparent through the genealogy that the notion of the classics has mutated depending on timeframe, politics, and culture. By complicating the idea of the classics, I hope to reshape the prism through which we view classical influence, particularly on black literature and esthetics.

## Antiquity

The formation of a classical tradition is not seamless; the narrative of the "eternal West" is a fiction.[7] The breaks and ruptures in "the classics" are indeed apparent from as early as classical times. In antiquity, the classical period, particularly of Athens from the fifth century into the fourth (and ending with the death of Alexander in 323 BCE), became a time of glory for the subsequent generation, and the Hellenistic world saw the establishment of a number of standards of reception.[8] That scholars in the Hellenistic period began to think in terms of tradition is evident in the redaction of Homeric epic, the creation of compendia and epitomes, or, more monumentally, the library at Alexandria. This is not to say, however, that the classics *as tradition* became a standard from the Hellenistic period forward. One rupture in the narrative of the classics as a fixed, inherited tradition—the eternal West—was that between Greek and Roman.

As is known to classical scholars, during the Roman Republic a portion of the nobility held a skeptical view of Greece and Greek influence.[9] Even when artistic, social, and political influences became inevitable—when, as the saying goes, "captured Greece held Rome captive"—the overall cultural view of Greece was at best ambivalent. Albert Henrichs (1995) cites the Roman statesman Cato, living in the third century BCE, as one who "despised and pilloried those members of the Roman aristocracy who in his view went too far in their emulation of the Greeks" (243). The seeds of Greece in Italy grow from the eighth century BCE on; cultural contact began early.[10] Classicists also know well that Livius Andronicus's translation of a Greek play in 240 BCE marks the first Roman literature. (Fragments exist of the Greek-slave-turned-author's Latin translation of Homer's *Odyssey.*) Yet, even as late as the first century BCE, Roman authors held the ambivalent position of resisting Greek influence while at the same time clearly and self-consciously being allusive to Greek literature—in fact permeating their writing with Greek philosophy, myth, and literary tropes and topoi.[11]

Henrichs captures a bit of the Roman ambivalence toward Greek influence, which is at core an issue of differences in cultural values:

> Indeed, while Virgil [or Vergil] allows that there were certain endeavours—sculpture, rhetoric, and astronomy, to be precise—in which Romans have made an effort but have failed to reach the superior level of Greek practitioners, the poet's immediate concern is with the comparatively grander and more useful Roman skill of defeating and pacifying other cultures. (257)

The Roman resistance to Greek influence came on the profound level of cultural values, of which artistic and literary esthetics are conduits. This is not to say that Romans had *higher* values than Greeks, unless we view "defeating and pacifying other cultures" as esthetically better than sculpture. Rome saw its primary value, Henrichs concurs, in the building of empire.

We can return to the figure of Ulysses as a way of distilling the problem of Greek influence on Roman esthetics and cultural values. The brief representation of Ulysses in Vergil's *Aeneid,* which was written at Rome between 29 BCE and 19 BCE, further illustrates the contrast between Greek and Roman at the time. This representation, although literary and not historical, is worth a closer look because to some extent the distinction between Ulysses and Vergil's Roman hero Aeneas—and thus between Greek and Roman—is characteristic of the reception of the classics for many subsequent generations. Even Dante seems keenly aware of why Ulysses, and thus Greek values, might not be fitting for the early modern Italian.

In Vergil's *Aeneid,* Ulysses is an implicit foil to Aeneas, who embodies the Roman quality of *pietas,* devotion to family, state, and the gods.[12] In *Aeneid* 2, where the Roman ancestor and subject of Vergil's epic begins to tell the tale of how he escaped Troy's destruction, he implicitly compares himself to Ulysses. Aeneas refers to the Greek hero no less than three times in the first one hundred lines of the book. This is a clear sign of Vergil's self-consciousness about his relationship to Homer and to Greek cultural influence. In Vergil's epic, Aeneas's audience is Dido, the African queen, who is also enamored of Greek achievement (in this case, military achievement).

(What is ironic, given our purpose here, is that Dido's infatuation with Aeneas destroys her imperial project. Yet fate destroys her not because the Greeks had influenced her. Greek influence inspired her project of Empire. Rather, *Italy* destroys Carthage because Dido's love for Aeneas overpowers her.)

Aeneas prefaces his narrative of *pietas*—how he carried his gods, his son, and his father from burning Troy—with the suggestion that even Ulysses, *dirus,* would cry at hearing the tale (line 7). In Lewis and Short's Latin dictionary, *dirus,* "fearful, awful," is synonymous with words for savageness, cruelty, and madness induced by anger, and in one word Aeneas communicates a different Ulysses from the Homer's *Odyssey,* where Odysseus is often empathetic, does in fact cry, and is far from savage.[13] Later in Aeneas's narrative, Ulysses is negatively implicated for his cunning (lines 44–45, and lines 97–99), as are the Greeks at large. ('Beware of Greeks even bearing gifts.') The Greeks dissimilate through Ulysses' idea of the wooden horse, presented to the Trojans as a gift, but bearing Greek soldiers who will empty its belly and sack Troy under the cover of night.

The contrasts and distinctions between Aeneas and Ulysses abound, and these distinctions mark alternative cultural esthetics. Aeneas is forced into wandering, while Ulysses, to some extent, wanders voluntarily. (Dante certainly read it this way, as we see in *Inferno,* Canto 26.[14]) Aeneas is devoted to family and state; Ulysses leaves these for heroic adventure. Ulysses returns home only to depart again to untold adventures. Through the Roman—and later Italian—prism, Ulysses, as Stanford confirms, would influence the European imagination for many subsequent centuries. That Ulyssean values were undesirable to many later Europeans parallels to some extent the ambivalence toward Greek influence at Rome. In later Europe, the supremacy of Roman esthetics over Hellenism held, for a time, because many readers, including Shakespeare, Chaucer, and Petrarch, could not read Greek and therefore saw the culture not through their own language but through the additional filter of Latin translation and Roman influence. And yet later, the Romantics would value Greek over Roman—and not necessarily the Greek of Euripidean tragedy.[15]

The Roman reception of the Greek classics in antiquity, as seen in Vergil's treatment of Ulysses, is worth considering in the context of a black Ulysses for at least two reasons. In the first place, the relationship between Greece and Rome in many respects parallels that between the classics and black authors. In each case, the former (Greek/classics) undeniably influences the latter (Roman/black), but Romans, similar to black American authors nearly two millennia later, are of two minds about this influence. Is the influence a fruitful insemination, or is it a shameful stain, a remnant of undesirable miscegenation? The bicultural (or multicultural) offspring of the mixture, which in the literary context are works like *Song of Solomon* and *Invisible Man,* contains artistic miscegenation despite any and every attempt to conceal it. These works are contaminated (borrowing from the Latin *contaminatio,* which refers to the weaving together of various Greek plays in the African Terence's Roman adaptations) despite their every attempt, if I may now borrow a common trope from African American (and American) literature, to "pass" (as in the American context, to "pass" as *black*).

The relationship between Greek and Roman traditions is important for at least a second reason: It causes a rupture in the narrative of the Western tradition, which is otherwise presented as seamless (Amin's eternal West). The notion of narrative, Aeneas's narrative of what is essentially the beginning of Rome in contrast to Ulysses' Greek narrative of adventure, which in some ways makes mythical Europe's (imperialistic?) interaction with the then-known world, is a fitting one in considering the classical tradition.[16] Vergil's *Aeneid,* with its rewriting of what it means to be Greek, along with its inscribing of Rome, is emblematic of the breaks and ruptures in a European reception that Bernal, for one, communicates as a fixed ideology.

## Black Athena: Revising the Europeanization of the Classics

The next period in the reception of the classics is the period of Europeanization. During this period Eurocentrism begins to take hold. With the rise of Eurocentrism we find, as Bernal argues, writers valorizing classical antiquity to affirm European ascendancy.[17] Without delving too deeply into discussions of medieval Europe, the Enlightenment and Renaissance, or Romanticism, it should be a sufficient corrective to the prevailing notion to speak of the Europeanization of the classics in terms of diversity (and ruptures and breaks as evidence of diversity). While the European author's identification with the classics, and the sense of identity that came with the recovery of classical texts, is undeniable, authors approached the classics with a greater diversity of perspectives than the ideologies of racism or Eurocentrism allow. (Again, this is not to negate the damaging and prevailing force of Eurocentric interpretation.)

Despite the obscurity of the classics to many at various times in European history, the fascination with a classical past, variously defined and reshaped, was a constant. What varied was how authors reconstructed the past, and what materials they had for that reconstruction. While Boethius, as one example, might have held Odysseus as type of the human being in his mortal, rational, and spiritual manifestation, Petrarch would view Ulysses in 1360 through the prism of a Latin translation.[18] Petrarch, who did not read Greek, asked Leontius Pilatus to translate Homer's *Odyssey* into Latin for him.[19] The esthetics would shift when learning Greek once again became the prevailing mode for scholars. With a new access to Greek texts, some European authors continued to hold Latin at a higher value than Greek literature, while others praised Greek esthetics, particularly in drama and poetry, over Roman.[20] In sum, the ideological prisms through which Europeans viewed the classical past included an ever-increasing Eurocentrism, Romanticism, and Christianity.[21] (In the latter case, the reader might recall that Christianity was not an exclusively European ideology; Christianity was known to African ideology from early on.)

It was during this period of Europeanization that, as Bernal argues, authors began to shape the classics as a hegemonic ideology that included racism. Bernal's argued that the view we currently hold of Greek civilization originated in the late eighteenth and early nineteenth century, in a racist Europe (Bernal 1987, 1–73):

> To recapitulate: it is certain that Locke and most eighteenth-century English-speaking thinkers like David Hume and Benjamin Franklin were racist: They openly expressed popular opinions that dark skin colour was linked to moral and mental inferiority. In Hume's case, racism so transcended conventional religion that he was a pioneer of the view that there had been not one creation of man but many different ones, because "Such a uniform and constant difference could not happen in so many countries and ages, if nature had not made an original distinction betwixt these breeds of men."

The centrality of racism to European society after 1700 is shown by the fact that this "polygenetic" view of human origins continued to grow in the early nineteenth century, even after the revival of Christianity. (203–4)

Bernal asserts that "whatever form it took, the new principle of ethnicity pervaded all areas of life and scholarship" (239). In the area of classical scholarship, Bernal sees the approach of Europe to the past as tantamount to what he calls the Aryan model, which resulted primarily from a Eurocentric unwillingness to acknowledge the influence of non-Indo-European peoples on ancient Greece.[22] Race in the modern world becomes one of the ideological prisms (and arguably the most important one) through which Europe would view the past. The effect of this prism on the modern psyche is a little acknowledged concern in circles that celebrate the classical heritage and its resultant literary canons.

Classical scholars concentrated on Bernal's errors in the area of philology, his approach to classical myth, and his errors in the area of source-criticism.[23] As we will see, the response to Bernal within the classics was at times infused with a curious protectiveness. Some of the response, however, raised legitimate concerns about ruptures in the narrative of Eurocentrism and racism that Bernal sought to advance. Suzanne Marchard and Anthony Grafton (1997), for example, argued that there was no Aryan model of viewing the classics but rather competing approaches to the past. Bernal attempted to show that the accepted connection in ancient Greece between Europe and Africa (particularly Egypt) was deliberately denied in modern Europe for racist reasons. In contrast, Marchard and Grafton see that while classicists such as K. F. Hermann (ca. 1830s) rejected the historicity of narratives linking Greece to Egypt, others, such as Jacob Bernays (1824–1881), looked consistently to the ancient Near East for their understanding of ancient Greek culture. Jacques Berlinerblau (1999) best characterized Bernal's efforts to revise, in a sweeping narrative, the European reception of the classics, his Aryan model, as "big picturism" (Berlinerblau 1999, 15, 23), a tendency to organize data in terms of systems of thought. Yet despite Bernal's factual errors and narrative approach, the response of some classical scholars, as we shall see, belied the posture of scholarly objectivity and reinforced the premise of racism.

Before looking at the response to Bernal, it is worth considering the way in which twentieth-century race-discourse influenced his narrative of Europe's reception of the classics. In other words, it is important to see the construction of narratives from all sides and not just from the perspective of the classics as a racist discourse. Bernal claimed that the Aryan model in Europe replaced an older model, the Ancient model. The restoration of the Ancient model, Bernal claimed, would show the extent to which Greece saw itself through the eyes of Africa.[24]

As we know, Bernal used myths, to a great extent, to support his premise of an Egyptian colonization of the Peloponnese in the second millennium BCE.[25] One particular myth (of the daughters of Danaus) gives an example of the seductiveness of this approach.[26] Danaus, who was the brother of Aegyptus (eponymous for Egypt), escaped to Argos with his fifty daughters, but Aegyptus's sons were still able to force the girls into marriage. The daughters, however, agreed among themselves to murder their cousins. Hypermestra was the only girl who did not follow through (Rankine 2005). The offspring of Hypermestra's union with Lynceus included many notable figures from Greek mythology, including Danae, the mother of Perseus, and, later, Herakles. Bernal uses myth of the daughters of Danaus to demonstrate the linkage between Greeks and Egyptians in myth, which he takes as evidence for actual colonization.

Building these arguments around the "source" Herodotus and what Bernal asserts to be linguistic and cultural links, the British scholar goes as far as to assert that Athena was in origin an Egyptian goddess and, as such, black. The outcry against Bernal's source-criticism and his general approach to mythology was resounding (Lefkowitz 1996), and his assertion of the blackness of ancient Egypt was, by his own admission, to a great extent a marketing ploy (Berlinerblau 1999). Thus whatever the merits of Bernal's narrative of eighteenth and nineteenth century Eurocentric classicism, the premise of race led him to a "fabrication" of his own, that of the Ancient and Aryan models, neither of which is necessarily a viable framework for studying the past. Rather, these models are inventions that aid Bernal in creating his "big picture." At the same time, Bernal's racially charged presentation met a response of equal valence.

While it would be unfair to ask classical scholars to take the moral high ground and avoid polemics, given Bernal's polemical stance toward the field, the general response to the Black Athena debate within the classics demonstrated the extent to which the twentieth century discourse of classics was now irrevocably mired in race. The Black Athena debate would not be the last word on race and the classics, as later writing in the classics and, more curiously, the advent of the study of black classicism would make clear.[27] Combatants in the Black Athena debate, however, demonstrated how deeply personal a stake was had in its outcome.

Of the most polemical classicists, Mary Lefkowitz was tantamount to Bernal's nemesis in a cosmic conflict, and she accused him being a bedfellow of Afrocentrists—clearly an insult in her eyes. As Berlinerblau attests, Afrocentrism, to name a counterhegemonic, affirmation of the black self in various articulations, is a perspective and a movement that has existed at least as long as the cultural hegemony of the West.[28] What I am suggesting here is the Afrocentric premise, which at core is an assertion of the black American's otherness, might govern any assertion of a black cultural experience independent of Western influence. Such pursuits as the tracing of non-European genealogy, for example, might even be labeled Afrocentric. Such an urge to connect to one's past is not questioned in the context of other American experiences, be it Irish, Italian, or Spanish. Yet for black genealogists the standard is somehow different.

As Stephen Howe (1998) demonstrates in his book, Afrocentrism, as an essentialist reality, is as troublesome as Eurocentrism. Afrocentrism, similar to its European counterpart, is an insufficient, often-flawed, human attempt to account for a given reality.[29] My corrective to the negative reception of Afrocentrism should not serve to dismiss the troublesome nature of any deliberately dishonest reconstruction of the past, which characterized a portion of Afrocentric thought.[30] Even in the nineteenth century, black writers, such as the classicist Wilmont Blyden, used their learning to revise the vision of blacks that many of their European counterparts held. The symbolic centrality of Africa to a particular worldview (once called Ethiopianism) was as important to black writers as was Indo-European and its symbolism to Western writers. As an expression of an African reality other than the one that scholars, political leaders, and slaveholders parlayed, an Afrocentric perspective might even be found in Phillis Wheatley's celebration of Terence in her poem.[31] Even as slaves, black people in the New World brought fragments of African cultures with them, reshaping them to fill the spaces left in the Middle Passage across the Atlantic Ocean.[32] These fragments, once reconstructed in the New World with their influences, formed some of the fundaments of modern American culture, finding expression everywhere, from Negro spirituals and the blues, to the idioms of American English and narratives of freedom penned by former slaves. African American and white American thinkers have for centuries, without trivializing or sensationalizing, accounted for the African contribution in the New World.

The New World—of modernity, industry, and exploration—would, by its very existence, color Ulysses black. This is not to say that Afrocentrism became an essential, black way of thinking in opposition to the mainstream. Similar to its European counterparts, Afrocentrism exists in many forms and degrees, sometimes as fractional truths, sometimes as falsehoods, but always as a way of viewing the world and organizing experience.[33] Nevertheless, Lefkowitz dismissed Afrocentrism, and Bernal with it, as a peripheral and dangerous monolith.[34]

Lefkowitz fell into a deep trap of race-bating. Her proverbial "shot heard round the world" came in a 1992 magazine article titled "Not Out of Africa: The Origins of Greece and the Illusions of Afrocentrists," in which she presents Afrocentrism as an unscholarly, often disingenuous, rewriting of the past resulting from a need for black Americans to see themselves as part of a legacy:[35]

> It was inevitable, therefore, that the black peoples in the English-speaking countries of this continent, as they developed a sense of their own identity, would want to show that they had a stake in the cultural legacy of Greece. (31)

For Lefkowitz, Afrocentrism is a way of revising history to fill a void in the present. She asserts that Marcus Garvey, who led a nationalist movement at the beginning of the twentieth century, "needed the past to show that it was not the fault of black people that they appeared to have no great historical achievements to look back on" (31).[36] Bernal's invention of an Ancient model, namely the idea that the ancient Greeks were well aware of their "Afroasiatic" origins, obscured later because of European racism, is to Lefkowitz's mind a dangerous tool in the hands of Afrocentrists: "To the extent that Bernal has helped to provide an apparently respectable underpinning for Afrocentric fantasies, he must be held culpable, even if his intentions are honorable and his motives are sincere" (35).

I will leave aside the demonizing of "Afrocentric fantasies," mostly articulated in the works of those *black* writers who also "must be held culpable," and the contrast in the potential exoneration of Bernal, a *white*, British scholar, as possibly having "honorable" intentions and "sincere" motives. Suffice it to say that by claiming that Bernal gave Afrocentrism the appearance of respectability, Lefkowitz more than suggests the opposite of Afrocentric scholars.[37]

Despite the fact that as a feature of modernity the classics are, for many, tantamount to a racist ideology, scholars in the culture wars and beyond continue to dismiss efforts at diversity in classical studies as more an issue of self-esteem and—that undesirable mongrel—multiculturalism.[38] As I will discuss in the next section, in the context of a black esthetic, the dismissal of the classics would hold form, the role of classical texts in the ongoing and changing construction of identity notwithstanding. Cornel West's linkage of modernity with race demonstrates the force of this argument:

> The notion that black people are human beings is a relatively new discovery in the modern West. The idea of black equality in beauty, culture and intellectual capacity remains problematic and controversial within prestigious halls of learning and sophisticated intellectual circles. The Afro-American encounter with the modern world has been shaped first and foremost by the doctrine of white supremacy, which is embodied in institutional practices and enacted in everyday folkways under varying circumstances and evolving conditions. (70)

West goes as far as to say that black humanity had to be discovered. (We might compare this to the invention of the printing press or the light bulb.) The contrary, black *lack of humanity,* was affirmed by notions of beauty and culture, the conglomerate of which West sees as tantamount to white supremacy. Given the polemical nature of race-discourse, rewriting the Europeanization of the classics has at times meant the complete evasion of discourse across racial lines.

## No Black Ulysses: The African American Evasion of the Classics

Throughout the twentieth century, and especially in America during segregation times, one literary response to modernity has been to deny mutual influence at all cost. On the white American side of things, authors failed to acknowledge black influence, even where that contact was, at least for African Americans, obvious. (In Europe, Pablo Picasso's cubism, with its indelible African mask, is a ready example.) T. S. Eliot (1965) could talk about "the American idiom" without mentioning how slavery and the presence of enslaved Africans in America were primary causes of these particular inflections in the local language. To Ellison's mind, however, the America of Twain and Faulkner was clearly as black inflected as it was classically trained (Ellison 1966a). The evasion of race would continue to be the case until at least the 1970s, after which point black was desirable, and Norman Mailer could appropriate blackness, or "coolness" and "the hip," through the "white Negro" (Mailer 1957).

In the area of black literature, the two dominant waves in the twentieth century—the New Negro and the Black Aesthetics movement—were to be assertions of artistic and cultural independence. Despite their schooling at elite American institutions and, at times, their own affinity for the material, black writers were, in many implicit and explicit ways, asked to pursue their esthetic projects as if they were independent from the broader culture—or at least their works were to be easily distinguished as *Negro*. (This is what Ellison inveighs against when he says he is a writer, not a *Negro* writer.)

In Alain Locke's 1925 essay, "The New Negro," the Howard University philosopher lays out a political, social, and esthetic agenda for blacks in a segregated America. He sees that, with the shift in Negro populations from the South to northern urban centers, of which New York's Harlem was emblematic, a new Negro was emerging. This Negro, who "seems suddenly to have slipped from under the tyranny of social intimidation and to be shaking off the psychology of imitation and implied inferiority" (4), would create a continuum from Negro spirituals and folk-music to twentieth-century art forms.[39] There are many noteworthy imperatives in Locke's essay, including the observation that it was "the rank and file who are leading, and the leaders who are following" (7). This statement comes in direct contrast to W. E. B. Du Bois' "talented tenth" notion, the idea that change would come not from the black masses but from the elite (Du Bois [1903] 2003). Most importantly here, Locke called for an unprecedented Negro independence: "However, this new phase of things is delicate; it will call for less charity but more justice; less help, but infinitely closer understanding" (Locke, 10). Politically, blacks would of necessity be what Locke calls "forced radicals" (11) because of the previous psychological and social oppression. He points to an international, "growing group consciousness of the dark-peoples" (15).

Although Locke does not say directly that the new Negro consciousness, to allow itself a separate, organic identity, would have to put aside white influence, at least ostensibly, this is more than implicit. The posture of independence is ironic, given on the one hand the role that white patrons played in the lives and works of such Harlem Renaissance artists as Langston Hughes.[40] The posture is also ironic given that classical influence, as one example of interdependence, permeated the works of African American writers from the previous generation. In her 1892 book, *A Voice from the South,* Anna Julia Cooper infuses her writing with classical references and allusions to support a radical thesis: Black women should be educated—even in Greek—in order to lead the education of Negroes. Cooper cites such examples as Sappho and Aspasia:

> Aspasia, the earliest queen of the drawing-room, a century later ministered to the intellectual entertainment of Socrates and the leading wits and philosophers of her time. Indeed, to her is attributed the authorship of one of the most noted speeches ever delivered by Pericles. (1998, 62–63)

Cooper supports the hypothesis that, even with the overwhelming, forced radicalism, to borrow Locke's notion, of blacks throughout the twentieth century, the classics were used in a previous generation to support radical political, social, and esthetic agendas. Works of black literature, such as W. E. B. Du Bois' *The Quest of the Silver Fleece* (1911), unabashedly adapted classical myth in strongly associative ways.

In addition to the shifts in educational priorities throughout America (discussed in chapter one), I attribute the move away from the black classicism of the late nineteenth to early twentieth century to the rise of a new African American esthetic that would develop throughout the twentieth century. Culturally and intellectually, segregation would reify the distinction between black and white esthetics, even as segregation reified a social and political reality. Even black authors who were classically trained explored the European esthetic in their work at great peril. In chapter 4, I speculate as to whether the return to a classical theme in his 1935 *Medea* was somehow symptomatic of the sudden demise of Countee Cullen, a poet and *infant terrible* of the Harlem Renaissance. Certainly by the time of Richard Wright's *Native Son* (1940), black literature was taking an even more radical turn than the New Negro could sustain.

The new direction of an esthetics marked, in part but not exclusively by violence and frustration, which we see in *Native Son,* was justified, given the ongoing and increasing violence against blacks throughout the twentieth century in segregation, urban poverty, and lynching.[41] If Locke merely suggested a rejection of classical esthetics in his 1925 essay, that rejection would be made emphatic in the Black Arts movement begun around 1965. In his suggestively titled essay, "Cultural Strangulation: Black Literature and the White Aesthetic," Addison Gayle Jr. anchored his rejection of the West in the classical period:

> Let us propose Greece as the logical starting point, bearing in mind Will Durant's observation that "all of Western Civilization is but a footnote to Plato," and take Plato as the first writer to attempt a systematic aesthetic. Two documents by Plato, *The Symposium* and *The Republic*, reveal twin components of Plato's aesthetic system. (40)

Gayle never clearly articulates what he means by the "twin components" of Plato's system, although he is likely referring to the distinction (which he does address) between the sphere of Forms, on the one hand, and the "earthy mirror" (40) of those Forms in the world around us. (Or perhaps he is directly referring to the dichotomy between black and white.) Gayle argues that while Plato "defines beauty" as a reflection of the Forms on earth, "only in ambiguous, mystical terms" (41), Western writers, as primarily white, "have defined beauty in terms of whiteness" (41). Gayle's critique locates the problem not in Plato or the classics per se but in their reception (in fact he speaks of the "distortion of the Platonic ideal," 44). Yet a general suspicion of the West had already been inscribed, and a new esthetic was being called for: "The acceptance of the phrase 'Black is Beautiful' is the first step in the destruction of the old table of laws and the construction of new ones, for the phrase flies in the face of the whole ethos of the white aesthetic" (46). The Black Aesthetics movement left an indelible mark on black literature, and we find that a Black Arts literary project continued for many writers after 1975 (Smethurst 2005).

Returning to Cornel West's notion of race and modernity, we find that, given the clear evidence of race-discourse in the construction of the "eternal West," a black writer's evasion of race would be tantamount to social death. Yet white writers could simply look the other way. Harold Bloom, in his exaltation of Ralph Ellison and Toni Morrison, praises these writers vis-à-vis the "Western tradition," yet he evades the issue of race—its relevance, how and why it matters, its social, political, and esthetic implications— almost entirely (as if these authors wrote magnificent works in a vacuum or just happened to be black). As Houston A. Baker (1984) and Jerry Gafio Watts (1994) intimate, the way in which Ralph Ellison handled the issue of race in his presentation of himself and his work had dire political— and esthetic—consequences. Critics more than suggest that if an African American makes bedfellows with the classics, he or she *must* care little about racial uplift. While I would like to rectify this misperception, the need for an aggressively self-conscious racial awareness is a caveat to black classicism. When Toni Morrison, in a discussion that touched upon her understanding of Ulysses (covered more fully in the next chapter), says that black men move (or travel) as well but "they don't have land, they don't have dominion" (Taylor-Guthrie 1994, 26), she is self-consciously moving the argument away from her work as an individual to its relevance *within community.*

Morrison's discussion comes up more fully in the next chapter, but suffice it to say in this context that Ellison somehow failed to inscribe his Ulysses *within community* in his discussions of race and *Invisible Man.* Within the novel, it might be argued that Ellison demonstrates his racial consciousness—though even this is arguable to some, given his negative depiction of the fictional black nationalist, Ras the Exhorter.[42] Ellison sets up what Morrison (as we see in her words above) might deem a false equality between his protagonist and Ulysses. Ulysses has power, or at least he will regain a power he once held, as king of Ithaca. But what political power does Ellison's protagonist have, as a descendant of slaves living in a segregated society? How can an integrationist posture be seen, in this context, as anything but accommodation? Ellison somehow wants his black Ulysses to speak as an individual, while Morrison wants to "trace" her Ulysses "historically," asserting that "one never knows what would have been the case if *we'd* never been tampered with at all" (26, my italics). For Morrison more explicitly than for Ellison, black humanism— the potential for a black heroism, and the question of tradition and influence for a black writer—is a direct byproduct of a broader collective experience.

Morrison embraces the classics in her fiction as much as Ellison does, but she is craftier in her public rejection of it in interviews. (In fairness to Ellison, Morrison might have had the luxury of hindsight and a more integrated space for public discourse than Ellison.) Both authors implicitly see that, despite the reality of race in the modern—and postmodern— world, to reject the classics as a monolith that is intrinsically racist and

nothing else is also an evasion, one that misreads the literature by ignoring the clandestine contact in black and white since the very beginning.

Some of the sociopolitical dynamics of the emersion of the classics
in race-discourse by the close of the twentieth century (and the evasion
from it prior to that) should be clear by now—first to begin to redefine
the scope of classicism, then to indicate some problems in dismissing the
classics wholesale as a racist discourse, and finally to give a framework
for why Western influence—the classics, tradition, the canon—might be
a touchy subject for African American authors. In the next chapter, I begin
to chart a way out of the abyss, to borrow again from the notion of the
heroic journey. Although discussions have at times devolved in polemics,
the experience of Western literature has been enhanced because of blackness, or what I ultimately refer to, borrowing a trope from Houston A.
Baker, as the black (w)hole. More specifically, I offer a reading of two particular works of African American literature before turning, in chapter 5,
to Ralph Ellison literary corpus. Those works are Countee Cullen's *Medea*
and Toni Morrison's *Song of Solomon.*

# ⇒ 4 ⇐

# The New Negro Ulysses

*Classicism in African American Literature
as a Return from the Black (W)hole*

CLARKE: I hope Mr. Hill can be brief with this exaggeration of the
   role of Ralph Ellison who has spent so much time in the last ten
   years in flight from his own people and has not even answered
   most mail addressed to him by his fellow black writers and has
   said positively that art and literature are not radical.

HILL: Let me say that I do not see how any intelligent person not
   committed to a previous bias can read *Invisible Man* and affirm
   that Mr. Ellison stands aside from the struggle for racial justice in
   the United States.

   —JOHN HENRIK CLARKE and HERBERT HILL,
      Negro Writers Conference, 1961. Excerpts from Harold
      Cruse, *The Crisis of the Negro Intellectual*

For African American authors, the use of classical motifs or emblems of
Western heritage has always had attendant political consequences. Since
Phillis Wheatley first showed "an inclination for the Latin tongue" in 1773,
black American authors who dabble in the classics have consistently met
a peculiar set of responses.[1] Wheatley's reception among critics is emblematic of the reaction to black classicism historically. The reactions, moreover, have fallen along racial lines. For white critics, African American
classicism has either been a proof of the educability of the black mind or
of its hopeless mediocrity, depending on the political orientation of the
analyst. Needless to say, many black critics would rather begin from the
starting point of an entirely new esthetics.

   In this chapter, I offer a close reading of Countee Cullen's *Medea* and
Toni Morrison's *Song of Solomon*. When not rejecting a black classicist text

as somehow washed-out, critics have read such works, under which rubric I am placing these texts of Cullen and Morrison, as somehow directly subversive—as expressly calling upon the classics only to reject them. The literary process, I believe, is more complicated than this. My reading of Cullen and Morrison draws from Houston A. Baker's concept of the black (w)hole, a trope for reading black literature, as a way of talking about a possible return from the readings of these texts that take into account race and little else. The reader will note that while I use reception, and particularly the reception of Phillis Wheatley's corpus, as a way of framing this chapter, I do not spend much time on the eighteenth-century poet. Instead, I focus on two specific works of twentieth-century fiction because Wheatley has already undergone substantial scrutiny in this area.[2]

The controversy surrounding Phillis Wheatley's classicism has been well documented.[3] The letter "To The Publik" that appeared in her volume signaled the need, on the part of Wheatley's master, to authenticate the body of poetry, suggesting that her primarily white audience would not otherwise credit the erudite verses of a black woman, who was formerly a slave.[4] The atmosphere surrounding the phenomenon of black literacy in general, and classicism more specifically, is perhaps best characterized in Thomas Jefferson's comment that Wheatley's poetry was "beneath the dignity of criticism."[5] Alternately, Wheatley's poetry, similar to the slave narratives that would emerge by the early nineteenth century as standard abolitionist reading, would help to build an argument against slavery and the unjust treatment of blacks.[6] But this would not occur without the significant personal expenditure on the part of the poet, who died in poverty in 1784.[7]

Nor would there be safe harbor for the black classicist among African Americans. The perception of classics as a hegemonic discourse would prevent black authors from being taken at face value as artists attempting to master their craft, whether that of lyric poetry, drama, or the novel, while at the same time being social and political persons, being "forced radicals," to borrow Alain Locke's notion from *The New Negro*. The black author who indulges in classical forms, as the reception would attest, must either be using them in outright protest, or that author has "sold out" to market forces. The dilemma is best summarized in Robert Kendrick's essay on Wheatley:

> Wheatley's critics are divided into two camps—those who contend that
> Wheatley critiques white oppression through the skillful use of biblical and

classical references, and those who contend that Wheatley used her poetry
to assimilate into the dominant culture. (1996, 71)

Indeed the reader of Wheatley is immediately confronted with her negoti-
ation of the symbolism of Western hegemony—both Christianity and the
classics. But these features of her poetic identity, along with what might
seem to some her disparagement of the African race, need not be set in a
Procrustean bed either of protest against or of complicity with mainstream
American currents.[8] Rather, Wheatley's language and attitude are inescapable characteristics of her time. Her dedication "To Maecenas," which
Cynthia J. Smith (1989) reads as her invocation to an "ideal reader" within
a flawed American society, is as much a classical, rhetorical strategy as it is
a self-conscious inscription of her identity, as a black slave, into that tradition.[9] Similar to Wheatley's idea of poetry as a "sacred flame," the classical
trope demonstrates Wheatley's acquaintance with the rhetorical strategies
of elegy. Nevertheless, Wheatley does present herself as a black poet, and
she inscribes herself (in "To Maecenas" and elsewhere) in a tradition that
knew Terence, the Afro-Roman comedian to whom "alone of *Afric's* fable
race" the Muses have bestowed their "partial grace."[10] Wheatley's self-
awareness as a black, female poet—and of her slave heritage—denies outright assimilation, but her visceral objection to her plight also falls well
short of Black Nationalism.[11] (It might be argued that from the moment
Wheatley gained literacy in English she had already, to some extent, begun
"to assimilate into the dominant culture" [Kendrick, 71]. Latin was only
another step in her cultural immersion.) Black critics perhaps ask a bit too
much of Wheatley, while white critics expect too little of her.
    The determining factors in Wheatley's reception among American crit-
ics would diminish only fractionally with time, as the nation moved from
slavery, to emancipation, reconstruction, segregation, and, later, the Civil
Rights movement. The critique of Wheatley's classicism would reverberate
through the twentieth century in the critical reception that Countee Cullen
met after 1935 to his *Medea*.[12] The circumstances surrounding Cullen's production of classical theater were certainly different, since he had already
gained a stellar reputation as one of the bright young talents of the Harlem
Renaissance.[13] Nevertheless, despite the fact that his classical training formerly recommended him among the literary elite (black and white alike),
his return to a classical theme would be concomitant with his artistic demise. Again, the rebukes would come from both white and black critics.

The *New York Times* review of Cullen's play was patronizing of what the reviewer saw as the folk adaptation of classical material (Corti 1998).[14] The reviewer did not see that the success or failure of Cullen's adaptation was to some extent a separate issue from the use of a folk idiom to translate the classics into a modern language. Folklore was in vogue, among black and white writers alike, as the expression of an authentic cultural reality.[15] The fragmentation of classical mythology into folk forms was central to the modernist literary outlook, as T. S. Eliot attested in America, James Joyce in Ireland, and numerous other writers worldwide. Cullen, as a writer of the *Negro* Renaissance, was not to be read squarely in the context of the modernists. Yet mainstream critics were in some regards more forgiving than those of the Harlem Renaissance. Writing about Cullen's late works, of which *Medea* is a part, one recent author concluded that "with his rejection of race, Cullen concentrates on the essentially fatuous literary artificialities which were, according to him, the poet's true concern."[16]

The reception of Wheatley and Cullen gives us a different insight (outside of, for example, Ralph Ellison's rejection of communism) into why *Invisible Man,* which the author himself advertises as a kind of crossover (or, equally troublesome, universal) novel, met such disparate responses. The quotation at the beginning of this chapter conveys the range of sentiments toward Ellison for his esthetic and political choices. Put otherwise, the idea of black classicism might be posed as the question of what happens when an African American author explicitly invokes his or her white audience, when he or she deliberately and self-consciously calls outside of a black audience.[17] While this question is worth considering in depth, it is also an unavoidable truth that even writers of the Harlem Renaissance would have correctly, and necessarily (Cruse 1984), imagined whites as part of—if not the major part of—their audience.

Perhaps an equally provocative question is how the black writer, since whites have always made up a great part of his or her audience, represents cultural experiences authentically so as to resonate with his or her black readership as well. Given this set of considerations, black classicism might be reimagined as the removal of a guise of cultural authenticity vis-à-vis a particular segment of American society. Nor does this reimagining mean the rejection of any real, or authentic, blackness on the artist's part. Rather, the black classicist has come clean with his or her audience. The black classicist has admitted that he or she can be committed both to his or her cultural identity and to the mastery of a certain craft. Such a confession would inevitably alienate some while inviting others.

Given the at-times self-imposed psychological and sociological isolation of some African American writers, such as the pose of authenticity that often means the rejection of overtly Western forms (and the rejection of a particular audience), the relationship between black authors and the classics might be envisioned as a return from the black (w)hole.[18] As we recall, in *Blues, Ideology, and Afro-American Literature,* Houston A. Baker (1984) characterized the core of black literature in terms of a black hole:

> A black hole is "an area of space which appears absolutely black because the gravitation there is so intense that not even light can escape into the surrounding areas." Such areas are posited by the General Theory of Relativity as unimaginably dense remains of stars. They may be only a few miles in diameter yet contain the entire mass of a star three times larger than the sun. The area marked by the black hole is dark because an initially luminescent star has, in its burning, converted energy to mass. (It has become a "massive concentration," one might say, invoking the term *Mascon,* first appropriated to Afro-American literary criticism by Stephen Henderson.) (Baker, 144)

The massive concentration of African American literature and its critique, as Baker sees it, has centered on two compelling motifs subsumed in the trope of the black (w)hole. First, the blues sensibility has been one of the pivotal sites of black cultural and literary expression.[19] As an organic art form that emerged from a particular condition and response, the blues is black, and black is beautiful. In his struggle to come to terms with Louis Armstrong's "what did I do to be so black and blue" (*Invisible Man,* 8), the protagonist of *Invisible Man* recognizes that this blues of blackness forms a great part of his identity (O'Meally 1980). Slavery, discrimination, and segregation were all features of his American odyssey. While these are negative, black (in its traditional sense) experiences, they have contributed to the formation of an African American self. Richard Wright, whom Baker argues is the quintessential example of writing in the black (w)hole, "linguistically structures desire—the vision and feeling of a *black blues life*—as universal symbol" (147). The blues symbol is forged from Wright's experiences growing up in Mississippi as characterized in *Black Boy.* Wright fashions his sense of self—and his personal integrity—from these experiences: "Further, in the script of Afro-America, the hole is the domain of *Wholeness,* an achieved relationality of black community in which desire recollects experience and sends it forth as blues" (Baker, 151).

A second motif within the black (w)hole is what Baker calls the "discourse of zero" (149). This discourse is a black esthetic response to the frustrated desire that is sometimes experienced within American society.[20] Here again, Baker uses Wright's narrative to characterize the categorical rejection from white society that the writer felt as a young man, and his response to it. The categorical rejection of African Americans, which historically occurred in Wright's case first in terms of segregation, amounts, Baker proffers, to a rite of passage. Indeed Elizabeth Alexander (1995) cataloged the feelings of young black men like Shelby Steele and Muhammad Ali to the lynching of Emmett Till in 1955. (We will return to Alexander's work and lynching in chapter 6, but for the time being it is important to realize that American practices such as lynching, historically, welcome blacks in America to the cultural markers of their identity and the obstacles to their success.) Lynching is certainly one of the rites of passages that result in the zero-sum discourse to which Baker refers. With the decline of lynching, police brutality and surveillance distinguish the black experience as at once wholly American and at the same time other (Thompson 1999). The esthetic response to living behind "the veil" of blackness, to borrow W. E. B. Du Bois' metaphor (from *The Souls of Black Folk*), has been a zero-sum game. When the black youth being initiated into American culture "becomes aware that he can never 'reintegrate' into a dominantly white society with a 'socially responsible' status," he moves toward a natural gravitational pull:

> What is possible is *entry* into the singularity at the black (W)hole's center. This *singularity* consists of an initiated, expressive black *community* that has "gotten the [white world's] picture," used it to fuel retreat, found the center of its own singular desire, and given expressive form to a new and meaningful *Black (W)holeness.* (Baker, 154)

It is a significant point that for Baker the trope of the black (w)hole in Ralph Ellison's *Invisible Man* appears in the character of Trueblood. Trueblood is the blues-singing sharecropper (a man who, it seems, has impregnated his own daughter), whom the protagonist and others try unsuccessfully to hide from the white gaze—and to whom the white philanthropist Mr. Norton is so powerfully drawn.[21] Trueblood is America's nightmare, the return of repressed, unconscious desire, but for the discerning reader he is also a blues hero, the badass, Bad Nigger (like Bigger Thomas) playing a zero-sum game on his own terms.[22]

Baker's theory of the black (w)hole is compelling, and it has relevance even nineteen years after its formulation. In America, the black (w)hole's most recent advent has been hip-hop culture (particularly gangster rap). An organic cultural form that finds its roots in inner-city life (Bob Marley's "concrete jungle"), hip-hop, with rap music as its centerpiece, boasts to be authentic black experience, born out of a blues, and engaged in zero-sum rites of passage (what Cornel West calls nihilism).[23] This is not to say that every expression of black culture conforms to the trope, or that hip-hop in its entirely is complicit in this esthetic. Nevertheless, the black (w)hole's has a palpable centrifugal force toward the characteristics Baker described. It is worth noting that the audience for black cultural expression (blues and jazz, literature, and rap music) remains primarily white. The paradox of an authentic black expression for a white audience suggests that for any honest interaction to take place each participant—black and white alike—would need (to borrow a phrase from hip-hop) to keep it real. Put otherwise, each party would have to encounter the black (w)hole but also imagine a return from it. Or again, white audiences should recognize much of the black esthetic as a trope, an artistic response to cultural and historical reality.

Even in his formulation of the black (w)hole, Baker posits the possibility of return. (The blues, after all, is not depressive, but emotive and uplifting.) Baker's trope is especially fitting today given that, scientifically, the notion that matter *does* return from black holes is only a recent hypothesis to which Baker would not have been privy in 1989.[24] Applying the metaphor to literature, Ellison's *Invisible Man* does not end with the protagonist's negative encounters. Battling nihilism or cynicism, Invisible Man returns from his coal-cellar, underworld experience to provide a document for an integral American audience. Although he announces himself as an invisible man, he concedes that "even an invisible man has a socially responsible role to play" (*Invisible Man*, 581). Reintegration, to use Baker's term, is perhaps a misnomer. Yet Ellison's protagonist comes to the realization that he is already an integral part of the American experience. (This perspective, as we will see, is difficult even for an author like Morrison, who claims that in her audience she was *not* writing for such an integral audience but for herself, as a black woman.)

Ellison's classicism conceives of a return from the black (w)hole, or, put otherwise, he imagines the American experience as being of a whole. That is, the cultural forms created through the black American experience, such as the blues, become wholly American. These forms were imagined with a collective, though separate or segregated, audience in mind. As Sandra Adell (1994) formulates it in her book, an "Other" cannot conceive of itself without its counterpart. The black (w)hole is a response to a certain isolation from the mainstream and the pull toward self-identification, yet as Ellison saw, American literature would don a black mask as the face of its alter ego.[25] For Ellison, the American idiom—its music, art, and literature—is, at core, *African American.* More specifically, from at least the seventeenth century, the presence of a large contingent of Africans in America colored its language, dialect, and folklore. In Ellison's words,

> [Walt] Whitman viewed the spoken idiom of Negro Americans as a source for a native grand opera. Its flexibility, its musicality, its rhythms, freewheeling diction, and metaphors, and projected in Negro American folklore, were absorbed by the creators of our great nineteenth-century literature even when the majority of blacks were still enslaved. Mark Twain celebrated it in the prose of *Huckleberry Finn;* without the presence of blacks, the book could not have been written. No Huck and Jim, no American novel as we know it. For not only is the black man a co-creator of the language that Mark Twain raised to the level of literary eloquence, but Jim's condition as American and Huck's commitment to freedom are at the moral center of the novel. (1986d, 109)

Ellison echoes T. S. Eliot in finding the universal, or a "grand opera" and "literary eloquence," in local idiom, but he colors American style with "Negro American folklore," an area that Eliot met with silence. In an earlier essay, Ellison goes as far as to argue that in American literature the Negro is in fact the "mask of humanity," a symbol both of local flavor and universal depth (1966a). In sum, black identity is already part of "white" American literature because each faction imagines itself vis-à-vis its counterpart, as an Other. There is no America without a ground zero of slavery; there is no America without the Negro, and, conversely, there is also no black American literature without its white audience. Metaphorically, there is no black (w)hole without the historical events against which it is conceived. The black (w)hole does not exist independently of the surrounding matter—including the classics—from which it pulls.

The easy (perhaps seemingly obvious) formulation of America's wholeness has not been a readily acceptable idea, despite its recent commoditization throughout the American marketplace.[26] White critics have been as dismissive of the integrity of the American idiom in terms of race as black critics have been reticent to accept the possibility that the classical form can be a spontaneous (though emerging from craft) feature of African American expression. In contrast to Ellison, T. S. Eliot was silent on the possibility of the black idiom as the folk expression for which he searched (Eliot 1927). Eliot's search for a distinctly American style, unique from the Queen's English, did not result in his embrace of African American culture. In this respect the distance between him and Ellison, who so emulated Eliot in his commitment to American erudition and to poetic form, could not be greater. In his address to Washington University, titled "American Literature and the American Language," Eliot claimed that "the strong local flavor combined with unconscious universality" distinguished American literature from other literature written in English (i.e. British literature).[27] He cites Mark Twain's *Huckleberry Finn* as a case in point, claiming that Twain was "strongly local" while at the same time conveying "a great unconscious depth." Yet in stark contrast to Ellison, there is no mention of race in Eliot's speech. Black critics, on the other hand, have also not been entirely accepting of the notion of America's cultural integrity, as the exchange quoted as the epigraph for the beginning of this chapter suggests. As Ellison would discover after the publication of *Invisible Man,* black critics would view classicism in black literature with a great degree of skepticism and hostility.

Despite the polarization of American life and thought, the argument that the American experience is of a whole rings true, especially when viewed from afar. For American authors, the return from racial frontiers would mean acknowledging the inextricable relationship between American cultural forms and the country's cultural and political history in a slave past. Race is as indelible a feature of American identity as is the classicism out of which the nation was born.[28] Race—as the justification for slavery in the New World—is important not only because of the significance of the past but also because the experience shook the foundations of American society. Race-thinking challenged the principles of freedom, democracy, and the pursuit of happiness for all. The American author responsible to history and tradition is forced to come to terms with the effects of slavery, segregation, and the struggle for civil rights on the psyche, culture, and life chances not only on African Americans but also on American society at large. We might characterize the engagement with these historical experiences as a heroic return. The return begins with an encounter with the racial other and leads to an understanding of the extent to which American identity is constructed through the prism of race. For the most part, this acknowledgement of race has been the province of African American authors. W. E. B. Du Bois' "double consciousness" is the ideological starting point of African American literature from the twentieth century forward, but it has not necessarily been a self-conscious starting point for American literature in general. Yet for the African American author, the encounter with the color line cannot reasonably be the beginning and end of his or her artistic expression. Put otherwise, the black author who remains in the (w)hole, or in the Underworld (to use the mythological motif), risks isolation from his or her own society. Since the call for a new Negro (Locke 1925), African American authors like Ralph Ellison have recognized that in finding themselves they must encounter the other, not only as a separate entity but also as an extension of themselves. The return from the black (w)hole is an inevitable point on the continuum of American identity.

Black authors have returned from the black (w)hole with a number of results. As we have seen, authors who engage the classics have, on the one hand, met the opprobrium of some African American critics. Black authors including Phillis Wheatley, Countee Cullen, and Ralph Ellison have all been labeled (implicitly and at times explicitly) "sell outs" for indulging white audiences rather than addressing with serious resolve, the argument goes, the social condition of black Americans at large. (Interestingly, Richard Wright's *Native Son,* which is harsh in its hyperrealistic portrayal of the black underclass, met the criticism of being "protest fiction."[29] There is no pleasing the critics.) On the other hand, these same black authors have at times been co-opted as protest writers, as we saw in the case of Wheatley. The classicist works of each has been read as radical in challenging white American hegemony. Nevertheless, each author's work rises above the critical reception to reveal its creator's artistry: a personal struggle not only to come to terms with sociopolitical reality but also an attempt to master artistic form. Ellison's proffered that the black artist, despite the at-times less-than-favorable social reality, could rise above sociological statistics to craft a way of being—and could do so eloquently. In Ellison's formulation, craft—not social condition—completes the individual, although Jerry Gafio Watts saw this as a "heroic individualism" that was troublesome for group identification.

We will return to Watts's objection to Ellison's formulation of black classicism later. For the time being, I offer that at least two things are gained from the black author's identification with the Western classics. In the first place, the return from the black (w)hole expands the African American author's artistic sensibilities. While he or she might work in an essentially black idiom of the blues form, engagement with the classics yields other metaphors. The correlative of antiquity deepens the artist's perspective on his or her social reality. (Perhaps any correlative would, which might explain many twentieth-century black writers' antithetical relationship to America through communism.) In addition, these authors, through their classicism, openly invite a broader audience to participate in their artistic journey. African American authors such as Ralph Ellison and Toni Morrison have gained name recognition beyond their local communities— despite the framework that views classicism as a gesture of assimilation. With awards such as the American Book Award for Fiction and the Nobel Prize for literature respectively, these authors have arrived at the pinnacle of success. They have achieved this success, moreover, because they bring something profound not only to white American audiences but to all reading audiences everywhere. These authors merge the beauty of the blues experience with the long-standing, humanistic motifs found throughout classical literature. Their artistic return achieves a particular sense of being in the world, one from which any modern reader can benefit. It might also be said that this sensibility was inevitable since the American experience is of a whole. To wit, the sensibility captured in these works was already being lived throughout the American frontier, as Gregory Stephens (1999) suggests.

In the pages that follow, I offer a reading of two black-classicist works: Countee Cullen's *Medea* and Toni Morrison's *Song of Solomon*. Cullen's play met a difficult critical reception. Once we move from the standard framing of criticism around his classicism, however, we find that Cullen's *Medea* is neither assimilationist, nor is the reading of the play as Black Nationalist protest tenable. Rather, Cullen, similar to other critics of his time, demonstrates an interest in the modernist interplay between folk forms and tradition. In his hands the interplay is specifically articulated as one between black identity and the classics. Cullen's Medea is not the strong, black woman who challenges patriarchy, as Lillian Corti (1998) argues. Rather, by working within inevitable racial stereotypes of the black woman, Cullen transports classical Medea into modern American culture. Once we read the play within the strikingly original frame of Cullen's "Byword for Evil," we find that Cullen accomplishes a deepening of Medea in the mode of Euripides while examining her core emotions, namely love and anger in its loss, in Senecan fashion. Similar to Cullen's *Medea*, Toni Morrison's *Song of Solomon*, which also features a number of women who are caught up in less-than-satisfying relationships with men, is replete with classical motifs and allusions to classical myth. Morrison, however, successfully negotiates her classicism with her black identity, primarily through her skepticism about the former and her outright advocacy of the latter. Unlike Ralph Ellison, who argued for the mastery of craft over all else (and who was absorbed in classical mythology), Morrison is not particularly overwhelmed with the motifs she uses to orient her work. Despite the abundance of classical motifs in her works, she often downplays their presence.

## Is Blackness the "Byword for Evil?": Countee Cullen's Translation of *Medea*

### *Medea*

Countee Cullen was born on March 30, 1903. His birthplace is uncertain, but Cullen would claim New York for himself as a way of asserting his central place in the Harlem Renaissance. He was indeed the Renaissance's most promising, most talented young poet. Raised by Methodist Episcopal minister Frederick A. Cullen and wife, Carolyn, from around 1918, Countee attended DeWitt Clinton High School from 1918 to 1921. He certainly learned Latin at DeWitt Clinton (his proficiency in classical Greek is not clear), and he also won a contest sponsored by the Federation of Women's Clubs for his poem "I Have a Rendezvous with Life." He attended New York University from 1921 to 1925, graduating Phi Beta Kappa, as attested in the *New York Times* caption of March 20, 1925. He was known to be proficient in writing ballads, sonnets, and quatrains. His poetic force lay in the fact that he often used these forms for black social expression, such as in his "Scottsboro, Too, Is Worth Its Song," which took the alleged rape of two white girls by twelve blacks in Chattanooga, Tennessee, in 1931 as its topic. (False claims of rape, as we will see in chapter 6, are a strong component of the racial environment in American throughout the twentieth century.[30])

It is also worth noting that both Gerald Early and Lillian Corti read Cullen as homosexual, or at least of "decidedly ambiguous sexual nature."[31] These scholars claim sexual ambiguity despite Cullen's (albeit failed) marriage to the daughter of W. E. B. Du Bois, Yolande, from 1928 to 30. (And he married a second time as well.) Cullen's sexuality, or at least his interest in gender dynamics, is a factor in the reading of his *Medea*. As it pertains to genre, Gerald Early labels Cullen's *Medea* "the first major *translation* of a classical work by a twentieth-century black American writer" (my italics).[32] The notion that Cullen's *Medea* works in the mode of translation is important for my reading here.

Given that a century and a half had passed between Phillis Wheatley's era and that of Countee Cullen, we might expect a markedly different reception for the classicism of the latter's work. In 1935, Cullen lived and breathed the rarified air of Harlem, where blacks and whites flocked to hear jazz and to dance together through the night. Writers of the Harlem Renaissance had wealthy white patrons who believed in their value, and America at large had shaken off the shackles of slavery. The broader political and social environment, however, was quite a different story, and the outlook on race affected even the most progressive Americans. By the end of his short literary career, Cullen struggled to negotiate his training in classical and modern languages with his identity as an African American.[33] Cullen's racial identity marked the early reception of his *Medea* (Corti 1998), and some critics, as we have seen, viewed the work as a rejection of his earlier positions on race. Cullen's foray outside of the strictly (if not explicitly) mandated confines of the New Negro esthetic rendered his work irrelevant (Kramer 1987). More recent criticism overlooks the poet's relationship to his contemporaries in terms of modernism (Corti 1998).

While critics tend to perceive Cullen's classicism negatively, it is precisely in the context of what Gerald Early called his classical credentials that we are able fully to come to terms with what is unique, or even subversive, about his play (Early 1991).[34] In addition to Latin at De Witt Clinton High School, there is some evidence that Cullen studied the classics at New York University with A. L. Sihler, who commented on Cullen's gifts as a student. Similar to T. S. Eliot and, later, Ralph Ellison, Cullen was interested in using local, folkloric idiom to come to terms with some of the broader themes he found in the classics. Despite the sense among critics that the dramatic structure of *Medea* might stifle his creativity (e.g., Gates 1987), Cullen, as Lilian Corti sees, clearly hoped throughout his work to use whatever training or knowledge he had to address artistic concerns as well as his identity as a Negro America.[35]

Two considerations should shift the reading of Cullen's *Medea*. Firstly, Cullen's training in the classics precludes a mere cursory knowledge of the originals. Cullen seemed to be well aware of the artistic and social concerns that inform an understanding of the classical character. Given this first consideration, reading Cullen's *Medea* as more of a translation than an adaptation changes how we approach the play. I am not suggesting that Cullen closely translated from the Greek original of Euripides or Seneca's Latin version, but he certainly knew these plays. I offer translation as a different paradigm for approaching Cullen's *Medea* than adaptation. While "translation" always takes into consideration the original languages and cultures, the latter model leaves room for looser treatments. As an adaptation of *Medea*, Cullen's play would certainly leave much to be desired, but if he were offering a play that was more intimately intertwined with its predecessors, he would have to stick closely to the original dramatic structure, language, and themes. This is, to my mind, exactly what he did.

A second consideration is Cullen's "Byword for Evil," the prologue and epilogue to *Medea*, published subsequent to the play.[36] Critics have not appreciated the differences between the play and "Byword," its frame. While Cullen's *Medea* is closer to a translation of Euripides' play than an adaptation of themes surrounding the character, "Byword" is almost entirely improvisational. Whether because of the critical reception or his own artistic impulses, Cullen was not satisfied with his Medea, as we might surmise in his return to the theme in the later framework that he writes. Through "Byword," Cullen gives his own personal improvisation on the themes of *Medea*, and by doing so he deepens the play's characters and adds insight to Medea's plight.

Euripides' *Medea*, a product of fifth-century Athenian theater, contains one of the central cultural dichotomies of the time, namely the conflict between Greeks and barbarians.[37] That is, in addition to the theme of a mother killing her children, *Medea* explores the psychology of a *foreign* woman. In the classical play Medea, a princess in the foreign land of Colchis, betrays her family for the love of Jason, the Greek prince who arrives at her country to steal a Golden Fleece, a sacred object that will secure his birthright.[38] Jason escapes to Corinth with Medea, who in the process has killed her father and brother. When the play opens some time after these events, Medea, now a mother, has learned that Jason has married the daughter of the Corinthian king. By the end of Euripides' play, Medea takes vengeance on Jason for his betrayal of her by killing his new bride and Jason's children by Medea. The tragic events occur only after Aegeus, the king of Athens, promised Medea safe refuge from exile for her acts. Aegeus has no idea what Medea is plotting. (Cullen's representation of this character, as we will see, is to my mind one of his strongest.) Athens figures in the play, as elsewhere in Greek tragedy, as an asylum for political exiles, but *Medea* also contains an implicit warning to the city-state against foreign influence.[39] Although Euripides humanizes Medea (another aspect of Greek tragedy being a female autonomy unusual for the time), he receives her as a witch; her representation is unavoidably framed in the politics of contemporary discourse.[40] If Medea kills Jason because he betrays her, her foreignness (vis-à-vis the Greek) is as much to blame for her reaction as is her gender (in its context) and her emotions.

Cullen is clearly aware of some of the salient features of the Greek play, and he presents the issue of race in America—blackness—as a parallel to the Greek-barbarian dichotomy. There is little reason to doubt the observation, made by the *Times* review and retold in Corti (1998), that Cullen had a black actress, Rose McClendon, in mind to play the role of Medea. Perhaps her death in 1936 would have deterred further interest in performing the drama.[41]

Cullen calls attention to Medea's foreignness, now as a black woman within the context of American society, from the very first words of the play, as the Nurse, who came to Greece from Colchis along with Medea, expresses frustration at "those Greeks!" (This perhaps suggests an inversion of the Greek/Other dichotomy.[42]) Medea is the black barbarian to America's white Greece. Seeking sympathy from the broader white audience, she laments "how difficult it can be for a stranger in a foreign land" (*Medea*, 11). In addition to the textual references to her Otherness, Cullen's black Medea would have accomplished more than the simple assimilation of his modern audience to the ancient setting of the play. McClendon, or whoever might have played Medea, would have transformed the play into a modern, and *American,* treatment of the classical theme.[43]

Cullen's Medea is far from the vehicle for social protest that Corti imagines her to be.[44] Although she is mostly conceived through the eyes of others, Medea remains, even to her sympathetic nurse, a "brooding" woman with "dark designs."[45] Corti's nationalist reading does not account for the negative imagery of blackness evident in these words and throughout the play. Creon, as another example, casts Medea as a "stubborn-browed sorceress and insubordinate wife." Although Creon's criticism might be read in terms of the overdetermining gaze of white society, Medea is, by her own admission, corrupt: "Dark is the path I tread but my foes shall tread a darker!"[46] She confesses to have betrayed her father and country. While Corti reads Medea as part of Cullen's social protest against American society and its rejection of interracial love, the playwright does nothing to save Medea from her own Otherness. In other words, Cullen uses the Manichean dichotomy of race in America to hone in on problems of morality, individual agency, and responsibility. As an African American woman who kills her biracial children to avenge her white husband's betrayal, Medea at best evokes pity. At worst, she serves to reinforce distrust by embodying in black the collective American angst regarding race during segregated times.

To aid her argument for the drama as protest, Corti reads Aegeus, who offers Medea safe harbor in Athens and thus unwittingly enables her to perform her acts of murder, as a figure for Paris, France, the home of black American ex-patriots and would-be nationalists. Suffice it to say that Aegeus's own softness, and the extent to which Medea takes advantage of him, makes this reading dubious, unless the comment is on the *impossibility* of France as a sensible alternative to the problem of race in America. Corti argues that

> Aegeus's sympathetic support recalls the solace which Cullen and other African Americans of his generation sought and found abroad, especially in Paris, during the period between the two World Wars. (629)

Paris, similar to the asylum that Athens offers in the ancient context, would provide a home for blacks who had grown weary with America's limitations (Stovall 1998). In this reading, Cullen offers his black American audience a strong alternative to life with a treacherous bedfellow. Although, only five years later, Richard Wright would use Bigger Thomas as a vehicle for confronting the ills of America in sociological terms, Corti's reading of Aegeus's relationship to Medea is inconsistent with the textual evidence.

Ironically, Cullen's Aegeus is one of his more creative characters. Since Cullen casts him as a weak man, given to sexual indulgence with women, Aegeus as Paris, France, would yield a critique *against* the virility of Black

Nationalism in Paris.[47] Rather than as a political symbol, Cullen's Aegeus might simply serve a similar dramatic function to that of his Greek model: namely, he enables Medea's vendetta against Jason. Aegeus's dilemma, also in keeping with Cullen's Greek model, is that he has not been able to have children.[48] When Medea asks if he has tried a wife, Aegeus replies, somewhat comically, that he has "tried *wives*." In Cullen's play, the oracle that Aegeus has consulted regarding his problem seems to suggest that he be careful, "drawing the wineskin tight, and saving the wine." In the context of Aegeus's weakness for women, "drawing the wineskin tight" can be read as a warning to Aegeus to avoid sexual liaisons "until [he] came to [his] own country again." Despite the warning, Aegeus accepts Medea's claim to "know charms and magic words to give life even to your seed." She promises Aegeus the very thing that he craves: "Believe me, Aegeus, I can raise up children to you." Aegeus allows Medea to draw him in, and the consequence for Cullen's character (quite a variation from the Greek), as we see in "Byword for Evil," is ultimately his own life.

Aegeus cannot serve as a strong symbol of African American expatriation to Paris. Nor does Corti's attempt to cast Medea's murders of her children in a neutral light diffuse the portrait. Indeed infanticide is a permanent—though heinous—feature even of modern society, and Corti is right to dismiss any claim that Medea's actions are out of step with Western civilization. The few examples of infanticide in the American context that Corti cites in 1998 could be augmented yearly. Social exigencies compound the problem, and Corti sees a link between infanticide and the conditions of slavery. But Cullen's deployment of the traditional language and symbols leaves the audience alienated from his main character, whether that audience was black or white.[49] The comparison to Toni Morrison's *Beloved* (which is Corti's) fails when we take into consideration motives and desired outcome. Sethe, the main character of *Beloved,* is explicitly set in the context of slavery and desperation regarding the life-chances of her children. *Beloved* gives voice to the social conditions that would cause a black woman to wish for the death of their own children, or even to enact this tragedy herself. If there is a connection between Medea and Sethe, it is in each author's attempt to situate his and her character in a broader psychological matrix than race alone will allow. The comparison, moreover, points to the moral dimension of the murder of one's children: motivation. Classical Medea murders her children because of inordinate erotic love and betrayal (i.e., vengeance), while Sethe and the historical character upon which she was modeled murder their children to save them from slavery (i.e., protective love).

To put this inquiry into Countee Cullen's *Medea* in other terms, it is likely that a black artist, even if he uses black life and black characters, is doing something other than simply pointing up broader historical or social plights. Medea allows Cullen a correlative not only to his own social condition but also to his emotional condition. A black American Medea, moreover, as the comparison to Sethe makes evident, might help readers to understand the classical character a bit better. Clues to Cullen's characterization of Medea might lie outside of the prism of race. Corti has already allowed for this possibility when she cites Cullen's own sexuality as an alternate prism. Corti makes a significant connection between her reading of Cullen's life and his choice of Medea as an artistic subject:

> No mere tribute to the art of Euripides, Cullen's *Medea* is an expression of fundamental autobiographical, aesthetic, and communal concerns. Dealing with the most obvious of these first, we may note that, as an abandoned child who was initially raised by his grandmother and later adopted by the Reverend Frederick Asbury Cullen (Perry 3–4), the poet may well have found in Euripides' forlorn protagonist an objective correlative for his peculiarly personal experiences and anxieties. The character Medea may represent Cullen's own abandoned mother, the son she deserted when his father disappeared, or the troubled adult inheritor of a childhood haunted by crises of desertion and abandonment. (622)

Given Cullen's abandonment by his mother, the "objective correlative" for his experience might well have been Medea, as Corti suggests. As we see in his ambivalent, if not negative, portrayal of Medea, the writer's underlying distrust of this particular black woman was as much a part of his dramatic character as any sympathy with her. Cullen's sexuality and his tried love life might well give a broader perspective on his choice of Medea than his racial identity alone will allow.

An example of this possible line of inquiry is Cullen's failed marriage to Nina Yolande. The couple married in 1928 and divorced in 1930, "although the actual time they spent together only amounted to several months" (Early 1991, 52). Given the personal connection, the possible links between Cullen's *Medea* and Du Bois' *The Quest of the Silver Fleece* would be a worthwhile project. Both works originate with the same mythological

quest: Jason's quest for a fleece. Could Cullen have been using classical
myth to work through more personal issues, or to dialogue with Du Bois
in covert terms?

From what we have seen thus far, Cullen's *Medea* is a rendition of the
Greek tragedy more akin to translation than loose adaptation. As is the
case with the ancient work, the play raises question about morality and
agency within a particular social context. Unlike *Medea,* which might at
times be deemed tedious because of its attention to original structure (i.e.,
the mode of translation), Cullen develops his treatment of *Medea* further
in "Byword for Evil," which is a truly improvisational work. Through adaptation, "Byword for Evil" gives us additional insights about Cullen's particular understanding of Medea. Corti factors "Byword" into her social-protest
reading of the play, drawing the curious conclusion that the broader text
insists "on the patriarchal brutality of a racially ambiguous society" (Corti
1998). Certainly a white lover, Jason, betrays Medea, and the utter destruction with which "Byword" ends might well be read as an apocalyptic vision
of American society.

## *"Byword for Evil"*

"Byword" is a "prolog" and "epilog" to *Medea.* The "Epilogue" is set in the
court of Athens, twenty years after Medea murdered her children by Jason.
Aegeus, old and blind, wants to bestow his realm to Pandion, ostensibly
his son with Medea, a character that Cullen completely invents. The character also serves a more important narrative function. In the "Epilogue,"
after an exchange in which Pandion claims that he does not want to rule,
a messenger reports that a stranger has been washed ashore. Pandion
leads in the battered sailor, whom Medea immediately recognizes as Jason.
Jason kills Pandion, only to have Medea suggest that he was in fact Jason's
son. Speaking to Jason, she says, "Could I have promised *him* [Aegeus] a
son had I not felt your seed stirring to life within me?" While *Medea* is
indeed a play about a lover's treachery (which I suppose one might interpret as "patriarchal brutality"), a racial reading alone does nothing to
account for the inner life, or agency, of Medea, whom Corti would reduce
to a female Bigger Thomas, overdetermined by her race.

Cullen's disparagement of his black, female protagonist results from his
synthesis of the classical and the new, but he redeems his character by
enlarging her psychological life in "Byword." Medea's excessive love for
Jason, paradoxically, causes her to kill their children in common once he

has betrayed her. Cullen's Medea suggests another parallel, not to Euripides' play but to Seneca's translation. As Martha Nussbaum (1994, 439–83) argues, Seneca's *Medea* is a Stoic study of what can happen once love is admitted into the human heart.[50] Seneca distills the themes of love and vengeance in a way that is consistent with Cullen's treatment. Cullen's "Prologue" allows the audience to see Medea's innocence *before* Jason's offense caused vengeance to overwhelm love.

Love, and not blackness, is Cullen's byword for evil. The emotion of love, which in excessive doses can transform its virtues into vices, helps us to understand even Seneca's Medea (although one is still shocked at her actions), who becomes the embodiment of evil. In the "Prologue" to *Medea,* Cullen presents us with a young Medea passionately in love with Jason. Cullen's creation of playful dialogues between Jason, Medea, and her innocent little brother, Absyrtus, affords us a perspective into the inner lives of these characters parallel to no classical playwright. By casting Medea as black, Cullen gives local, American flair to a universal tale of lost innocence, betrayal, and revenge. Perhaps Medea becomes evil, and here again is Seneca's *fiam Medea*—"I should become Medea." Evil, however, is not the person's essence. Rather, through "Byword for Evil" we witness Medea's progression from innocence to corruption, once she has let love into her heart. (Medea's transition, or corruption, is not unlike that of Hecuba, and both characters raise questions about the destructive nature of some of the emotions a human being lets into his or her being.)

So Cullen's *Medea* might be read as a sonnet to love, but the sonnet would crystallize love's corrupting power—its evil—rather than its good. Love is a byword for evil because of its potential to injure whoever admits it into the self. Cullen manipulates preconceived notions about race in American society to expand Medea's inner life. As a symbol, Medea reaches the final stage of love's corrupting process. "Byword for Evil" ends with every character dead, in the mode of a Shakespearean tragedy. In philosophical terms, one might use Cullen's *Medea* to engage the Stoic sages on the extent to which such an emotion is even beneficial in human affairs. In poetic terms, the writer eulogizes love through the dramatic form much as he would in elegiac couplets. Such utter destruction as we find at the end of the "Epilogue" does not allow for any heroes or villains. As in Shakespeare's *Romeo and Juliet,* no one emerges victorious. Were Cullen's *Medea* to be readable solely in racial terms, we might expect justice to be served in the end, perhaps through Jason's (white society's) punishment. Without the "Epilogue," Medea escapes at the end of the drama unpunished, and we might read her flight as the vindication of a scorned, black woman who allowed herself to be seduced by a white lover. With "Byword for Evil," Cullen's *Medea* becomes a play not about a black woman, per se, but about the conflagration of a treacherous emotion, one that every race of man, whether black or white, has known, must account for, and must struggle to overcome. Read in this light, "Byword for Evil" is somewhat exceptional as an adaptation of classical drama for modern American culture. Through it, Cullen arrived at a uniting metaphor for what is at core a translation of Euripides' *Medea*.

As Ralph Ellison would later argue of his mastery of the novel, it is the task of the artist to employ all of the resources at his disposal to come to terms with his personal and social reality. Mastery of craft, for Ellison, went along with racial identity. Modernist writers like Cullen offer a classical frame through which to express local culture. Success in articulating their individual plights for a broader, increasingly global culture meant their immortality as writers. Cullen does not evade race through *Medea*, as some critics have claimed, nor is he using the character for radical social protest. Rather, Cullen embraces race as a way of understanding Medea—and Medea as a way of diffusing a focus on race. Cullen's treatment is more dynamic that Corti's reading will allow—black classicism more radical than either/or dichotomies will allow. And yet for the Negro writer, race would continue to be an obstacle to the reception of his or her craft. To their African American audience, "universalism" was a synonym for assimilation and the betrayal of racial solidarity. For the white audience, despite the attempts to co-opt a universal idiom, Cullen's *Medea* would remain, perhaps, beneath the dignity of criticism, at least for a time.

### The New Negro Ulysses: Is Toni Morrison's *Song of Solomon* a (W)holy Black Text?

#### *Toni Morrison's Ulysses*

Earlier in the chapter, I formulated African American classicism as a return from Baker's black (w)hole. It is time to return to the trope of Ulysses in black. Outside of Ellison's writing, the Ulysses theme in African American literature is most profound in Toni Morrison's *Song of Solomon* (1977). Morrison, born Chloe Anthony Wofford to a working-class family in Lorain, Ohio, wrote two novels before *Song of Solomon*—*The Bluest Eye*

(1970), and *Sula* (1973). The presence of the Ulysses theme in *Song of Solomon* is noteworthy especially when we consider Morrison's claim, which we will explore, that in her earlier novels she wrote primarily for herself and not for any broader white audience. Along with Morrison's biographical statements, John Duvall (2000) argues that an essential, or authentic, black identity was most forcefully articulated in Morrison's early novels and interviews. By early novels, Duvall means the three including *Song of Solomon;* he sees a different, less class-based and race-based approach beginning in *Tar Baby* (1981). (To date, Morrison has written nine novels.) The presence of Ulysses in the early novel *Song of Solomon* (1977) points to the deeper reality behind the veil of racial identification. A reading of *Song of Solomon* helps us to some extent in understanding where African American classicism had reached by the 1970s. As a strongly black-identified writer, Morrison offers a parallel to Ellison as an author who is equally comfortable within the Western canon as in African and African American folklore. In a manner more evident than with Ellison, moreover, Morrison's framing of the question of classicism results in the privileging of neither.

Morrison's own approach to the either/or framework for black classicism gives deeper perspective to the issues and concerns of black classicism. Her treatment of classical themes in the novel and in her interviews allowed her to create autonomous characters. As she put it in a 1981 interview:

> Ralph Ellison and Richard Wright—all of whose books I admire enormously—I didn't feel were telling *me* something. I thought they were saying something about *it* [the black experience] or *us* that revealed something about *us* to *you*, to others, to white people, to men. Just in terms of the style, I missed something in the fiction that I felt in a real sense in the music and poetry of black artists. When I began writing I was writing as though there was nobody in the world but me and the characters, as though I was talking to them, or us, and it just had a different sound to it. (Taylor-Guthrie 1994, 96)

Morrison's esthetic choices, evident in this interview, caused Timothy B. Powell to claim that in *Song of Solomon* she had written the "(w)holy black text" (T. Powell 1990, 759).[51]

Before analyzing Powell's assertion, it is worth offering a brief summary of *Song of Solomon,* or at least of the narrative points that will become important to the analysis here. *Song of Solomon* opens with the suicide of Robert Smith. Smith's suicide is tied to the novel's plot in that it coincides with the birth of Macon Dead III (or Milkman), and, later in the novel, we find that Smith had organizational ties to Guitar, Milkman's best friend. (Smith was part of Seven Days, the brotherhood that practices reciprocal violence against whites.) Smith's suicide also introduces the theme of flight early on, and we find that each character's desire for flight—freedom, adventure, identity—culminates in the novel's musical/biblical homage, the Song of Solomon, to the folkloric flight of black slaves back to Africa. Morrison makes the explicit point, moreover, that her flight metaphor does not hearken to the Greek Icarus but to African folklore (Taylor-Guthrie 1994).

Although Morrison develops all of her characters well (with the exception of Reba), Milkman is the ostensible protagonist, or hero, of the novel. Macon III's nickname, Milkman, which puzzles his father, in part indicates the broken relationship between the patriarch (Macon II) and his wife, Ruth, who nurses her son well past the appropriate time. Macon lives a fairly uneventful life at home until the age of thirty-two, which is 1962 in the novel's timeframe. Milkman's main boyhood adventures include wandering off to the home of his aunt, Pilate, his father's estranged sister. He enters an affair with his older second cousin, Hagar, Pilate's granddaughter. Pilate, her daughter, and her granddaughter live relatively autonomously from the rest of society because they make and sell wine. The well-told, though uneventful, life of Milkman sours to new heights when his father suggests that Pilate might be hoarding gold that they discovered years earlier. (The senior Macon's belief that Pilate has stolen the gold is the primary cause of the estrangement between brother and sister.) The quest for this gold leads Milkman on an adventure through geographical space and time, as he comes to discover a family history leading all the way back to the flying slaves of folklore, legendary figures who, in certain figurative ways similar to Robert Smith, escaped life's bondages through flight.

Powell's argument that *Song of Solomon* is a (w)holy black text does not leave much room for the fact that characters like Circe, the midwife about whom both Pilate and Macon tell Milkman, situate the novel in the classical, Western past.[52] He argues that Morrison's Circe is "a figure so utterly beyond the pale of the white logos that Milkman finds himself having to 'take a chance' when he invokes 'logic' to try to understand even her very existence" (757). Despite the fact that Morrison transforms Circe, the character's origin as a multivalent female figure in Homer's *Odyssey* is undeniable.[53] Morrison exploits Circe's ambivalence in her own artistic creation. From the novelist's entrenchment in classical mythology, which will become even more apparent later, we might argue that the wholly back text does not exist—cannot exist—either in a black (w)hole or outside of it. Rather, Morrison's novel is able to speak for black Americans, and Americans at large, because of the way in which it affirms the integrity of a wholly American literary and cultural enterprise.

Despite the critical reception of *Song of Solomon*, Morrison's statements regarding figures in Western mythology and their role in her novels reveal a somewhat complex psychology around the issue of classicism. Throughout these statements, she returns, time and again, to two aspects of her own identity that structure her thoughts on the classical past: race and gender. On the one hand, Morrison expresses admiration for figures like Ulysses, whose wanderlust deepened his experiences and his wisdom. She finds "the Ulysses theme, the leaving home" (Taylor-Guthrie 1994, 26) to be central to black male writing:

> They are moving. Trains—you hear those men talk about trains like they were their first lover—the names of the trains, the times of the trains! And, boy, you know, they spread their seed all over the world. They are really moving! Perhaps it's because they don't have a land, they don't have dominion. You can trace that historically, and one never knows what would have been the case if we'd never been tampered with at all. (Taylor-Guthrie 1994, 26)

Morrison sees this wandering as a process through which the self is made complete: "And in the process of finding, they are also making themselves" (26). Morrison's statement is compelling for several reasons, not the least of which is the fact that, similar to Ellison, she gives a theory of the self—one not *determined* strictly by race. While for Ellison *craft* "completes" an individual (Ellison 1986a, which I will discuss in chapter 7), Morrison speaks of black men "making themselves" through travel. In addition to this, Morrison draws a clear distinction between black males in literature, who "don't have dominion," and Ulysses, who apparently does have dominion and who leaves home without seriously adverse consequence to himself (as opposed to the consequences for those he leaves behind). (Of course Odysseus suffers a great deal in Homer's *Odyssey*, but I believe Morrison's point has to do with a certain impunity around the fulfillment of desire, e.g. his affairs, etc.) Morrison seems to question whether or not Ulysses is so grand a figure after all, one to be emulated by black men, with dire consequences to black women.

Although Morrison admires the adventure, "the leaving home," she recognizes a difficulty with it, and she asserts a complexity around the issue of travel:

> Although in sociological terms that is described as a major failing of black men—they do not stay home and take care of their children, they are not there—that has been to me one of the most attractive features about black male life. (Taylor-Guthrie 1994, 26)

Morrison offers a multivalent treatment of classical themes in black literature. She does not find particularly commendable what she characterizes as Ulysses' twenty-year abandonment of his wife and child.[54] Nevertheless, she sees the journey, which Joseph Campbell calls the monomyth, as pivotal to the formation of self. Morrison asserts that while black men have embraced the idea of exploration, black women had to struggle, for a number of social and cultural reasons, with the issue of self-discovery. Yet contrary to some treatments, Morrison does not announce a rejection of Ulysses; she admires his mobility. At the same time, she sees it necessary to reconstitute Ulysses, grafting blackness onto a broader Western identity while at the same time cultivating a black identity for men and women that has an inner integrity.

It is also worth pausing on Morrison's claim that she was not writing for a white audience. What use would a black audience, therefore, have for the profuse play not only on biblical themes, but also on European folklore (Goldilocks, Hansel and Gretel, and perhaps Jack in the Beanstalk), and on the Ulysses theme? Is Morrison's claim to be writing for herself a subterfuge (Duvall 2000)? By deploying classical motifs, is Morrison conceding that the wholly black text is impossible, that it cannot exist on a Western frontier?

Before turning to Milkman's odyssey, I should frame the discussion around Morrison's use of myth and folklore generally. Given her identity and her themes, it is not surprising that gender and race are the two main ideological prisms through which *Song of Solomon* has been received. The deeper reaches of Morrison's improvisation on classical myth in the novel, however, have been attenuated because of these prisms.[55] Timothy Powell,

for example, is right to see that one of the main struggles of black identity—and hence black literature—is the question of how to construct
from inside outward an autonomous identity, which finds its roots in slavery, that is not over-determined by otherness, or the white gaze. Powell
speaks of "the inadequacies of the white mythology for representing the
black self" (752). He also sees that such an identity cannot productively be
constructed around hatred or with its view trained exclusively on the past.
In this respect, Powell sees that Pecola, the protagonist of *The Bluest Eye*,
is trapped in society's view of her: "These figures of the white mythology
to which she compares herself are the catalysts which precipitate Pecola's
psychic disintegration, leaving her alienated from any sense of authentic
black self" (752). Powell's rejection of what he calls "white logos," however, denies the reality that the project of African American identity is
contained within a broader American one. The either/or paradigm—the
necessity of rejecting white logos for a black one—misleads on many
counts. A purely race-based analysis does not fully capture the nuances of
Morrison's esthetic.

Nor is gender the only prism through which Morrison conceives her
work, as we have seen in her own statements. Rather than rejecting what
has been perceived as a male hegemony (classical mythology), Morrison
constructs her characters—male and female—out of inherited material.
Past treatments of Morrison's approach to classical myth do not acknowledge this possibility. In his article on *Song of Solomon*, Michael Awkward
(1990) forged a link between the role of gender in the novel on the one
hand and mythology on the other. Awkward's essay is a useful attempt to
frame a discussion of the novel's mythic dimension. The essay includes,
for example, a treatment of Joseph Campbell's idea of the monomyth as
it pertains to Morrison's novel. Awkward's general argument is as follows:

> To read *Song of Solomon* in terms of its informing ideologies facilitates the
> reader's discernment of the ways in which the novel offers a disruption of
> the androcentric sequence both of Western sacred narrative in general, and,
> specifically, of (appropriated) Afro-American myth. (487)

To this end, Awkward casts mythology as, generally, "androcentric." His
analysis extends to Campbell's monomyth: "Campbell validates the phallocentric belief that women's role is to complete—to make whole—the
heretofore psychologically fragmented and defeminized male hero" (487).

Awkward seems generally correct that Morrison at times "breaks the (sacred) narrative sequence" in order to inscribe "usefully transcendent possibilities for the female" (494), as she does by interrupting the story of Milkman's progress with that of Hagar's demise. Morrison's contribution here is to question heroism itself by disrupting a standard heroic narrative. As a female novelist, Morrison certainly amplifies the mythological dimensions of women's lives in general, and that of African American women specifically. Morrison makes clear that as a successful hero, Milkman would have to understand feminine principles as much as he does masculine.

Although Awkward's critique is an important contribution to understanding *Song of Solomon,* he betrays an inclination against classical myth, particular in what he reads as its gender bias, its misogyny. Awkward's claim that Campbell "inscribe[s] woman as supplement and object" (487) obscures the context of the latter author's framework. Awkward seems to ignore the very opening of his citation of Campbell: "Woman, in the picture language of mythology, represents the totality of what can be known" (Awkward quoting Campbell, 486). Put otherwise, classical myth, especially earlier myths surrounding the notion of a Great Goddess, the pre-Western privileging of female deity over male (such as in Isis and Osiris of Egypt), articulated something about the feminine principle that later Western culture had certainly forgotten (or repressed).[56] The dichotomy between male and female in mythology is dynamic even *within* classical mythology. Pre-Homeric society, for example, seems to have represented women somewhat differently from post-Homeric society, and this obfuscates the claim that mythology is, in and of itself, "androcentric." Rather than rejecting classical myth, Morrison taps into the primal possibility of myth to structure reality. By doing so, she amplifies the role of the feminine in her stories, even in her representation of male characters.

The scholarship on *Song of Solomon* has contributed to our understanding of the novel, but a reading built primarily around gender and race obscures the significance of Morrison's contribution, and her genius. By deploying myth in the way that she does, Morrison implicitly asserts, as Richard Heyman (1995) claims of the novel's main character, Milkman, that an otherwise external history can be part of her own personal memory.[57] In other words, the objective correlative of the classics (and their hegemony) is part of Morrison's personal experience. Just as the recovered history of Milkman's family helps him to come to terms with his personal struggles, so Morrison's recovery of classical mythology helps her to represent complex characters. To reject the Western heritage is to deny part of her identity.

The reading that I offer here of *Song of Solomon* relies on a different understanding of classical mythology than that of the authors I have presented. It may be conceded that classics have come to represent a hegemonic discourse—Amin's "eternal West."[58] This being the case, classical mythology may well, for many critics, be part of a binary opposition between power, on the one hand, and the ongoing struggle against it, on the other. This struggle can be parsed in terms of class, as the elite versus the masses, or in terms of race, as master versus the oppressed. Polarity, however, does not account for the fact that at the core of classical mythology is folklore. In this respect, classical mythology can be aligned with, on the one hand, folklore throughout the world, and, on the other hand, with African American folklore (as Ellison does). Morrison's deployment of classical myth is similar to what we will see of Ralph Ellison in that her riffs on the classical tales are to some extent indistinguishable from her use of fairy tales and African American folklore. Morrison is first and foremost a storyteller—a fabulist or folklorist. If there is a hierarchy of tales in *Song of Solomon,* it is one that privileges the personal. If African American folklore is privileged in the novel, this is the case because Morrison is a black author; her personal experiences and cultural memory take precedent over any notion of a Western heritage. Yet similar to classical authors like Euripides and Seneca, she works with received motifs and symbols. In addition to this, Morrison is able to bring a different understanding to myth as a black, female author—or even as an American author. As such, Morrison forces classical mythology to speak for her.

Mythology, moreover, is a study that encompasses psychology, religion, and sociology, to name only a few of its associated disciplines. It is no more productive to label mythology racist or misogynist than it would be to label psychology, religion, or sociology as racist. Indeed the cultural prisms through which these disciplines are reflected take on the vices of their culture, so that Freudian psychology, as an example, might be deemed misogynist or homophobic. Likewise, religion becomes sexist (or racist) in the hands of the cultures that practice it, so that the intrinsically misogynist nature of Pauline Christianity, for example, might be viewed as a marker for religion in general, but it is not.

In *Song of Solomon,* Morrison confronts some intrinsically misogynistic markers of culture and transforms them. For example, the evil witch is a

hallmark of Western mythology. In Jungian psychology, witches represent destructive forces in the unconscious (Jung 1972). Along with the evil
stepmother in fairytales, the witch is a destructive feminine force whom
the social order—read male, hegemonic, and good—must overthrow.
Morrison takes the traditional understanding of witches and inverts it, so
that while representing a power outside of the male, hegemonic culture
witches—if this is what we must label Circe and Pilate for the sake of talking about them—are a necessary and productive aspect of society.[59] While
to the European mind witches might conjure powers traditionally linked
with evil, Morrison restores a preclassical notion of chthonic and creative
potential linked to earth and the moon.

   An example of Morrison's inversion of traditional mythological symbols is her treatment of Hagar. The protagonist Milkman's second cousin
and his lover, Hagar's playful sensuality turns destructive when he ends
their relationship coldly. For one year—or twelve moons—following their
breakup, Hagar in her "lunacy" (*luna,* the moon) stalks Milkman but comes
to her senses each time before she is able to inflict a fatal blow. Morrison
evokes the traditional fairy tale symbols in Hagar's characterization:

> The calculated violence of a shark grew in her, and *like every witch that ever*
> *rode a broom straight through the night to a ceremonial infanticide* as thrilled
> by the black wind as by the rod between her legs; like every fed-up-to-the-
> teeth bride who worried about the consistency of the grits she threw at her
> husband as well as the potency of the lye she had stirred in them . . . Hagar
> was energized by the details of her mission. She stalked him. (Morrison 1977,
> 128, my italics)

Morrison's portrayal humanizes the archetypal witch who rides the broom-
stick. In the first place, we find that the witch, contrary to what we learn
in fairy tales, is sexual. She is "as thrilled by the black wind as by the rod
between her legs." The acknowledgment of the witch's sexual desire re-
moves her from the depravity of "ceremonial infanticide." In addition
to this, the idea of the "fed-up-to-the-teeth bride" links the witch's desire
both to the frustrations that women in general might sometimes feel and
to that of specific characters in the novel. We recall that Ruth, Milkman's
mother, had to repress her sexual desire for a lifetime because of her
husband's rejection of her. His complaints about her cooking—echoed in
the fed-up bride "worried about the consistency of the grits"—feed the

frustrated desire that she feels toward him. Finally, Hagar makes material the fact that a person—male or female—can take only so much; the witch in Hagar, similar to the "witch" of frustrated desire in such male characters as Guitar, is the vengeful potential contained in every person. Hagar is Medea, who in turn is Hecuba, and so on.

Morrison's use of folklore and mythology is also multivalent. While Hagar is the furious woman scorned, she is also the girl—an uninitiated female—trying to find her place in the world. When her mother Reba and grandmother Pilate hold a mirror up to her, she believes she has found the reason why Milkman does not want her. She determines to "fix myself up" by going on a shopping spree for designer clothes and makeup. Unfortunately, she is caught in a rainstorm that ruins her purchases. Nevertheless, Hagar makes every effort to put on this new—ruined—attire and is only shocked into reality upon seeing the look on her mother's and grandmother's faces when she emerges. Michael Awkward's analysis of why Hagar weeps herself literally to death is worth evoking here: "Hagar comes to the bitter realization that her efforts to achieve American society's ideal of female beauty are utterly fruitless" (494). It is also true that "her (ruined) society will never provide her opportunities for the types of transformations necessary to win the love of the man with whom she feels she belongs" (494). Yet Morrison is not satisfied to place the responsibility of transformation in society, per se. Rather, she challenges the individual's resistance to some desires, and engendering of others. When Hagar really sees herself (perhaps for the first time), not through Milkman's eyes or through those of her mother and grandmother, she is broken: "She lay in her little *Goldilocks'-choice* bed, her eyes sand dry and as quiet as glass" (314–15, my italics). Similar to Goldilocks, Hagar has extended her desire into troublesome territory by seeking to possess something that never belonged to her.[60]

While Morrison's association of Hagar to Goldilocks might be read in terms of the troublesome desire of African American women to gain esthetic acceptance (or acceptance in other areas) in a society that values blond hair and blue eyes, the analog does not only mark difference.[61] That is, Goldilocks here is not merely objective correlative, or the standard against which others are judged. Rather, Goldilocks is herself a bundle of misplaced desires.[62] Put otherwise, even the blond, blue-eyed woman brings herself harm by succumbing to externally manufactured desire. In this respect Hagar and the fairytale character are exactly alike. Both women tried to fit themselves into a Procrustian (to borrow another motif) bed that did not belong to them. Both women were trapped in a narcissistic bubble. After trying to fulfill her desires with things that were "too hot" or "too big," Goldilocks learns that even those things belonging to the poor little bear could suit her just fine. In a similar fashion, Hagar was initially confident in her ability to win Milkman, who was younger and less exposed than she. In the end, her overconfidence destroys her, as Milkman grew tired of her games. The fairy tale ends well (being a fairy tale), but Hagar's self-destruction in *Song of Solomon* marks the tragic results of misplaced desire intimated even in Goldilocks's story.

## Milkman's Odyssey

At the core of *Song of Solomon* are fragmented images of Ulysses' journey and return, particularly as it relates to Milkman. The critical reception of *Song of Solomon* within Black Studies, as we have seen, was generally to assert black (and female) over what is read as white, male hegemonic power, which Milkman and his father Macon imitate in their desire for dominion (over property, people, places). Harris argues that "Morrison ultimately intends Milkman as a heroic figure whose heroism can only be defined through dualistic, sometimes ambiguous actions, and whose qualifications for heroism do not depend on his goodness" (1991, 88). Within the context of Milkman's own polarities—his rejection of Hagar along with his defense of his mother, for example—Greek myth, or Powell's "white logos," becomes that which has to be rejected for an essential black identity; it represents the bad that Milkman must come to terms with. (We will see this again later in the criticism of Ellison's black Ulysses.) For Harris, "the dichotomies between good and evil are usually fairly clearly delineated" (87). It is perhaps not possible (and perhaps not desirable) to break away from binary oppositions in thought and criticism, yet the binary opposition between black and white, or male and female, has prevented readers from, as it were, reading between the lines. Morrison blurs the lines between the classical and the folkloric, or white and black, so that the reader asserts, along with Milkman, that everything and everybody "kept changing right in front of him" (*Song of Solomon*, 321). Homer's *Odyssey* is an indelible feature of Morrison's jazzlike riffs on tradition—on naming. Readings that seek to privilege an essential identity in the novel, whether male, female, or black, prove unsustainable. Morrison, as we will see, even critiques the folkloric premise of the novel, the tale of the glorious flight of slaves back to the homeland of Africa.

As with Morrison's use of folklore in the novel, allusions to myth, and in particular to the *Odyssey*, are both implicit and explicit, and the latter references allow some leeway to speculate about the former. As has already been touched upon, Circe, while clearly a strong, black woman, who is perhaps neither dead nor alive, is an explicit reference to the character from Homeric epic, and it will be necessary in closing to tease out more of her significance. Meanwhile, it might be argued that *Song of Solomon* in its entirety rewrites—riffs on—Homer's *Odyssey*. Hints of the proverbial hero's journey come as early in the novel as Milkman's first encounter with Pilate, and later in his awakening to selfhood when he prevents his father from hitting his mother. Homer's *Odyssey* is more strongly at hand in part 2 of the novel, which Morrison, ironically, begins with what might be read as an invocation to European folklore: "When Hansel and Gretel stood in the forest and saw the house in the clearing before them, the little hairs at the nape of their necks must have shivered" (220). Milkman is now squarely set in the context of his heroic journey, through the forest, on a quest for his father's gold.

As we saw in chapter 2, issues of hospitality, Greek *xenia*, are pivotal to the Homeric epic. Characters throughout the epic, such as Odysseus's son Telemachus, rely on hospitality to facilitate their journeys. Failure to observe hospitality was the cardinal sin of Penelope's suitors, and even Odysseus can learn a thing or two about the proper behavior of both guests and hosts. In *Song of Solomon* part 2, Milkman might initially be read as similar to Telemachus in search of his father's fame. Here Milkman is searching for his father Macon's gold but finds his fame, or his legacy. Morrison could well have had Telemachus in mind when she places Milkman in the home of Reverend and Mrs. Cooper, the hosts in Danville who direct Milkman to Circe, midwife and keeper of information vital to the Deads (and the dead). Similar to Nestor in Homer's *Odyssey*, who equips Telemachus with a convoy, including his son Peisistratus, to Sparta, where he will learn more about his father from Menelaus, Mr. Cooper sends his nephew to drive Milkman to Circe's home. We later learn that Milkman must walk much of the way alone because Circe's house cannot be accessed by automobiles, a fact that evokes the long-ago feeling of Homer's epic.

Later Milkman, similar to Odysseus in Polyphemus's cave, violates decorum and proper Southern hospitality in Virginia. Milkman is taken to be condescending when he, arrogantly, intimates his desire to find a woman:

"Nice around here. Peaceful. Pretty women too."

A young man sitting on a chair tilted to the wall pushed his hat back from his forehead and let the front legs of the chair hit the floor. His lips were open, exposing the absence of four front teeth. The other men moved their feet. Mr. Solomon smiled but didn't say anything. Milkman sensed that he'd struck a wrong note. (265)

A fight ensues between Milkman and Saul, the young man whom Milkman reads as having "hostility" toward him. Saul is no more an ogre than is Polyphemus in Homer's humanizing hands.[63] We learn from the third-person omniscient voice that these country folks "looked with hatred at the city Negro who could buy a car as if it were a bottle of whiskey because the one he had was broken" (266). Just as Odysseus has to learn proper hospitality, so Milkman undergoes a transformation in Virginia. The townsmen take him on a hunt, and while he enters Virginia in his tan suit, he emerges with the fatigues of a hunter and a sensibility, born in his unconscious, that makes him in essence a new man.

Hospitality is only one of several themes—and allusions implicit and explicit—that tie *Song of Solomon* to the *Odyssey*. Another is the idea of cunning intelligence, Greek *metis*. In the Homeric epic, we will recall that Odysseus accomplishes the blinding of the Cyclops, and the defeat of the suitors, through *metis*. The hero has to outwit both his antagonist and his environment—such as the sea/Poseidon—to find success. The same applies to Morrison's characters, and she is explicit in her play on *metis*. When Milkman tells Guitar his idea of stealing Pilate's gold, which we later discover is a bag of bones, the response recalls Homeric epic:

"You're forgetting, Guitar, how Pilate got the gold in the first place. She waited in a cave with a dead man for three days to haul it out, and that was when she was twelve. If she did that at twelve to get it, what you think she'll do now when she's almost seventy to keep it?"

"We don't have to be rough. *Cunning is all we need to be.*" (180, my italics)

Again, Morrison would not be content simply to allude to her Greek antecedent. Rather, she introduces the idea of cunning intelligence within the broader critique not only of male agency throughout the novel but also of the actions of her female characters. Milkman's cunning intelligence, on the one hand, fails because heroism itself is troublesome. (He gets the bag from Pilate's house, but there is no gold in it.) Heroism, contrary to some readings of the novel, does not seem to rest in the female characters any more than in the males. While Hagar could have killed Milkman many times and proven to be a heroine of sorts (in the mode of Medea), her actions were taken with a "*complete lack of cunning or intelligence* even of conviction" (301, my italics). Morrison more than implies that heroism—for men and women—might include an unconscious urgency that exists outside of the intellect. Cunning intelligence and hospitality are only two of the Homeric riffs in *Song of Solomon*.

As I have already suggested, Circe, the midwife who delivered Pilate, is a Homeric figure transformed into a racially charged icon. Circe points the reader to the realm of the unconscious, the place where dream images reside and play freely without regard to social constructions of race, gender, or even life and death. Circe's centrality to Morrison's literary project, whatever we conclude that it is or is not, is evident in references to her from early in the novel, even before we know who she is. Pilate mentions Circe when the boy Milkman first goes to the former's home: "So when we left Circe's big house we didn't have no place to go, so we just walked around and lived in them woods" (40). Macon had forbidden Milkman from going to his aunt's house. Milkman learns more from his father upon his return from his encounter with Pilate. Through Macon, we learn of the livestock at Lincoln's Heaven, the farm that his grandfather (also Macon, father of Macon II and Pilate) owned. The livestock, with their historical, human names—Mary Todd, Ulysses S. Grant, General Lee—elicit irrepressible comparisons to the men in Homer's *Odyssey* whom Circe transforms into pigs. The reader finally encounters Circe in flesh (and alive?) when Milkman travels to Danville. The woman who was midwife to Milkman's seventy-year-old aunt is witchlike, though not evil, and the reader is aware that this character is well over one hundred years old (if she is indeed alive and not a ghost). Circe's life, in fact, extends over a few thousand years, back to Homer.

Significantly, Circe in *Song of Solomon* serves a role parallel to that of her appearance in Homer; she directs Milkman toward the dead. Morrison's Circe informs Milkman that his grandfather's bones are in the cave where Macon and his sister Pilate first severed ties, and she suggests that he collect those bones and give them a proper burial. (Homer's Circe directs Odysseus to the realm of the dead, the Underworld, where he will encounter an unburied comrade, his mother, and others who facilitate his journey.) Milkman travels to the cave (the Underworld) to collect the bones of his grandfather. He later makes the connection between these bones and those that Pilate keeps in her home. At the end of the novel, Milkman and Pilate return to Virginia to give the bones a proper burial. So Circe is not only midwife to the Dead family, she is also a literary midwife: a figure that has something to tell the reader about the hermeneutics of the past—the dead—in living, American literature.

Returning to one of the earlier introductions to Circe in the novel, Macon tells his son of a horse on Lincoln's Heaven named President Lincoln, as well as "her foal, Mary Todd; Ulysses S. Grant, their cow; General Lee, their hog" (52). Milkman's father told him fragments of the tale to which Circe is central, and through his travels the protagonist learns more himself. Powell mistook Circe for an essential figure for blackness, rather than as a hybrid and protean symbol of hermeneutics, because of the extent to which the character speaks to certain issues of collective memory, selfhood, and the familial. Yet as is evident in Morrison's riffs on names—Macon Dead, Milkman Dead, Not Doctor Street, Song of Sugarman/Solomon/Shalimar—things are not always what they seem. Individuals have the power to alter narratives through their constant reinscription of self into the past. Through Circe, Morrison insists upon the ongoing transformation of American culture and society—in this case through a hermeneutics that is not static but that taps into a broader, collective unconscious. The Civil War changed America. But in order to understand the significance of that transformation, the American individual has to return to and apprehend President Lincoln, Mary Todd, Ulysses S. Grant, and Robert E. Lee. Through this return, the American is able to transpose history onto him- or herself, changing both irrevocably. This is as much the case with the African American's encounter with classical myth as it is with an American's reflection on the national past.

Some readers might reject the interpretation of *Song of Solomon* offered here, preferring a more essential, explicitly Afrocentric prism. Certainly, it might be argued, African and African American folklores have roles to play in the novel as well, even if we allow for Circe's centrality. The theme of flight with which the novel opens recurs throughout, and we close with the majestic folklore of flying slaves returning to Africa from their bondage in America. Morrison explicitly moves the reader away from the Western metaphor for flight, namely Icarus. I would caution readers, however, against privileging the folkloric motif of the slave's flight home. Morrison is as critical of this folklore as she is of Western mythology. We learn, for example, that Milkman's great-grandfather Solomon tries unsuccessfully to fly off with one child, Jake (Macon I), while leaving behind his other twenty. Throughout the novel, we are told of the danger of such escape. As the ghost of Macon I (Jake) first tells Pilate, "you just can't fly on off and leave a body" (147). The idea is repeated explicitly at least twice later in the novel (208, 332), and as an overarching theme flight as trouble-some—and not just as a glorious celebration of blackness—permeates the novel. As a criticism of Solomon's flight, the warning not to fly off and leave people behind might find echo in futile, suicidal-homicidal flight of Milkman and Guitar at the novel's close. Nothing in the novel is more patriarchal (and phallocentric) than Solomon's flight: the wife left behind becomes an Echo, and Milkman mimics his ancestor's flight in his aban-donment of Hagar. Morrison points to the legitimate and illegitimate chil-dren that Solomon leaves behind in his flight. The warning against flying off and leaving bodies behind calls into question the priority of the black, folkloric tale of Solomon, but it also makes a black flight from the body of Western texts an equally troublesome evasion.

For an American Ulysses, therefore, heroic return is not possible with-out the encounter with the classical (and American historic) past. The black and white individual, moreover, share in a common past, although their particular ethnic experiences differ. The critic or reader caught in an either/or dichotomy cannot fully appreciate either Morrison's classical motifs, which permeate her fiction, or the depth and breadth of American identity. The construction of any white identity that denies a black past—through the ideas of slavery, freedom, and a continuing democracy—fails, in mythological terms, to enter the abyss, the *katabasis* or "descent" into the Underworld. On the other hand, by opening herself up to the classical past Morrison gains perspective on her own identity. The African Amer-ican writer or critic who does not emerge from the black (w)hole forfeits his or her broader cultural identity. In addition, the classics are enriched and imbued with new life as they are transformed to speak to contempo-rary psychological and social needs. Morrison clearly represents the integ-rity of the American experience in her fiction, and particularly in *Song of Solomon*. As we will see again in the analysis of Ralph Ellison's writing, the process of coming to terms with this integrity can yield surprising results.

# ✤ Ralph Ellison's
# Black American Ulysses ✦

# ❧ 5 ❦

# "Ulysses alone in Polly-what's-his-name's cave"

*Ralph Ellison and the Uses of Myth*

His hands reached out, seized two of them [my men], and smashed
them to the ground like puppies. Their brains spattered out and
oozed into the dirt. He tore them limb from limb to make his
supper, gulping them down like a mountain lion, leaving nothing
behind—guts, flesh, or marrowy bones.

—Homer's *Odyssey* 9.287–93 (translated by Stanley Lombardo)

On his deathbed [the narrator's grandfather] called my father to him
and said, "Son, after I'm gone I want you to keep up the good fight.
I never told you, but our life is a war and I have been a traitor all my
born days, a spy in the enemy's country ever since I give up my gun
back in the Reconstruction. Live with your head in the lion's mouth.
I want you to overcome 'em with yesses, undermine 'em with grins,
agree 'em to death and destruction, let 'em swoller you till they
vomit or bust wide open."

—RALPH ELLISON, *Invisible Man*

In *Emergence of Genius*, Ellison biographer Lawrence Jackson reports an
episode in which young Ralph witnessed the white children of the local
corner grocer dressed in ceremonious white sheets and hoods for a mock
parade (2002, 45). The episode was one of the larger-than-life (or mythic)
experiences that shaped Ellison's childhood. Through his studies, Ellison
came to a particular awareness of how an experience such as this con-
tributes in forming an individual and collective consciousness, becoming
the stuff of myth.[1] Ellison concurred with the Jungian view that myth,

classical mythology, and for Ellison, African American folklore as well, permeates our collective unconscious. In a speech that he delivered at the United States Military Academy at West Point, Ellison related his understanding of myth, derived in part from his reading of Lord Raglan's *The Hero*. Ellison believed that, because of the way in which myth functions, we have the ability not only to tell our stories but also to retell and to reshape them so that they reflect our ideals—and guide our actions. The classical hero Ulysses was as much an icon for Ellison as any figure from African American folklore or American history.[2]

In this chapter, I examine Ellison's deployment of the Ulysses motif in *Invisible Man* and *Juneteenth* in light of the discussion of myth throughout his essays. The reader unfamiliar with the plot of either novel will find summaries along the way. Suffice it to say for now that many scenes in *Invisible Man*, and particularly the battle royal scene in the novel's first chapter, represent an unrelenting violence against the black protagonist that Ellison would distill to the simplicity of the Cyclops episode in this chapter's epigraph. The nameless protagonist, Invisible Man, must find a way not only to cope with this violence but also to master it, to overcome it, and perhaps use it to his advantage.

Little has been written specifically regarding the role of classical myth in Ellison's writings, and particularly not in light of his prose. An emblematic example of the treatment of Ellison's classicism (in his novels only) is John Stark's 1973 essay, "*Invisible Man:* Ellison's Black Odyssey," in which the author claims that the "comparison [of Invisible Man to Ulysses] suggests that for the ancient Greeks, but not for contemporary Black Americans, heroic aspirations can be achieved" (60). Ellison certainly would have cringed at Stark's conclusion, one that is consistent with the response to black classicism that we saw in the previous chapter. Other critics (Sanders 1970, for example), while noting Ellison's celebration of Western literature in general, and the classics in particular, miss subtler riffs on classical myth in *Invisible Man*, such as particular images in the battle royal scene, which I analyze here. These more covert allusions to classical myth, and particularly to Homer's *Odyssey*, convey a pervasive classicism throughout Ellison's fiction *and* prose.

In contrast to previous treatments, I offer a reading of *Invisible Man* and *Juneteenth* based in Ellison's myth analysis, which we find throughout his essays, interviews, and speeches, but especially in his illuminating essays, "Change the Joke and Slip the Yoke" (1966b), and "On Initiation

Rites and Power: Ralph Ellison Speaks at West Point" (1986b). By turning to Ellison's prose, I concur with Ray Black (1999), who asserts that much of the excitement over the publication of *Juneteenth* obscures Ellison's achievements as not only a novelist but also as an essayist. From these two essays we learn that Ellison was steeped in a ritual approach to myth, which his literary companion Stanley Edgar Hyman (1963) traced to the work of James Frazer, or the Cambridge School.[3]

Most illuminating to the discussion of his use of myth was Ellison's fixation on the Ulysses theme. In "Change the Joke," Ellison suggests a connection between the grandfather character in *Invisible Man* and Ulysses in the Cyclops's cave. Using Ellison's directive as a point of departure, we find that the grandfather in the novel is constructed around the drunken ogre motif, the folkloric model that informs the Homeric episode of Odysseus and the Cyclops.[4] What is more, the protagonist of *Invisible Man*, as Floyd Horowitz (1970, 32) and Robert O'Meally (1980, 95) intimate, can be read as a would-be Ulysses. What these authors do not explore, however, is the extent to which the Ulysses theme informs characterization throughout the novel, as the protagonist is initially myopic (a sort of ogre) and develops into a kind of hero (compared implicitly and explicitly to Ulysses). In addition to this, American society at large is depicted throughout the novel as a type of Cyclops, or the drunken ogre. A close reading of the novel vis-à-vis the Ulysses theme demonstrates the extent to which Ellison was steeped in symbolism of Ulysses' encounter with Polyphemus, the one-eyed ogre. In addition to this, Ellison returns to the Ulysses theme in the posthumous novel, *Juneteenth*. The novelist's creative deployment of classical mythology was characteristic of modernistic approaches to literature. This is not to say, contrary to Baker's suggestion (1984), that Ellison valued the classical tradition higher than African American culture or folklore. Rather, Ellison demonstrates a desire to make the classical heritage, and myth in particular, speak for him.

## An Ellisonian Journey

Ralph Waldo Ellison (1914–94) was born and raised in Oklahoma in times of segregation.[5] The Civil War had ended just forty-nine years before his birth, ushering in the defeat of slavery in America and the inauspicious rise of segregation throughout much of the United States. Indeed, Ellison's own grandfather had been a slave, had endured Emancipation, and had witnessed firsthand the gradual retreat of his rights as an American citizen.[6] Ellison's grandfather belonged to that generation that he speaks of in his essays "Going to the Territory" (1986e), a generation that journeyed to Oklahoma with great hope because the "territory" had not known slavery. Nevertheless, despite his description of Oklahoma in the essay as a mythic place, "a territory of hope" that for Negroes "had a traditional association with freedom which had entered their folklore" (132), Ellison's place of birth would gradually become a jim-crow society. Oklahoma, a territory that had been incorporated only in 1907, would come to resemble the South in its approach to blacks and Native Americans. Ellison felt the reality of life in America for Negroes under jim crow firsthand, and he saw its humiliating effects on others. In Oklahoma, Native Americans were lynched in the early twentieth century (Littlefield 1996), and the circumstances of lynching led to the Oklahoma riots of 1921. Ironically, Ellison did not write about such memories in his essays. As his writing developed, he would revisit the experiences that scarred him, not in prose but in his fiction. He seems to have felt that he could make the dehumanizing experiences of blacks in segregated America palatable through myth. For Ellison, myth was an essential emotional screen both for himself and his audience. For Ellison, myth functioned, like dreams, as a site of transference for conscious experiences (Jung 1972).

The battle royal scene in *Invisible Man* is one of the most memorable portrayals of violence against blacks in American fiction. Even before the publication of the novel, the episode, published as a short story, had captured the attention of some of the most prominent literary critics of the time (O'Meally 1980; Jackson 2002). The scene, in which the novel's protagonist is made to fight other black boys for coins to entertain white Southerners that comprised "some of the most important men in the town" (Ellison 1952; 1995, 18), opens the novel. In his discussion of the scene in his speech "On Initiation Rites and Power," Ellison explains the battle royal's underlying ritual and mythic features:

> No one had ever told me that the "battle royal" was a rite, but I came to see that it was. It was a rite which could be used to project certain racial divisions into the society and reinforce the idea of white racial superiority. On the other hand, as a literary person trying to make up stories out of recognizable experience, and as one who was reading a lot about myth and the function of myth and ritual in literature, it was necessary that I see the

"battle royal" situation as something more than a group of white men having sadistic fun with a group of Negro boys. Indeed, I would have to see it
for what it was beyond the question of the racial identities of the actors
involved: a ritual through which important social values were projected and
reinforced. (Ellison 1986b, 50–51)

In this passage, Ellison lays out his thesis that, first, the battle royal, and
by extension the practices found throughout the jim-crow South, was a
ritual belonging to a particular type of society, and second, that the novelist would have to understand the underlying, mythic dimension of the
practice in order to represent it meaningfully. In the same essay, Ellison
claims to have been reading Lord Raglan's *The Hero,* a work substantially
influenced by James Frazer's ritual approach to classical myth.

The ritual approach to myth, most exhaustively articulated in Sir James
George Frazer's *The Golden Bough* (1890), linked the customs and beliefs
of a number of traditional, premodern societies to underlying patterns
in magic and religion.[7] Most importantly, since all societies based their
stories on these patterns, classical myths could also be understood in terms
of magical and religious rituals. Frazer's work takes its name from the
branch that allows Aeneas entry into the Underworld in Vergil's *Aeneid*
(6.137). Frazer believed that Aeneas's Golden Bough shared the same symbolic value as mistletoe, a semiparasitic shrub with yellowish flowers,
because of the magical quality that many societies in Europe, Asia, and
Africa attributed to it. Aeneas's Golden Bough serves a ritualistic function,
as does mistletoe in other myths, allowing him entry into the Underworld
and thus symbolizing the ritual patterns of life and death—and the quest
for immortality—known to all societies.

Frazer believed that stories like Aeneas's quest for the Golden Bough
are, at core, tales about fertility and mortality (Campbell 1973). The quest
is repeated in such ancient myths as Theseus and the Minotaur, or Jason
and the Golden Fleece.[8] Frazer's contribution was that of encouraging
readers to examine these tales across cultures so as to tap into their universal, transcultural themes. The ritual approach to myth came to influence
Sigmund Freud, who used Frazer's research in part to explain what he
saw as underlying patterns of unconscious thought, such as the Oedipus
complex, the prepubescent male's symbolic overthrow of the father-figure.
Jung would develop this foundation toward the notion of the collective
unconscious. Although some of the less systematic, less scholarly aspects

of Frazer's work have been modified, *The Golden Bough* is still foundational to understanding one of the primary approaches to mythology, as
well as to sociology and anthropology. The ritual approach to myth was
pivotal to Ellison's thinking on American society and identity.[9]

Although Ralph Ellison came to mythology from outside of the formal,
academic disciplines of Classical Studies, he valued the work of classicists as he grappled with the experience of Negroes in America.[10] Most
significantly, Ellison seemed to believe, as Martin Luther King Jr. did,
that a certain emotional distance from lived experience would be critical
to understanding racism and white supremacy, and hence to overcoming
these vices.[11] In America, as in all other cultures, rituals safeguard life. The
stories Americans tell, whether in mass media or in novels, help to organize society and the expectations of individuals therein. Specifically, Ellison
saw that America (particularly the South) practiced lynching, one particularly brutal ritual, as a way of safeguarding a certain (white-supremacist)
worldview. If racist institutions can serve a ritual function, then through
an understanding of myth, or the stories that narrate the rites, Americans,
Ellison believed, could tap into the unconscious workings of our society
to restructure the collective unconscious. As we will see more clearly in
the next chapter, which looks more closely at lynching, Ellison's deployment of classical mythology was not a retreat from contemporary American concerns, as some critics would have it.

The ritual approach to myth is apparent in many of episodes throughout *Invisible Man*, including the battle royal, as "On Initiation Rites and
Power" indicates. *Invisible Man* has a lasting impact on the American
audience (and was an international success) in part because of the author's
mastery of myth and folklore in casting a local, black hero. And although
Ellison's modernistic approach represented the avant-garde, his interest
in mythology was more than decorative. As he reveals in "On Initiation
Rites and Power," myth could "enlarge" characters in *Invisible Man* (Ellison
1986b). Through myth, Ellison came to terms with "the nature of leadership, and thus with the nature of the hero" (44). The writer argued that
through mythological paradigms he was able to understand "just what
[there was] about the structure of American society that prevented Negroes
from throwing up effective leaders" (44). Ellison's hope was that his fictional personalities would come to be viewed outside of the customary
paradigm of race in American society. The Negro in America, Ellison saw,
had experienced something uniquely painful, but this experience could gain

meaning—and possible solutions—only through its relationship to that of others, as Richard Wright also believed.[12] Mythology and folklore, like fiction in the novel form, allowed Ellison, a black writer in pre-Civil Rights, segregated America, to construct black identity from outside of a limited, contemporary framework. Although his approach garnered him much criticism, Ellison, through folklore and fiction, constructed human characters whose possibilities transcended the limitations that society placed upon them.

Ellison himself provides the framework for our reading of classical mythology in his novels, and specifically the theme of Ulysses and the Cyclops, in the essay "Change the Joke and Slip the Yoke." In it Ellison links the grandfather character in *Invisible Man* to Ulysses:

> I knew the trickster Ulysses just as early as I knew the wily rabbit of Negro American lore, and I could easily imagine myself a pint-sized Ulysses but hardly a rabbit, no matter how human and resourceful or Negro. (1966b, 72)

Although it might be argued that there is a hierarchical relationship between African American folklore and classical myth in this quote, it is also possible that Ellison was simply employing a strategy, albeit one prone to criticism, to explain the role of myth and its associations in the human imagination. As a reading of *Invisible Man* vis-à-vis the Ulysses theme reveals, Ellison uses Ulysses and the Cyclops, which is based on the folkloric drunken ogre motif, to structure his protagonist's experiences.[13] Similar to Ulysses, who encounters many people and places on his journey home from Troy, Invisible Man travels throughout America, from the South to New York City's Harlem, in search of "home," a physical and emotional place of belonging. While war, wandering, and upstart suitors of his wife Penelope displace Ulysses from home, myopic antagonists, some of whom practice distinctly American rituals of exclusion, would keep the unnamed, African American narrator of *Invisible Man* from recognizing America as his homeland. Ellison returns to Ulysses' encounter with the one-eyed ogre in *Juneteenth*. In this context, the protagonist is not black but, similar to his invisible counterpart, he is an individual searching for "home" within the American context. For Bliss, the protagonist of *Juneteenth*, the Ulysses theme points to the individual soul's longing for balance and integrity, a spiritual home, in a materialist, racist culture.

Ulysses and the Cyclops: The Drunken Ogre Motif in *Invisible Man*

Ellison's discussion of Ulysses and the Cyclops in prose centers on the grandfather in *Invisible Man,* and for this reason the old man is a fitting place to begin. In "Change the Joke and Slip the Yoke," the writer uses the Ulysses figure to take issue with Stanley Edgar Hyman's characterization of the grandfather in *Invisible Man* as a minstrel (Ellison 1966b). Minstrelsy, made popular initially in the "blackface" performances of white actors in the nineteenth century (Lhamon 1997), reifies the racial polarities of American society, with blacks represented as buffoons to their orderly white counterparts. As Orlando Patterson (1998) observes in his discussion of the representation of black men in twentieth-century American media, the appropriation of the form among blacks can bear ambivalent meaning.[14] Similar to a folkloric trickster's guise of innocence, blacks appropriate minstrelsy for material gain, thus in some ways undermining its surface message of ignorance. The grandfather character, with his seemingly sycophantic grins, would at first glance seem to submit willingly to the Manichean category imposed upon him. Hyman had argued that *Invisible Man* contained "the fullest development I know of the darky act in fiction" (Hyman 1963, 299). For Ellison, the reduction of his characters (and in particular the grandfather) to minstrelsy attenuates their personalities to one extremely limited (and to his mind inaccurate) reading. In his observations, we see the extent to which the mythological drunken ogre motif (Ulysses and the Cyclops) helped Ellison to explore the broader, epic dimension of his character.

We learn of Ellison's thoughts on the grandfather's relationship to Ulysses in his response to Hyman:

> So intense is Hyman's search for archetypal forms that he doesn't see that the narrator's grandfather in *Invisible Man* is no more involved in a "darky" act than was Ulysses in Polyphemus' cave. Nor is he so much a "smart-man-playing-dumb" as a weak man who knows the nature of his oppressor's weakness. There is a good deal of spite in the old man, as there comes to be in his grandson, and the strategy he advises is a kind of jiujitsu of the spirit, a denial and rejection through agreement. (Ellison 1966b, 70)

Ellison suggests that, similar to Ulysses, who himself demonstrates qualities of the trickster in Greek mythology (Stanford 1963), the grandfather offers more than comic buffoonery. By comparing the grandfather to Ulysses in Polyphemus's cave, Ellison points to the epic dimension of the character, which is displayed in his cunning intelligence (marked by self-awareness and wit), long-suffering, and courage.[15] In other words, cunning intelligence (Greek *metis*), which might at times have a comic effect, is only one of the qualities that the epic hero demonstrates. While the trickster figure is at times deployed comically (Ulysses garners many laughs disguised as a poor beggar in his own home), in the epic he is part of a broader array of human qualities. Because the trickster figure became nothing more than an archetype for Hyman, he could read the grandfather in *Invisible Man* only as a "darky," a smart-man-playing dumb. For Ellison, there was much more to this character, just as there is a great deal more than a trickster in Ulysses.

By revealing the Ulyssean quality of the grandfather in *Invisible Man*, Ellison shifts the interpretation of the character away from particularly comic readings. While Hyman associates the grandfather with minstrelsy, Ellison moves his characters beyond this archetype, claiming that

> between [archetypes and literature] there must needs be the living human being in a specific texture of time, place and circumstance; who must respond, make choices, achieve eloquence and create specific works of art. (Ellison 1966b, 62)

In this quote, Ellison again points to the use of myth and literature to represent full, human beings exploring their possibilities. Ellison argues that, despite the overdetermining gaze of at large American society, blacks were still responsible agents.[16] Within any social context, the individual's struggle, his choices, amount to, in Ellison's view, a striving for eloquence. "Eloquence" and "work of art" do not refer only to the achievement of a novelist or musician, both crafts that Ellison himself strove to master (Ellison 1986b). In Ellison's worldview, even the layperson has his or her own area of eloquence and art (whether as a mother or father, janitor or salesperson). In America's social discourse, built around race, the perceptions of outsiders could affect one's own striving for eloquence. The struggle of individual African Americans—as with any other overdetermined group—would be that of maintaining his or her self-awareness in the face of an overdetermining, external gaze, or antagonism. (In Ulysses' case, these external antagonists include nature, or the gods, and even culture.)

Through self-awareness, the grandfather in *Invisible Man* came to his own eloquent mode of living. The figure of Ulysses, to Ellison's mind, complicated a reductive archetype, that of minstrelsy, that rendered his character subhuman. Odysseus, although at times a comical, trickster figure, is also at times cunningly intelligent and deeply emotional. As an unfaithful husband, he is not always the epitome of goodness. Nevertheless, he knows the pain of homesickness, and a goddess's love cannot assuage the longing for his own wife.[17] Ulysses is a complete human character, making mistakes but also demonstrating the ability to learn from them. The hero is the embodiment of human possibilities.

Such possibilities, as Ellison recognizes, were historically denied to African Americans. In American entertainment, for example, blacks were— and still are—often reduced to the archetype of minstrelsy. Ellison saw that this archetype, which Hyman applied to his grandfather character, belonged not to the black imagination, but to the realm of

> white America's Manichean fascination with the symbolism of blackness and whiteness expressed in such contradictions as the conflict between the white American's Judeo-Christian morality, his democratic political ideals and his daily conduct—indeed his general anti-tragic approach to experience. (Ellison 1966b, 63)

As white American, comic entertainment, the archetype has nothing to do with African American identity intrinsically, and the Negro who knows this is able to enact a "profound rejection of the image created to usurp his identity" (Ellison 1966b, 69–70).[18] Minstrelsy, moreover, steeped in the symbolism of white America, has a predominantly comic value and therefore attenuates epic heroism, which is as tragic and serious as it is comedic.

When Ellison's reflections on the grandfather as a Ulysses figure are read alongside the novel and within the context of *American* sociopolitical concerns, we come to understand the role of the Ulysses motif in restoring a somewhat concealed dimension of the character. Although "Change the Joke and Slip the Yoke" was initially presented in *Partisan Review* six years after the publication of *Invisible Man*, the Ulysses theme was no afterthought to the novel or to the development of the grandfather character. A reading of the perplexing scene at the opening of the novel, in which the dying grandfather, himself a pivotal character, utters his last words, reveals the extent to which the drunken ogre motif shapes the character's representation.

In the beginning of the novel's first chapter, the unnamed narrator conveys his dying grandfather's last words:

> On his deathbed he called my father to him and said, "Son, after I'm gone I want you to keep up the good fight. I never told you, but our life is a war and I have been a traitor all my born days, a spy in the enemy's country ever since I give up my gun back in the Reconstruction. Live with your head in the lion's mouth. I want you to overcome 'em with yesses, undermine 'em with grins, agree 'em to death and destruction, let 'em swoller you till they vomit or bust wide open." (Ellison 1952; 1995, 16)

While the idea of "over[coming] 'em with yesses, undermin[ing] 'em with grins" might indeed conjure up images of a buffoon, these closing words are somewhat incongruous with what precedes. The old man's advice is deathly serious. It reverberates deeply with the metaphor of war, as Joseph F. Trimmer (1978) asserts in his article on the grandfather's riddle. The grandfather, a man who might have fought in the Civil War and surrendered his gun "in the Reconstruction," understands that war is not confined to the battlefield. The war might be actual (as the Civil War) or symbolic of the slave's struggle for freedom. "Life is a war," the old man warns his grandson, and one must "keep up the good fight." What we immediately encounter are not the jesting words of a minstrel but rather the reflections of a man that endured local struggles and wants to communicate their ongoing significance.

The idea of Reconstruction is critical to the grandfather's characterization. Although life is at times war for all who live it, life's war was in some ways particularly cruel for the Negroes confined to a world of segregation after the Civil War, and later to jim-crow laws (Woodward 1974; Nadel 1988). Such American Negroes had their "head[s] in the lion's mouth," not unlike the biblical hero Daniel, who was thrown into the lion's den for worshipping a god other than the Babylonian king, in whose land he was held captive. Trimmer argues that the grandfather is a traitor to his own people. But the old man is as likely to be a parallel to Daniel, who serves a foreign king but never fully adapts to the manners and mores of the land. The grandfather lives as a spy in the enemy's country because he preserves an inner self separate from the citizen who conforms to social expectations. He is a self-styled "traitor," one whose compulsory outward compliance belies inner treason. This is double-consciousness, the conflict between inner reality and outer presentation, that segregation, stemming from Reconstruction, created.[19]

Ellison suggests this deep symbolism in his comparison of the grandfather to Ulysses in his debate with Hyman. By reducing the grandfather figure to the role of minstrel, Hyman misses the complexity of a figure that becomes a Sphinx-like oracle for the main character (Trimmer 1978). In addition to conveying an atmosphere of conflicts actual and transcendent, including the Civil War, biblical conflicts, and given Ellison's comparison, Ulysses' Trojan War, the old man's war metaphor affords the reader an intimate sense of the speaker's heroic struggle. Wars are fought to be won, and if the speaker tells his son to "keep up the good fight," it is clear that the war continues even after his own death. He hands down his particular brand of struggle as a heritage and an ongoing legacy. A life styled as war, moreover, is removed from the realm of minstrelsy, taking on epic depths. Yet lighter tones still remain in the grandfather's advice. "Overcome" and "undermine" suggest a final victory, one expressed in the enemy's eventual self-destruction: "Let 'em swoller you till they vomit or bust wide open."

If, as Ellison argued, a reading of the grandfather as a minstrel is incongruous with the character's own words and the symbols connected to them, then we ought to read the idea of "overcom[ing] 'em with yesses" within a broader context than has been commonly accepted. The grandfather in *Invisible Man* resembles a buffoon in his gestures, but his private reflections reveal his epic struggle within a society that demands of him an intellect, patience, and courage equal to that of the mythological hero Ulysses. In his portrayal of the grandfather Ellison points to a folkloric motif present in the mythological tale of Ulysses, namely the comic demise of the hero's cannibalistic antagonist, who will eventually "bust wide open."

The grandfather episode in *Invisible Man* contains all of the themes of Odysseus's encounter with Polyphemus in Homer's *Odyssey*. Itself patterned after the folkloric motif of the drunken ogre, the Homeric episode consists of several movements: (1) the drunken ogre eats Odysseus's companions alive; (2) Odysseus conceals his name from the Cyclops (calling himself "Nobody"), outwitting the ogre but also raising the central issue of identity; and (3) Odysseus blinds the ogre and escapes from his cave victorious (Schein 1970). The hero triumphs through the heroic qualities of cunning intelligence (he premeditates his actions and comes to a well-thought-out solution), craftiness, and long-suffering. The drunken ogre motif is present in the grandfather's call to "let 'em swoller you till they vomit or bust wide open," an allusion (albeit elusive) to Polyphemus's cannibalism (swallowing Odysseus's companions) and to his final defeat (*Odyssey* 9.252–306). The motif of naming is contained in the grandfather's concealment of his identity through guile; he is not what he appears to be. Although Polyphemus does not "bust wide open," Odysseus is able to blind the Cyclops because of his senseless gluttony.

Within an American context, society's inability to see individuals like Invisible Man's grandfather as full human subjects parallels the Cyclops's blindness. As a one-eyed giant, one of America's weaknesses historically has been the legacy of slavery, the holocaust of Africans in the New World. The remnants of slavery were present throughout the twentieth century in the struggle of African Americans to gain full citizenship. Southern Negroes like the grandfather relied on American institutions (the courts, schools) to protect their freedom and humanity, yet America at large continuously violated the norms of civility.[20] Individuals like the grandfather, a Negro in the postbellum South, anticipated Reconstruction, but these individuals came to face an ongoing process of segregation and second-class citizenship. Some of America's most severe barbarism (such as the institution of lynching) would increase in frequency after 1877.[21] Within this context, Ellison represents American society as the antagonist, the Cyclops. The would-be hero is faced with the prospects of a heroic reversal, a "jiujitsu of the spirit" (Ellison 1966b, 70) represented in folklore through the ogre's blinding. Taking American society as the Cyclops in its late nineteenth- and early twentieth-century institutions, the old man's strategy is one of undermining those institutions through self-affirmation. He hands over his epic struggle to his grandson, the young protagonist of the novel, who strives to come to terms with his grandfather's principle of conduct within a hostile, violent America. The grandfather in *Invisible Man* counsels his progeny to overcome his foes by, in Ellison's words, "knowing the nature of his oppressor's weakness," just as Ulysses does in the case of Polyphemus.

The deeper reading of the Ulysses figure in *Invisible Man* for which I am arguing aids our understanding of the novel and of Ellison's broader work, including *Juneteenth*, in several important ways. The grandfather's riddle is itself a structuring device (Schafer 1970), and although the character might be read as a minstrel-type for the protagonist to reject, the deeper symbolism Ellison offers would resist such easy dismissal. The folkloric motif of the drunken ogre strengthens the link between Ulysses' heroism and heroic struggles in *Invisible Man* and thus affirms Ellison's classicism. Each character in *Invisible Man* achieves eloquence for his time; the grandfather's self-awareness will not be that of the main character, any more than will Invisible Man's antagonist be the same as that of Ulysses. Invisible Man's heroic struggle is particular to his place in time. By the end of the novel, he comes to his own interpretation of his grandfather's apparent sycophancy (his grins and "yesses").

Similar to the riddle of "overcom[ing] 'em with yesses," the centrality of the Ulysses figure in structuring *Invisible Man* can be traced throughout the novel. The mythological motif becomes a marker of the protagonist's epic struggle in American society. A similar use of the Ulysses theme is at play in *Juneteenth*, where the question of the hero Bliss's triumph, his blinding of the Cyclops, is presented but left unresolved.

The motif of the hero's encounter with a drunken ogre, figured as Ulysses and the Cyclops, recurs in at least three key moments in *Invisible Man:* (1) during the battle royal episode (chapter 1), where Ellison casts the protagonist himself as the ogre; (2) in a hospital scene (chapter 11), where the drunken ogre motif works in tandem with improvisations on Brer Rabbit tales of African American folklore; and (3) in the protagonist's final encounter with Brother Jack (chapter 22), a leader in the novel's Brotherhood, which resembles the Communist Party in America in the early twentieth century. These passages correspond, respectively, to (1) the hero's initial encounter with the drunken ogre, (2) naming and identity in the cave, and (3) the blinding of the Cyclops. The motif structures *Invisible Man*, and in each case, along with the attendant symbols of sight and blindness, visibility and invisibility, the folkloric and mythic dimensions of the narrative highlight the epic nature of Invisible Man's struggle. A reading of the motif in these passages aids our understanding of Invisible Man who, like Brer Rabbit in fables, taps into "our sense of both identification and spectatorship" (Dauer 1948, 131). The character himself is both narrator and spectator of his own life (Steele 2000). Classical myth, along with African American folklore, helps to convey the comic and tragic complexity of Invisible Man's American odyssey.

The first passage in *Invisible Man* that features the folkloric motif in relation to the main character is the battle royal, which corresponds to the hero's encounter with the drunken ogre. In this passage, the white Southerners that exploit Invisible Man and the other black boys are Cyclopes because of their intoxication and disregard for human life (particularly when it is contained in a black body). Yet there is no hero in the passage. Invisible Man is at the same time cast as a Cyclops. He lacks the understanding (the sight) to accomplish the ogre's (the white Southerners') blinding. Concerning the battle royal episode, Ellison stated that he was interested in symbolizing lived experience through ritual and myth (Ellison 1986a). As we have seen, the battle royal was for Ellison "a rite which could be used to project certain racial divisions into the society and reinforce the idea of white racial superiority." Similar to lynching, the battle royal is "a ritual through which important social values were projected and reinforced" (Ellison 1986a, 49, 50). Ellison situates the battle royal, as with all of the protagonist's encounters throughout the novel, within the context of a ritual approach to myth, which emphasizes the genesis of heroic and legendary narratives from encounters within societies (Hyman 1963). Ellison saw that in American society lynching, as one example of an insidious racial habit like the fictional battle royal, becomes ritualized. That is, lynching was a celebrated moment in the lives of the Southerners that practiced it (Patterson 1998). In addition to this, lynching was a rite of passage for young black men coming of age in American society. For them, the practice reinforced a sense of alienation and hopelessness (Alexander 1995). Social habits like lynching become mythical in that they help to structure the individual and collective conscience.

In the battle royal episode, Invisible Man faces objectification at the hands of racist Southerners, and he hopes to overcome their mockery through restraint and his skill as an orator. The passage contains a number of perspectives (Steele 2000). The character narrates his experience in the first person, but it is also the case that he is telling the reader about these events after some time. This temporal distance affords him a third-person perspective, which affords him a cool ability to convey both the painful emotions it elicited *and* its comedy. Here again, we see echoes of Ellison's practice of representing extremely painful experiences for blacks in America from the distance of classicism.

The drunken ogre motif is an undercurrent throughout the battle royal scene. Similar to Homer's Cyclops, whose drunkenness is a minor infraction only in comparison to his eating of human beings, the men who indulge in the spectacle boarder on cannibalistic excess. One such figure, who readily recalls the Cyclops, is "a certain merchant who followed [the woman] hungrily, his lips loose and drooling" (*Invisible Man*, 20). An obese and comic bloke, who like the Cyclops would devour human flesh, the merchant is "a large man who wore diamond studs in a shirt front which swelled with the ample paunch underneath." Demonstrative of his excessive desire, the merchant "wound his belly in a slow and obscene grind." His intoxication, like that of the other men present, uncovers the barbarity that lies beneath the veneer of daily civility in America. As the narrator comments earlier in the passage, "I was shocked to see some of the most important men of the town quite tipsy. They were all there—bankers, lawyers, judges, doctors, fire chiefs, teachers, merchants" (18). Drunkenness helps to reveal the Southerners' unconscious states; the man described as an "intoxicated panda" is now cast as more bestial than human: "This *creature* was completely hypnotized" (my italics). The merchant is linked to symbols of barbarism: the ostentatious display, drunkenness, and gluttony.

The Southerners clearly act as Cyclopes in their cannibalistic excess. They are creatures with ample paunches, following the dancer hungrily, and drooling. The protagonist, similar to Ulysses in the Cyclops's cave, faces the prospect of being "swoller[ed]" up. One man expresses a desire to "tear" the "ginger-colored" protagonist "limb from limb" (21). But unlike Ulysses, Invisible Man has little hope of effecting a heroic reversal, of forcing the antagonist to "bust wide open": "I stood against the rope trembling. For in those days I was what they called ginger-colored, and he sounded as though he might crunch me between his teeth like a crisp ginger cookie."

The story of Ulysses' encounter with the Cyclops is an important subtext to the battle royal. In the passage, Ellison uses comedy to create an objective distance from a racial and sexual objectification that historically has led to tragic American rituals. The Southerners, however, are not the only agents with attenuated vision.

With the perspective that time and distance brings, Invisible Man is able to see that he lacked understanding in his early days. Although ogres surrounded him at the battle royal, he is able later to reflect on his own Cyclops-like blindness during that time. At the time, he believed that these Southerners would listen to reason and would see him as in some ways a peer (Callahan 1990, 158). He does not fully recognize the barbarity that some Southerners during the time embodied. His grandfather concealed his true identity because of the Southerners' ignorance, not his own. In the battle royal scene the protagonist is closer to the one-eyed ogre than to Ulysses. He attempts to deliver his speech after a boxing spectacle that nearly renders him blind, literally. The protagonist dramatizes a central aspect of the Cyclops figure, the ogre's limited, one-eyed vision (Glickman

1970). Invisible Man's adoration of a blond woman earlier in the passage (his objectification of her), for example, is emblematic of the Cyclops's uncontrolled desire: "Had the price of looking been blindness, I would have looked" (*Invisible Man,* 19). Later in the episode, when the boys are forced into the ring, "blindfolds were put on" (21). They "grope about" and fight one another, "like blind, cautious crabs" (23). A boy named Tatlock, who is finally left in the ring with the protagonist, effectively blinds him in one eye: "A blow to my head as I danced about sent my right eye popping like a jack-in-the box and settled my dilemma" (25). The idea of vision, represented literally and in the figure of the Cyclops (his limited vision and the hero's blinding of him), underscores Invisible Man's trust in men that would entangle him in a dehumanizing exhibition.

In the battle royal scene, Invisible Man fails at eloquence, to borrow again from Ellison's creative lexicon, because he does not properly assess his circumstance (Callahan 1990; O'Meally 1980, 7–25). As the novel progresses and his experiences broaden (traveling North to Harlem), his challenge of eloquence, that of "living human being in a specific texture of time, place and circumstance" (Ellison 1966b, 62) continues. Invisible Man is increasingly capable of meeting this challenge. As O'Meally sees, the exploration of folk forms, such as the oratory of black preachers, folkloric narratives, and the eloquence of the blues, are critical to his success. From a narrative perspective, improvised Brer Rabbit tales become an important symbol of the character's development. Here I would like to uncover the coupling, as opposed to hierarchy that Baker (1984) suggests, of black folklore with the Ulysses theme that I read in the novel. Invisible Man comes to a realization that African American folklore is an indelible feature of identity. If he is to achieve the mastery of self that is emblematic of Ulysses, he must come to terms both with his broader (classically influenced) context and with his identity in an African American texture of time, place, and circumstance.

In "Change the Joke and Slip the Yoke," in addition to outlining the link between Ulysses and the grandfather in *Invisible Man,* Ellison suggests the relationship between Brer Rabbit (the African American texture of folklore) and Ulysses. Ellison claims that he "knew the trickster Ulysses just as early as [he] knew the wily rabbit of Negro American lore, and [he] could easily imagine [himself] a pint-sized Ulysses but hardly a rabbit, no matter how human and resourceful or Negro" (Ellison 1966b, 72). Far from rejecting the African American, Ellison saw Brer Rabbit and Ulysses as equally important components to his understanding of folklore and mythology, and to his own self-awareness as an American. Houston Baker (1984) misreads Ellison's juxtaposition of the Western and the folkloric as a hierarchy. (Or perhaps those who evaluate things this way misread Baker.) Ellison's apparent privileging of Ulysses might be read as Euro-centric. It might as easily, however, served as a rhetorical strategy that he deemed necessary in order to appropriate the figure from his Eurocen-tric audience. While outsiders might limit the Negro to what they see as simplistic ("lowbrow") folklore, Ellison shifts the focus by claims that an African American can have as much sympathy for the classical hero as any other human being. The novelist, to my mind, performs his own "jiujitsu of the spirit" by linking local folklore to (ostensibly) loftier classical myth-ology. As the final episode of *Juneteenth* demonstrates, Ellison felt that mythological motifs such as Ulysses and the Cyclops were themselves only local manifestations of folkloric tendencies in all human societies. African American folklore was no exception. Black identity, and American iden-tity by intimate association, is for Ellison part of an integral fabric.

The deployment of the Ulysses theme in the battle royal scene shows what readers of *Invisible Man* had already recognized, but now with new symbolism. While an undeveloped hero (an antihero of sorts) in the first half of the novel, Invisible Man's self-awareness increases through his ex-periences. Within the American context, self-awareness for the black pro-tagonist involves coming to terms with a distinct past, and for this reason African American folklore becomes a necessary counterpart to the Ulysses theme. The beginning of heroism for Invisible Man is the hospital scene, in which the interplay between the drunken ogre motif and Brer Rabbit tales point to the harmonious integration of his identity. Overcome by Lucius Brockway, himself cast as a trickster like Brer Rabbit in chapter 10 (Horowitz 1970), the protagonist awakens from a concussion in the hos-pital.[22] In the novel, the hospital serves as a symbol, a place of recupera-tion, reflection, and recollection of the self. Thus the hospital is the site of the protagonist's awakening to social and personal realities.

The first impression that Invisible Man has as he gains consciousness at the hospital might recall to the reader the Cyclops: "I was sitting in a cold, white rigid chair and a man was looking at me out of a bright third eye that glowed from the center of his forehead" (*Invisible Man*, 231). A three-eyed doctor (the "bright third eye" being the doctor's reflector) disorients the protagonist, and the mythical Cyclops is sometimes depicted with three eyes (Mondi 1983). The transformation of the reflector into a mythical third eye evokes a heightened attentiveness on the reader's part. (The symbol has a jarring effect.) As the local concerns of sanity, identity, and agency are rendered symbolically, the mythical dimension now dominates the narrative.

The return to the myth of Ulysses and the Cyclops is central to the narrative in chapter 11.[23] The passage draws on the preoccupation with naming and identity found throughout the drunken ogre motif. In many versions of the tale, the giant asks the hero his name, and the hero responds with "Myself" (Brown 1966). An affirmation of personhood that echoes the biblical burning bush—the God-claim of being (*I AM*), there is likely another play on this motif later on in *Invisible Man* in chapter 13, where the protagonist concedes to being a yam eater: "They're my birthmark," I said. "I yam what I am!"[24] In Homer's *Odyssey,* Odysseus is able to escape the Cyclops's cave through improvisation on the theme of naming, claiming to be "Nobody" (*Odyssey* 9.360–67). As a result of this, the Cyclops is only able to assert: "Nobody has blinded me" (*Odyssey* 9.401–8). The heroic achievement ultimately brings Odysseus fame, since he lives to recount his deeds for posterity.

Through the drunken ogre motif in chapter 11, particularly the naming of the hero, Ellison moves the narrative toward an anatomy of the African American protagonist. The distortion of vision and disorientation of a "bright third eye" conveys, on the one hand, the antagonism that the character feels from the white doctors. For the protagonist, the objectification that he feels is similar to the more overt racism of Southerners at the battle royal. On the other hand, Invisible Man begins to discover his own possibilities for overcoming adversity. Rendered as "Nobody" through invisibility, the character faces the question of his identity, which the "cyclops-eyed" (O'Meally 1980, 95) doctor poses:

"What is your name?" a voice said.
"My head . . ." I said.
"Yes, but your name. Address?"
"My head—that burning eye . . ." I said.
"Eye?"
"Inside," I said. (232)

The Homeric epic provides an illuminating backdrop to this passage. As we recall from *Odyssey,* Odysseus blinds Polyphemus with an olive beam, blazed until burning hot. In *Invisible Man* the protagonist, somewhat of a

Cyclops himself through the earlier chapters, now feels "the bright third eye still burning into [his own]."

As with the battle royal scene, Ellison's deployment of the mythological motif yields a number of points of view. The Cyclops's gaze belongs to the doctors, but the protagonist feels "that burning eye," as though he himself had been blinded "inside." The symbol communicates an antagonism directed toward the protagonist. Invisible Man tells his reader that "[the doctor] reached out, touching my skull gingerly, and said something encouraging, as though I were a child" (*Invisible Man,* 231). The doctors are "laughing down," and the nurses, "in white," are "looking down" at the protagonist. At this point in the narrative, the symbols have not yet been reversed, that is, the protagonist still has not learned how to overcome his adversaries. He has not yet discovered how to avert the overdetermining gaze. As Invisible Man reminds us, the doctors' purpose should be to comfort him: "They would care for me. It was all geared toward the easing of pain. I felt thankful" (177). Nevertheless, Invisible Man experiences confinement and pain, which result in his disorientation. He finds himself "sitting in a cold, white rigid chair."[25]

Although the scene is narrated from the perspective of Invisible Man's objectification, the symbols deployed throughout shift attention to heroic possibilities, contrary to Stark's reading. Invisible Man is moving away from the blind faith that he had in Southerners earlier in the novel. He begins to realize that his own heroic reversal, similar to his grandfather's treason, must emerge from "deep inside" himself. African American folklore symbolizes his possibilities for heroism. The protagonist, as we have seen, is potentially the blinded ogre, since succumbing to his external limitations would render him blind, or invisible. But, as Invisible Man himself ironically asserts in the novel's prologue, "even the invisible victim is responsible for the fate of all." If he is to survive the "electric chair" to which the hospital chair is assimilated, he is compelled to become a responsible human being. Ellison offers the recollection of the past as the beginning of the protagonist's transformation. Folklore, which in the scene is an ironic response to a dehumanizing gaze of (antagonistic) racial identity, is the central symbol for cultural memory.

Similar to Ulysses, Invisible Man must arrive at self- and cultural-awareness to escape confinement. Ellison's improvisation on the motif of the hero's identity underscores the character's unique, personal reaction to his circumstances:

WHO WAS YOUR MOTHER?
    I looked at him, feeling a quick dislike and thinking, half in amusement,
I don't play the dozens. And how's *your* old lady today? (241)

In response to the question of identity, the protagonist reaches back into his childhood, and although he claims that he does not "play the dozens," he begins to do just that: "And how's *your* old lady today?"[26] His ironic amusement, his memory of childhood games, suggests that through the recollection of the past blackness in America can be as sweet as it is bitter. (This is Louis Armstrong's blues of blackness, "What did I do to be so black and blue?") Bittersweet memories situate the character's reaction to objectification within the context of local, African American folk forms, such as singing the blues (Baker 1989; Murray 1973).

The reader already senses the local coloring of the blues earlier in the chapter when the protagonist first awakens:

Oh doctors, I thought drowsily, did you ever wade in a brook before breakfast? Ever chew on sugar cane? You know, doc, the same fall day I first saw
the hounds chasing black men in stripes and chains my grandmother sat
with me and sang with twinkling eyes. (234)

The passage conveys a complexity of experience that might be localized as African American, although human suffering and folk responses are universals. To "wade in a brook before breakfast" reminds again of child's play, while "chew[ing] on sugar cane" evokes a mixed response, as we recall both the sweetness of sugar and the trash that we cannot swallow and must spit out. The image of sugar cane also calls back the experience of black slaves, who chop on—"chew on"—sugar cane on Southern plantations. The multivalent sugar cane merges into the horrific image of "hounds chasing black men in stripes and chains," which is the flight and chase of runaway slaves, or the escape and recapture of a chain gang. Invisible Man anchors his recollection in childhood, as he offers both laughter and a loss of innocence in the blues that his grandmother "sang with twinkling eyes."

Invisible Man's plunge into memory, a plunge perhaps outside of history, to borrow Tod Clifton's idea (Ellison 1952; 1995, 376–77, 434–35), culminates in the symbol of Brer Rabbit (Horowitz 1970), which, like the blues, localizes human struggle within the context of African American

cultural experience.[27] For Ellison, Brer Rabbit and Ulysses are akin. As we
have seen, *Invisible Man*'s protagonist is himself Cyclops early in the novel,
unable to accomplish heroism because of his inexperience. In like manner,
throughout the first half of the novel the antagonist is often Brer Rabbit,
while the main character is Jack the Bear, duped continuously by his wilier
opponent (Horowitz 1970). In other words, the association of the protagonist with Ulysses in the factory hospital extends the already-attested
reversal of symbols found throughout the scene. Through self-awareness
and a consciousness of his cultural history (his "specific texture of time,
place and circumstance," Ellison 1966b, 62), Invisible Man in chapter 11
becomes Brer Rabbit, an African American Ulysses figure, and later he is
able to accomplish the blinding of the Cyclops.

Late in chapter 11, one doctor asks, "Boy, who was Brer Rabbit?" Earlier
in the passage, Invisible Man could not answer the question, "What is your
name?" His response to "who is Brer Rabbit" suggests that identity is more
permanent than a forgotten name. Similar to a wily rabbit, or to the cunning hero Ulysses, Invisible Man answers as though he were now in fact
being asked his name:

> I laughed, deep, deep inside me, giddy with the delight of self-discovery and
> the desire to hide it. Somehow *I* was Buckeye the Rabbit . . . or had been,
> when as children we danced and sang barefoot in the dusty streets. (241)

The laughter that emerges from "deep, deep inside" counters the burning
that the protagonist earlier feels "inside," and he characterizes the moment
as one of identification, or "self-discovery." Being Buckeye the Rabbit
means having the ability to draw upon the joyous experience of a child
that "danced and sang," but it also means deploying cunning intelligence.
Invisible Man would have somehow to adapt the mode of life for which
African American folklore is representative, his grandfather's mode of life,
in order to overcome adversaries. From this we see that the hospital scene,
which falls in the middle of the novel at chapter 11, is the beginning of a
deep self-awareness for the main character.

In *Invisible Man*, the protagonist does emerge from his coal cellar with
the tools necessary to blind the Cyclops, or to master American society.
Mastery of any society involves a high degree of self-awareness and awareness of one's social institutions. We begin to see this perspective in Invisible Man during the second half of the novel, in Harlem. After a short time

in Harlem, Invisible Man becomes involved with a political organization, the Brotherhood. The Brotherhood, which bears a striking resemblance to the Communist Party in American in the first half of the twentieth century (Howe 1973; Watts 1994), provides Invisible Man with an oratorical platform for the concerns of poor Harlemites. Brother Jack, the leader of the Brotherhood, begins to close Invisible Man out of the inner politics of the organization when the latter fails to conform completely to its ideology. Invisible Man's independence is most apparent when he gives a funeral to Tod Clifton, a black Brother gunned down by police officers.[28] The protagonist realizes that the Brotherhood could not "speak for [him]," or Tod, because it did not fully regard his humanity. The leaders of the Brotherhood are as likely to be as corrupt as white Southerners, black university presidents, or distinguished doctors. This realization frees Invisible Man from naïve trust in organizations. Here we see Ellison's privileging of the individual over groups, what Watts calls the novelist's heroic individualism.

The protagonist's hostile encounter with Jack (who is associated with Jack the Bear, the bear being one of Brer Rabbit's nemeses) is the climax of the drunken ogre motif, the blinding of the Cyclops. As we have seen, the giant's blinding is prefigured earlier in the novel in the battle royal scene and in the factory hospital, where the image reinforces the symbolism of invisibility as the protagonist struggles to be acknowledged among people that deny his essential humanity. In chapter 22, Invisible Man has angered Brother Jack. Despite the fact that the organization is indifferent to Tod's murder, Invisible Man leads a funeral for Tod without the Brotherhood's consent. Although Brother Jack's opposition to Invisible Man's actions might reasonably lead to the young protagonist's further disillusionment, it is Jack that falls apart—literally—in chapter 22. When Invisible Man verbally provokes him ("But are you sure you aren't [the] great white father?"), Jack "leap[s] to his feet to lean across the table . . . spluttering and lapsing into a foreign language, choking and coughing and shaking his hand" (473). The altercation approaches the intensity of a physical fight. The protagonist's autonomy is at stake, the fight to make choices based upon conscience and not on faith in others.

As in the earlier passages, Ellison points up the emergence of the hero through the drunken ogre motif. Invisible Man's provocation exposes the potential blindness of organizations such as the Brotherhood. In this way his piercing vision exposes the Cyclops's blindness. Jack can now be read as the embodiment of the blinded ogre. Observing him closely, Invisible Man sees that "one of his eyes glowed brighter than the other." After he causes Jack to stumble, the protagonist notices that "something seemed to erupt out of his face." He expresses disbelief at what he sees falling into a glass: "I stared at the glass . . . and there on the bottom of the glass lay a glass eye. A glass eye. A buttermilk white eye distorted by the light rays" (474). As in the case of Ulysses' blinding of the Cyclops, the protagonist of *Invisible Man* effects a metaphorical blinding of his opponent, or the antagonist's self-generated dismemberment. The eye, which is "distorted by the light rays," appears different under the clarity of the glass, through which "a transparent, precisely fluted shadow" is cast. Now one-eyed without his glass eye, Jack "stopped, squinting at me with *Cyclopean* irritation" [my italics].

Jack's limited vision suggests the myopia of the Brotherhood, which offers an unrealistic solution to the broader American issues that the organization seeks to address. Jack urges discipline and sacrifice in forging a "new society" of future time, but without a humanistic vision inclusive of all factions, invisibility is likely to be a feature of that society as well: "But what kind of society will make him see me, I thought." Invisible Man emerges from his encounter with Jack with a better understanding of himself and the world around him.

Invisible Man's transition from naïveté to self-consciousness marks the final third of the novel. The reader is able to discern the protagonist's growth through his irony. The childlike play that equates the protagonist to Brer Rabbit in chapter 11 is resonant with Invisible Man's mocking of Jack in chapter 22: "'If [I should lose my eye], maybe you'll recommend me to your oculist,' I said, 'then I may not-see myself as others see-me-not.'" The word play suggests Odysseus's taunting of Polyphemus. ("You were blinded by Odysseus," Homer, *Odyssey* 9.504.) If Invisible Man's adversaries throughout the novel's first half were Brer Rabbit (while he was Brer Bear), then chapter 22 completes the inversion of symbols begun in chapter 11. Invisible Man is now symbolically Brer Rabbit (Horowitz 1970). Similar to the animal in Uncle Remus fables (and Ulysses), Invisible Man overcomes antagonism through intellect, patience, and courage. Jack "the Bear" is his immediate opponent, but American society at large challenges the black protagonist (as it does others) to safeguard his individual identity while engaging in the collective.

## "Ulysses alone in Polly-what's-his-name's cave:"
### Ralph Ellison's *Juneteenth*

Although *Invisible Man* was the only novel published in Ellison's lifetime, his life's work included a body of essays on American society and identity, many of which discuss folklore and the ritual approach to myth, and a forty-year work-in-progress, amounting to thousands of pages, his unpublished second novel. In 1999, John F. Callahan, Ellison's literary executor, published a portion of this work as the novel *Juneteenth*. In it Ellison represents America's pluralism through the relationship between Alonzo "Daddy" Hickman, an African American preacher, and the racially mixed, surrogate son that he raises, Bliss, or Adam Sunraider (his incarnation as a racist senator). In *Juneteenth*, Ellison returned to the Ulysses theme. Similar to Odysseus in the postwar, Homeric epic, Bliss wanders throughout the American frontier in search of adventure, love, and ultimately "home," and he encounters an antagonist named "One-eyed" along the way.

Ellison's treatment of the Ulysses theme in *Juneteenth* is even more irreverent than that of *Invisible Man*. In the posthumous novel, the writer seems to ask not only what Ulysses has to say to an American audience but also what an American audience has to say to Ulysses.[29] In the final episode of the novel, a contemporary, oral (perhaps illiterate) storyteller demonstrates little knowledge of—or regard for—classical myth. He goes "toe-to-toe" with Homer in creating suspense and drama. The storyteller (Choc Charlie), despite his lack of knowledge, challenges the stability of the classical myth. Choc Charlie's rewriting of the Ulysses tale echoes Ellison's recasting of the same motif through Bliss, since the novelist focuses on the classical hero's spiritual quest, the antimaterialistic nature of Ulysses' homecoming.[30] The hero seeks his epic return in spite of the abundance of wealth and pleasure available to him on the frontier. In other words, Ellison offers a relatively unexplored interpretation of the Ulysses theme, one that capitalism (or Michael Clark's bourgeoisie materialism) affords.[31] More broadly, Bliss is presented with the question "what is your name" in existential, even theological, terms. To borrow from Ann Astell's (1994) discussion of the medieval writer Boethius's approach to Ulysses, Bliss, through the traditions of the black church, reiterates the existential question, "What is man?" The black preacher represents a part of the answer.

Early in the novel, Bliss (as he moves in and out of consciousness after being shot down on the senate floor in his manifestation as Senator

Sunraider) recalls his travels through the American frontier early in his life taking footage to be featured in a movie. He happens upon a town that he wants to put "on the map," perceiving that its richness and adventure will titillate audiences. The place has the excitement of an American city, along with its attending vices:

> But what a town, everything in our grasp: gunplay and Indians, dance-hall girls, cowboys and gamblers, gunmen, bandits, rustlers and law officers, the real frontier atmosphere and Wild Bill acting himself right off a circus poster. (*Juneteenth*, 77)

The town is described in terms of a frontier.[32] The unexplored place (at least from Bliss's perspective) offers Bliss both the excitement of "gunplay and Indians" and the pleasure of "dance-hall girls." He and his companions have "everything in [their] grasp," and the location provides the rich environment that an individual excited by "the sheer bliss of impersonation"—or the filmmaker looking for drama—might exploit. The seductive element of this materialism echoes the Siren's song in the Homeric context, or even the intoxicating allure of the Lotus-eaters, whose plant allows Ulysses' men to forget their troubles and their longing for home.[33]

Ellison deploys the theme of Ulysses and the Cyclops throughout the scene in tandem with the frontier imagery. Bliss recalls the episode as one that was "all too real," and he tells how when "we set up the camera on the street [people] gathered around, looking from everywhere." The spectacle is brought to a head when the people, "understanding," "knocked us down and fifteen .45s were looking us dead in the eye" (78). The threat of violence invokes the suspense of the Cyclops episode in Homer's *Odyssey*. A heated exchange follows:

> What's the big idea, I said.
> What's your name, the one-eyed one said.
> We told him and what we were about.
> *Pictures*, he said. We don't need any dam' pictures around here.

Although there is no single allusion to the *Odyssey*, two features of the episode recall the motif of Ulysses and the Cyclops. First, the question "what's your name" suggests the drunken ogre scene and Odysseus's response, "Nobody." Here the antagonist, One-eyed, mockingly offers Bliss and Donaldson (one of Bliss's companions) the names "Hear-No-Evil" and "Mister Speak-No-Evil." Ellison's improvisation on the theme of naming suggests that he is now taking a different direction from that of a simple, one-to-one correspondence between vehicle and tenor, or the myth and its direct application.

The second feature of the motif of Ulysses and the Cyclops is the (quite forthright) representation of the antagonist as a one-eyed ogre. In the scene, One-eyed's hostility is immediately felt. (One-eyed could represent any number of "types" on the American frontier; he is a provincial afraid of outside influence.) When Bliss presents him with the idea of making a film, the ogre's response is, "We don't need any dam' pictures around here." In the first place, an antagonist of limited vision is unable to imagine the possibility of learning from an encounter with a stranger. Bliss offers that film could "put [the] town on the map." One-eyed's response shows his provincialism: "Map? The one-eyed one said. We don't want it on any goddam map. You want to ruin everything?" One-eyed is lost to cynicism and materialism. His outlook is held to stereotyped views, as the epithets he gives to others suggest: "Fact we got Frenchies, we got Poles, we got Irishers, Limeys, Eskimos, Yids, and even a few coal-shuttle blondies" (80). The character offers that the correct approach to the abundance on the American frontier is to lose oneself to blissful abandon:

> Drink up . . . Now you got the right idea, One-eyed said. You're getting the hang of how to live in this town. This here's a good town, you monkeys; the best town in the West. All you have to know is how to live in it. (80)

In these few lines, Ellison represents the American vices of a provincial, racially inflected outlook (Poles, Yids, etc.), and an intoxicating, materialistic abandon ("Drink up . . . Now you got the right idea"). One-eyed, like the Homeric ogre, is similar to the Southerner—the "intoxicated panda"— in the battle royal scene of *Invisible Man*.

Throughout *Juneteenth*, the epic symbolism is infused with the images and metaphors of the Christian church through Daddy Hickman, the black preacher. Early in the novel Bliss, just a boy and already an assistant preacher to his surrogate father Hickman, practices his emergence from a box (symbolic of Jesus's resurrection from the tomb), which is to take place on-stage during the Juneteenth sermon.[34] Bliss is explicitly transformed into a Christ figure. Christ's resurrection from the dead is an epic, heroic return similar to that of Ulysses (Astell 1994), and a heroic return marking the primacy of the longing for home over the abandon of the frontier. (This is a counter to the Ulyssean acquisitiveness we discussed in chapter 2.) Furthermore, in Daddy Hickman's Juneteenth sermon, Christ's resurrection is an analog to the triumph of black Americans over slavery and its legacy, a triumph that called upon all of the spiritual resources of African American religious practice. "We shall overcome" marked a declaration of homecoming; the statement, and the tradition from which it comes, are deeply connected to spiritual outlooks filtered through Christian language and symbols. That the narrative of blacks in the New World is for Bliss foundational suggests that for the American protagonist in general, black or white, slavery and emancipation are significant times culturally and personally. That is to say, even the non-black protagonist must come to terms with America's ideals, its spiritual quest, so to speak, in an effort to make the country his or her home (Rankine 2001).

Within the frame of human wandering, suffering, and triumph, Hickman embodies a redemptive potential, or the possibility of homecoming. Alonzo (read "So Alone") Hickman was himself given to a "wild and reckless" life (Juneteenth, 394). Nevertheless, as a preacher he finds purpose in serving the needs of a broader community. Daddy Hickman, as the godlike, loving father, is a foil to Bliss, the prodigal son. Ellison's Christian symbols are concomitant with the Ulysses' homecoming (which, as we have seen, can be interpreted in terms of a soulful rather than physical longing). Ulysses understands that, to continue the religious imagery, man cannot live by bread alone. The American frontier might be a place of materialism and indulgence, but as Hickman knows, the American value of liberty (for all) runs counter to the excess of the frontier. Hickman's return from a moral abyss signifies a human obligation to find meaning even in chaos, and as such the character is a foil to Bliss.

In the episode early in Juneteenth, One-eyed does not see the need for any personal responsibility on the American frontier. Bliss finds this outlook early in his life, and as Adam Sunraider, he comes to adopt it himself.[35] He recalls the episode as he lies in the hospital: "For I was in the kingdom of the dead, tight and enclosed. Back in the box . . ." (79). Bliss has the responsibility of using his craft to uphold his personal and cultural values. The "kingdom of the dead," however, opposes him. Unlike Odysseus, who escapes the Cyclops's cave and later returns home, One-eyed represents myopia, which leaves the individual perpetually stuck "in the box." A society of "one-eyed" citizens encourages individuals to act as "monkeys," imitating the Cyclops in their immoderation and lack of reflection on the alternatives to a frontier lifestyle. Ulysses offers a heroic contrast to this. By continuing to strive to return home despite the seductive alternatives or the suffering it entails, he asserts the importance of homecoming. Bliss's journey, however, is an endless wandering, as he represses any return home (even in memory) to the culture and values that Daddy Hickman offered him as a child.

*Juneteenth* ends with the central question of Bliss's return home, his rejection of materialism, cynicism, and racism for a personal and cultural integrity that involves race, unresolved. At the same, Ellison deploys symbols taken from Homeric epic, Christianity, and African American folklore in order to address the concern. In doing so, the novelist offers that the resolution of America's ideals, its heroic return, rests in these symbols.

Toward the close of *Juneteenth,* Bliss has a dream that takes him back to his days as a filmmaker when he encountered Choc Charlie. Choc, as a creative storyteller whose drunkenness belies his artistic potential, is himself a product of the American frontier. The folksy narrator tells Bliss the Brer Rabbit story, to which one character will assimilate Ulysses. Choc Charlie narrates a scene in which a "hound"

> was so hot on Brer Rabbit's trail that he had to do something real quick because that hound was chasing him come hell for breakfast. So 'bout that time Brer Rabbit sees him a hole in some rocks—and blip! he shoots into it like a streak of greased lightning—and too bad for him. (323)

The tale, which functions as allegory or fable, is one of flight, reversals, and a return home. The wily rabbit runs from danger, but once he is in a hole "in some rocks" Brer Bear traps him. At first glance, the tale rings of trivial entertainment. Beneath the surface, however, is the problem of heroism found throughout *Juneteenth.*

Bliss's companion Donaldson highlights the heroic cycle of the journey, conquest, and return:

> "Dramatic as hell, isn't it," Donaldson said. "A turn in the plot; a 'reversal.' David and Goliath . . . Daniel in the goddamned lion's den! Ole J. C. couldn't do better."

Donaldson compares the tale to the biblical story of Daniel in the lion's den. In doing so, he offers a link between Christian symbols and the Ulysses theme that the grandfather in *Invisible Man* had intimated. Donaldson sees Brer Rabbit's persecution at the hands of the hound and the bear as on par with the struggles of "ole J. C.," Jesus Christ. Finally, Donaldson draws a Homeric parallel: "Ulysses alone in Polly-what's-his-name's cave. . . . And without companions."[36]

Through the triad of African American folklore, biblical heroic narratives from Daniel to Christ, and the Ulysses tale, Ellison offers a pluralistic mythology. The apparent incongruity of the many tales upon which the novelist draws is expressed comically through Choc Charlie:

> "Man," Choc Charlie said. "you drinking too fast.—And sit back out of that sun—Anyway, don't nobody name of Polly mess with Brer Bear, male or female. Not when he's trying to get his rest . . ."
>
> "That's his name," Donaldson said, "Polly-fee-mess."

Choc Charlie, a man unschooled in the classics, lacks the information needed to make the association between his local cultural forms and those of the broader society. But, although he is somewhat hostile to Donaldson's intrusion onto his tale, his point that "don't nobody name of Polly mess with Brer Bear, male or female" is precisely the crux of Donaldson's observation. Like Daniel and Ulysses, both of whom faced menacing giants, the rabbit will overcome his foes because of a resolve that makes him seem "like he's all of a sudden ten feet tall and weighing a ton." Brer Rabbit beguiles the bear and the hound with trickster qualities similar to those that Ulysses possesses: "Poor Brer Bear thought Brer Rabbit's tail was a pearl-handled pistol grip and he felt so bad he started to cry like a baby" (326). The merging of these three spheres of influence, the Homeric, the biblical, and the folkloric, is a polyphonic point-of-reference for the novel's would-be hero.

The extent to which the folkloric motifs of the drunken ogre (Ulysses and the Cyclops) and African American folklore (specifically improvised Brer Rabbit tales) permeate Ellison's work is beyond question. An exploration of these motifs in Ellison's essays, *Invisible Man*, and *Juneteenth* reveals a skillful deployment comparable to James Joyce's use of the Ulysses theme in his novel. Far from a traditional literary allusion (or even a complicated simile), Ellison disintegrates the tale of Ulysses in the Cyclops's cave throughout *Invisible Man* and *Juneteenth*. He nevertheless retains the key elements of the epic encounter: the hero's entrapment in the cave of a drunken, cannibalistic ogre, his assertion of his identity as "Myself" ("I yam what I yam") or, in Ulysses' case, "Nobody," and the ogre's blinding. The motif is at play throughout *Invisible Man* and again in at least two passages of *Juneteenth*.

In the posthumous novel, the interplay between classical myth and African American folklore is suggestive of Bliss's own need to integrate seemingly conflicting aspects of his past (as American, as hybrid) into a composite whole. In both *Invisible Man* and *Juneteenth,* the drunken ogre motif serves the novelist to expand upon the hero's wiliness, his long-suffering, and his bravery, both in his retreat to the past, represented as the memory of folk forms, and in his assertion of his selfhood despite opposition. Through these symbols the reader gains third-person omniscience even in first-person narratives.[37] This perspective yields complex, three-dimensional characters. We are brought into intimacy with the fictional personalities even as they themselves struggle to understand their actions and motivations.

Ellison's approach to classical mythology brought him a great deal of criticism, primarily from critics who, on the one hand, felt that African Americans should reject European philosophical, esthetic, and cultural models, as formerly the sources of oppression. On the other hand, classicists often tend toward more sterile, scholarly approaches to the field. As a self-made intellectual, uninitiated into the tribe of readers and preservers of Greek and Latin, Ellison was for most of his life an outsider to the hallowed halls of academic institutions. Nevertheless, Ralph Ellison has much to offer both classicists and students of African American literature.

Ellison undertook the shaping of heroic possibilities within an American social context through his exploration of classical myth in his writings and, in his novels specifically, through his construction of characters that were part of a broader epic struggle. As in the classical genre of epic, the hero's failure at a given moment does not preclude his eventual triumph. Epic characters are part of an ongoing journey of adventure, failure, and eventual success—a return home. This return, Ellison offers, is as much a soulful journey as it is a physical one. In the next chapter, we enter an abyss of racial violence to see how Ellison deploys classical symbols to suggest a heroic return.

## ☙ 6 ❧

# Ulysses in Black

### *Lynching, Dismemberment, Dionysiac Rites*

Ralph Ellison is among the few Americans to have recognized the
stark fact that lynching was human sacrifice, laden with religious and
political significance for his culture.

> —ORLANDO PATTERSON, "Feast of Blood,"
> in *Rituals of Blood*

The fantastic vision of a lily-white America appeared as early as
1713, with the suggestion of a white "native American," thought to be
from New Jersey, that all Negroes be given freedom and returned
to Africa. In 1773, Thomas Jefferson, while serving in the Virginia
legislature, began drafting a plan for the gradual emancipation and
exportation of the slaves. . . . What is ultimately intriguing about the
fantasy of "getting shut" of the Negro American is the fact that no
one who entertains it seems to have considered what the nation
would have become had Africans *not* been brought to the New
World, and had their descendants not played such a complex and
confounding role in the creation of American history and culture.

> —RALPH ELLISON, "What America Would Be Like
> without Blacks," *Going to the Territory*

Ralph Ellison's curious, often-repeated notion that the literary artist is better off keeping silent on political issues peppered the reception of *Invisible
Man* throughout the twenty years that followed that novel's publication,
as William Walling's article (1973) "Art and Protest" attests. In the wake of
the Civil Rights movement of the 1950s and '60s, black artists turned to

an esthetic agenda that would match the fervency found in the political arena. Even before the rise of an esthetic response in the mode of Amiri Baraka, writers such as James Baldwin, who spoke publicly during the 1960s, often and eloquently, made the push for civil rights part and parcel of their artistic output. For Baldwin, racial matters were of the utmost urgency despite his earlier criticism of Richard Wright's *Native Son* as "protest fiction," a novel that, while addressing the plight of blacks in sociological terms, did not allow for the full humanity, and dignity, of the Negro.[1] Ellison's evasion of politics, coupled with the classical Western esthetic found in *Invisible Man* and, later, in *Juneteenth,* would alienate him from many African Americans whom he undoubtedly conceived as part of his audience.

In this chapter, I show, contrary to the overwhelming critical response in the opposite direction, that Ellison's public statements on race and politics belie his grappling with race, American institutions, and the violence against blacks throughout the society found in his writing.[2] Ellison's classical esthetic was not an evasion of race, as a reading of his novel through the lens of his polemical statements might suggest. Rather, through classical ideas, such as the motif of ritual dismemberment found in mythology, Ellison hoped to come to terms with his own racial identity.[3] Certainly an aggressive, black esthetic agenda might call for the complete rejection of the "eternal West," yet even Addison Gayle does not situate a racist, Eurocentric esthetic in the classics per se.[4] It might even be argued that Ellison's approach to Western literature brought him to somewhat radical conclusions about race, such as his idea, expressed in the quote of Patterson in the epigraph, that lynching was human sacrifice.

Ellison's classicism, moreover, was not universalism. He saw that blacks, owing to their unique perspective on humanity, had an essential role to play both in American society and in letters. In the case of America, Ellison argued that the country's core values—its expression of freedom, its idiom in language, and its cultural composition—were black, in that their quintessential articulation came with the odyssey of Africans in the New World. The American evasion of race, what Ellison called "the fantasy of 'getting shut' of the Negro American," belied the indelible role of blacks in forging a national identity. In the area of literature, Ellison saw that authors such as Mark Twain and William Faulkner expressed a native humanity *through the Negro.* American literature would be nothing without the presence of blacks:

This conception of the Negro as a symbol of Man—the reversal of what he represents in most contemporary thought—was organic to nineteenth-century literature. . . . But by the twentieth century this attitude of tragic responsibility had disappeared from our literature along with that broad conception of democracy which vitalized the work of our greatest writers. . . . It is not accidental that the disappearance of the human Negro from our fiction coincides with the disappearance of deep-probing doubts about a sense of evil. (1966a, 49, 50, 52)

Critics might well take issue with what might appear to be Ellison's rendering of an essential, symbolic identity to the Negro. He sees in Twain and Faulkner the reversal, to some extent, of Manichean dichotomies, and the Negro's archetypal value, as "a symbol of Man," has more to do with white identity than anything else. Similar to the protagonist of the slave narratives, the Negro, for Ellison, somehow urges the American audience toward loftier ideals. In this case, Ellison's treatment of race would be as reductive of black humanity as Norman Mailer's later reading of the black male as the essential hipster.[5]

What salvages Ellison from the indictment of racial evasion, of "stand-[ing] aside from the struggle for racial justice in the United States" (Cruse 1984, 507) is, ironically, his classicism. Owing in part to his understanding of myth and ritual, Ellison endows his characters with a profound sensibility. Nor should this sensibility be read as a universal humanity. Rather, through his ritualizing of black life in America in fiction, Ellison shows the unique perspective on human affairs that the presence of African Americans brought to the world. Ellison taps into the mythic dimension of race in America, as I argue here, through one of the most disturbing challenges that African Americans faced in the twentieth century: violence—and *literal* dismemberment—through lynching. The ritual dismemberment that blacks, and primarily males, faced in America during Ellison's life echoed the *sparagmos* (or *sparagma*), the dismembering of sacrificial victims, expressed most profoundly in Euripides' *Bacchae*.[6]

Momentarily, I will offer a reading of Orlando Patterson's assessment of lynching in *Rituals of Blood* for two reasons. In the first place, Patterson gives a sense of the centrality of lynching to Ellison's outlook on America, a centrality that yielded a perspective paralleled in "few Americans." Second, Patterson's treatment of lynching hints at the link between classical Dionysus and the black protagonist, figuratively, on the American stage.

Before turning to Patterson, however, I would like to weave together the connection between the *Bacchae* and Ellison's notion of ritual dismemberment. As I will show later in the chapter, Ellison read such figures as Charlie Parker, the black, jazz saxophone player whose inability to reconcile in his own mind his integral role in American society led to his effective suicide by drug overdose, as a victim of ritual dismemberment. To Ellison's mind, Parker faced *symbolic* dismemberment—"a man dismembering himself"—in front of a "ravenous, sensation-starved" public. Although Ellison's allusion to Bacchus is not as self-conscious as that to Ulysses, Ellison wrote these words with a clear understanding of classical myth and ritual. There is no evident trace, no smoking gun, as it were, of where Ellison derived his understanding of the motif of dismemberment in classical myth. (This is a sharp contrast to his outright evocation of Ulysses.) Ellison might certainly have read the *Bacchae*, Frazer's passages on dismemberment, or E. R. Dodds's *The Greeks and the Irrational,* as he had read so many other classical works and criticism from his time.[7] Dismemberment for Ellison was *both* an actual and symbolic result of miscegenation, a repercussion for the violation of the taboo against racial mixing. The association with *sparagmos,* the "rending" of the body that is connected with Dionysus in classical myth, is Ellison's insightful reading of what it means, to many, to be black in America—what it means to face ritual violence in one's own backyard, as it were.

Dismemberment, *sparagmos,* amounts to a sacrificial ritual intended to reify a social order, but it also, as we will see, suggests the possibility of the disruption of this order: protest, or even revolution. Euripides' *Bacchae,* for the Nigerian playwright Wole Soyinka, is the quintessential expression of protest, and thus to him an affinity for the play among artists that Alain Locke conceived in terms of forced radicalism would be natural.[8] By protest, I take Soyinka to mean the opposition to societal norms fundamental to the nature of Dionysus. While conventional wisdom looks to Dionysus as a god of sexual ecstasy and liberation, we find, at least in Euripides' *Bacchae,* that Bacchic revolution is really more of a *social* than a *sexual* kind. For example, from a *social* standpoint, it is significant in the play that, at Dionysus's instigation, the women of Thebes have left the shuttle and loom, symbols of a woman's role in Greek society, for Bacchic revelry (lines 117–19). This revelry, moreover, despite perceptions from the outside, is decidedly not sexual. As Teiresias the prophet claims in the play, "the modest woman will not be corrupted in the Dionysiac rites" (317–18).

In the characterization of the Theban women we begin to see why, for Soyinka, Dionysus is a symbol of protest and perhaps even social revolution. In addition to ritual dismemberment, which I read in the context of lynching in America, the idea of protest renders Euripides' Dionysus a fitting symbol for any marginalized group, including blacks in America. And similar to the Negro from whom Ellison sees that America wants to "get shut," Dionysus, as we will also see, is simultaneously Greek and Other, the desired and the scorned.

In the *Bacchae*, the god Dionysus arrives to the Greek city of Thebes and insists that his worship be instituted there. From the first words of the play, Dionysus presents himself as a foreigner, who has already established his cult elsewhere, in Asia: "I come first, of the Greek cities, to this city [of Thebes], since I have danced far away and set up my rites so that I may be a god manifest to mankind" (20–22). Yet despite what might seem to be a foreign intrusion, Dionysus is Greek, and his ancestry is already Theban. Dionysus is a son of Zeus by Semele, daughter of Cadmus, Thebes's founder. Dionysus represents the return of native, repressed desire. Pentheus, the king of Thebes, seeks to rid the city of Dionysus in the play, and in this respect he might be read in the context of those who, in Ellison's mind, sought to "get shut" of blacks in America. As Patterson's reading of "American Dionysus" will show, African Americans might be aligned to Dionysus in their ambiguous role as at once American and other.

Along with the ambivalence regarding Dionysus's otherness, ritual dismemberment is a recurrent theme throughout *Bacchae*, and, as I suggest in my analysis of Patterson's text, it would not be extreme to associate this *sparagmos*, the "rending" of the body, to the practice of lynching. There are at least four striking references to *sparagmos* in the *Bacchae*, and in each case the rending of the body stems from the violation of a taboo. Lynching in America is always linked to a violation of the social injunction against miscegenation (even if the racial mixing is not explicitly of a sexual nature). One of the first references to *sparagmos* in the *Bacchae* comes from Cadmus, founder of Thebes and bacchant, who warns Pentheus to accept Dionysus into the city as part of him, as it were. Pentheus's transgression, his taboo, would be that of failing to recognize Dionysus as a god, an integral, sacred part of the community. Cadmus references another figure that violated a taboo, namely Actaeon, who boasted that he excelled the goddess Artemis in hunting. For his transgression Actaeon was "thoroughly torn apart" by flesh-eating dogs. In Greek mythology outside of the play, Actaeon is guilty of an even more scandalous act, that of seeing Artemis, a virgin goddess who presides over the rites of *korai* (virgin girls) naked.[9] The hunter Actaeon becomes a human, sacrificial victim, as his own dogs rip him apart on behalf of the goddess because of his violation of a taboo.

Pentheus's dismemberment at the hands of his mother Agave at the play's close follows at least two additional warnings about taboo violation. The chorus urges that Pentheus accept the bacchants and their god, and one ode contains an allusion to Orpheus. The musician plays in the context of wilderness, and Orpheus's ability to tame through music is highlighted when he loses his love Eurydice. Orpheus descends into the underworld to retrieve Eurydice, but he loses her to eternity when he fails to heed the warning not to look at her. Perhaps we might read the association to Orpheus in terms of the singer's descent into the underworld, itself a violation of the taboo boundary between the living and the dead.[10] In the end, Orpheus himself is a victim of ritual dismemberment, also perhaps stemming from his taboo, when female revelers tear him apart. Later in the *Bacchae,* the bacchant "ripped through young cows with rending," an image that recalls Orpheus's dismemberment. These references to *sparagmata* (plural for *sparagma*) are warnings to Pentheus not to violate the worship of Bacchus, and, more likely, a foreshadowing of his impending, sacrificial death. In this last reference, the herdsman reports to Pentheus that his mother, Agave, "ripped apart a groaning calf with her [bare] hands." At last the messenger reports Pentheus's *sparagmos:* "His ribs were stripped naked with rendings" (1134–35).

Pentheus's transgression was his failure to worship Dionysus, his repression of an integral part of his community, what Friedrich Nietzsche abstracted as "the Dionysiac spirit" (1956, 119) that balanced Apollonian, ordered aspects of Western thought. For Nietzsche, the Dionysiac spirit represented something "potent and hostile" (119) that for the Greeks was part—albeit a necessarily contained aspect—of a balanced cosmos. Pentheus, through the taboo *sparagma* of human flesh, becomes a symbol of frustration: the consequences both of repressed desire and of taboo violation.

In the American context, Patterson reads aspects of black culture in terms of a "Dionysiac ethos," and certainly Ellison's notion of the desire in the broader culture to "get shut" of African Americans elicits worthwhile parallels (here Pentheus being cast in the role of white America).

As we will see, however, Patterson's reading of blacks as "American Diony-sus" perhaps owes too much to Nietzsche's dichotomy. The association of black culture *just* with desire is reductive, and it plays into the very esthetic that African American authors such as Addison Gayle saw as trou-blesome. Nevertheless, the motif of *sparagma* allows for something deeper than desire, an aspect of the American experience that undeniably affected the lived experience of blacks, as the abysmal reality of ritual violence through lynching shows.

To complicate the common association, owing in part to Nietzsche, of the Dionysiac spirit and desire, it is worth recalling that Pentheus's dis-memberment might to some extent be read as a ritual reenactment of the *sparagma* of Dionysus himself, a god Wole Soyinka associates directly with *revolution*.[11] In some stories, Dionysus was originally the son Zeus by Persephone, and upon his birth the Titans *dismember him;* in this ren-dition, Zeus's impregnation of Semele (Dionysus's mortal mother) was an attempt to reconstitute the broken body. The *Bacchae* does not tell this version of Dionysus's story, but the allusions to Orpheus and Persephone suggest in Euripides' narrative an even more radical manifestation of Dionysus than is immediately apparent. As sacrificial victim, Dionysus transcends the Manichean dichotomy between black and white, desire and the control of it (i.e., the Dionysiac and the Apollonian). Perhaps his dis-memberment points to the aspect of Dionysus that Soyinka sees, an aspect discernable in Ellison's esthetics of violence against blacks. Similar to Dionysus, blacks in twentieth century America are potential victims of rit-ual dismemberment through lynching. In the myth, the Titans disrupt a social order in their attempt to do away with the son of their antagonist, Zeus. The social order that the Titans oppose is that of Zeus's generation, which established itself when Zeus overthrew his father Cronos and the Titans.[12] Dionysus's reconstitution represents a revolutionary spirit, the same spirit through which Zeus conquered the Titans. Thus in classical myth Dionysus embodies the spirit of revolution, change, and a sacrificial rite of dismemberment that symbolizes these as much as it results from taboo violation. Although he never discusses it explicitly, Ralph Ellison makes the connection between Dionysus and black culture through his association of ritual dismemberment with lynching.

Certainly the possibility of Dionysus as a symbol of revolution did not occur to writers of the Black Arts movement. Nevertheless, my reading of Dionysus, and Ellison's associations with him, helps to call into question

John Henrik Clark's claim that the novelist was unconcerned with the plight of "his own people."[13]

In the pages that follow, I expand upon Patterson's metaphor of American Dionysus by tightening the link between the black victim of lynching and the Greek god. In the study of lynching provided in Patterson's book *Rituals of Blood*, the sociologist makes strong connections between Christian ritual and lynching. (He suggests parallels between the victim of lynching and Christ.) He reads "American Dionysus," later in the book, primarily in the context of contemporary black youth culture (specifically hip-hop) and desire. There is a stronger association to be made, however, with Dionysus as the lynched. Once I have built upon the Dionysiac framework for Patterson's sociological study of lynching, I return to Ellison's notion of taboo violations, lynching, and ritual dismemberment. Three Ellisonian samples shape the later portion of this chapter: (1) the early short story "A Coupla Scalped Indians"; (2) Ellison's treatment of Charlie Parker's life in the essay "On Bird, Bird-Watching, and Jazz," originally published in 1962; and (3) the lynching motif in the posthumous *Juneteenth*.

I have chosen these passages as a map of Ellison's approach to ritual and myth, particularly as it pertains to taboo violation and dismemberment. Although neither race nor lynching is a predominant motif in "Scalped Indians," the story gives another perspective on Ellison's approach to myth, ritual, and taboo. Transgression and taboo violation are apparently important themes to Ellison from early on. In the 1962 essay, sacrifice and dismemberment are shown to be strong undercurrents even in Ellison's nonfiction writing. Finally, the lynching motif is dominant in *Juneteenth*, which is an important point given the novel's protagonist is not black.[14] Here Ellison seems to be thinking through the significance of ritual violence against blacks—through slavery and later through lynching—in America as a rite of passage even *for whites*. That is, since the culture is of a whole, lynching affects whites to the same extent as it does blacks, even if in a different way. In the end, Ellison's esthetic is far from separatist, but he calls for a Bacchic revolution that would involve his entire, imagined audience of Americans.

## The Blood Ritual and American Dionysus

In *Rituals of Blood*, Orlando Patterson sees that the black body within American society has undergone an alienating gaze, and he uses the figure

of "American Dionysus" explicitly in his discussion of representations of
the black male in the mass media. He claims that three central images
accompany the iconography of masculinity vis-à-vis African American
men,

> the age-old image of the Afro-American man as demon; the twentieth-
> century image of him as athletic demigod; and the more recent and rapidly
> growing fin de siècle image of him as the American epiphany of Dionysus.
> (Patterson 1998, 241)

Regarding the first, men like Willie Horton and O. J. Simpson provide
good examples of Patterson's claim. Separate from their guilt or innocence, the images of these men were drawn from an age-old reservoir of
racial stereotypes, as Toni Morrison corroborates in her discussion of the
Simpson trial.[15] These stereotypes, moreover, impact the everyday lives
and imagination of all Americans. The racial stereotype is not, however,
one-dimensional. Regarding the black man as athletic demigod, Patterson
cites such examples from popular culture as references throughout the
media to Michael Jordan as supernatural—somehow a god. While such
hyperbole might be dismissed out of turn, within a historical context it
reveals America's consistent tendency to "embrace Afro-American heroes
and cultural productions even as it segregates and demonizes the people
that have produced them" (245). From blackface performance to rap music,
the black figure has amused and delighted American audiences for centuries.[16] Herein lies some of the associative power of Dionysus, a figure at
times linked to the buffoon.[17] In Patterson's America, Dionysus brings
ecstasy to a society that has sold out its selfhood for mechanical order and
the sacredness of productivity.

For Patterson, American Dionysus is a symbol for the Otherness of black
identity within a race-conscious society. Despite the fundamental integrity
of American society, race remains a veil, or a dividing line, that separates
black from white. Although the races interact, "we should be careful never
to confuse interaction with mutuality" (241). That is, blacks and whites still
look across the dividing line, the veil, and see each other as something radically different.[18] As Gregory Stephens sees in his analysis of the symbol
of "straight white line" in the episode of *Invisible Man* where Mr. Norton
travels to his fateful meeting with Trueblood, crossing this line can prove
dangerous and destructive (even in postsegregation times).[19] Emmett Till,

who was lynched in 1955 for a passing comment to a white woman in Mississippi, would not have to be convinced of the reality of his Otherness or of the racial taboo. Ellison, as we have also seen, traced the roots of the racial polarity to "white America's Manichean fascination with the symbolism of blackness and whiteness" (1966a, 63). Patterson's "American Dionysus" updates Ellison's observations, confirming that, despite great progress on racial frontiers, America's sociocultural and political matrices still fall along racial lines.[20] Similar to Dionysus, the black figure is ambiguous; he (or she) is wholly same (as Greek, as American) yet somehow entirely Other, acceptable only in extremely proscribed and restricted ways.[21]

I have already suggested that Patterson should have explored the Dionysus connection, which he sees in Nietzschean terms, in his analysis of lynching. The sociologist moves from Christ as the uniting symbol in his lynching chapter to Dionysus in his chapter on black men in contemporary American society. Dionysus helps Patterson to distill the themes of Otherness, minstrelsy, and boundary crossing, all of which are traceable to the classical god and applicable, at points, to blackness in America. What Patterson's analysis does not expand upon is the extent to which Dionysus, similar to Christ, brings us to a critical moment of the hero's journey, one delineated by sacrifice, physical dismemberment, and the possibility of reintegration (resurrection in Christian terms).[22]

The overview of the classical myth of Dionysus shows that Patterson overlooks certain aspects of the narrative that would have complicated his own analysis of American Dionysus. In particular, Dionysus's ritual dismemberment, which is suggestive of his association with taboo violation later in classical myth, deepens the connection to blackness and lynching in the American context. Lynching, America's ritual *sparagmos,* results from the crossing of the taboo boundary that separates (white) American society from (black) Dionysiac desire. Certainly lynching comes to be read in black literature as a result of sexual transgression.[23] Patterson cautions against seeing lynching as directly related to miscegenation between blacks and whites, asserting that "of the reasons given by those who took part in lynchings, rape or attempted rape was mentioned in only a quarter of the cases occurring between 1882 and 1968" (Patterson 1998, 174).[24] In contrast to the statistical and historical evidence, however, it is clear from representations of lynching in fiction that, at least within the African American imagination, miscegenation is the underlying cause of all lynching.[25] Even the allegation of stealing from a white person might be read in the context of miscegenation since it presupposes a taboo contact, during segregated times, between white and black persons.

Emmett Till's case, which lays bare the taboo of miscegenation, was emblematic, and it became legendary. The fifteen-year-old "Chicago Negro," who traveled to Greenwood, Mississippi, to visit relatives, was said to have made an offensive comment to the wife of Roy Bryant, one of his assailants.[26] Till's lynching provides a blueprint for the representation of the sacrificial ritual in such works as James Baldwin's *Blues for Mister Charlie*. Even if the miscegenation taboo, the illicit—whether by law or custom—contact between blacks and whites, is not overtly sexual, sexuality, in particular the incest taboo (with miscegenation as the taboo), is always a strong trope for the ritual of lynching. This is evident in the concentration on genitalia, as the centerpiece for dismemberment, in many of the cases of lynching (Klotman 1985).[27]

Because of the black male's transgression of the miscegenation taboo, the community undertakes what Patterson calls "a sacred ritual," which "was often presided over by a clergyman" (Patterson 1998, 173). In several cases, he asserts, the lynch-victim was burned after being hanged and dismembered. (Till was not burned but instead hanged from a 125-pound machine and submerged in water.) Burning moves the lynching ritual toward consumption, with eating, as Marcel Detienne (1989) asserts, as the ultimate purpose of sacrifice. Patterson offers that "taste and smell stimulants add up to the same sensation," and that "their effects are not perceived differently by the brain" (198). Once the sacrifice was complete, the perpetrators often spoke of their hunger. They sometimes followed the ritual with a meal: "Eating barbecued cow's steak while savoring the smell from a piece of barbecued human flesh that one has carried away as a memento clearly crosses the line between ritual and actual cannibalism" (199).

Patterson conveys the connection between lynching in America and aspects of the ritual of sacrifice. (Of course, the cooking of the meat distinguishes this ritual process from *ōmophagia*, which is the consumption of uncooked meat.) The sacrifice of animals might find its origin in totemism (Lévi-Strauss 1971), but human sacrifice contains the most profound of ritual symbols.[28] Put otherwise, the eating of the gods (Detienne 1989) is conceived as something that brings social order and well-being to the community.

Ironically, the life-giving (Bacchic) potential of lynching in the unconscious imagination is seen in the fact that the members of the lynch mob carry off a token from the victim's body. The token is the penis, often literally, sometimes symbolically (such as the victim's fingers).[29] As a sacrificial victim, American Dionysus makes the local, white (and Southern) community whole while it contemplates his disparate parts. Outsiders might look upon lynching as itself a violation of civil laws—as the abduction and murder of someone who becomes now a *victim* as opposed to a suspect, but the social practice often met the tacit consent of American society (or at least the Southern community). The ritual nature of the act and its role in community-building point to the extent to which the practice of lynching reified a Southern worldview, which, as Patterson demonstrates, was built on a racially charged, Christian imagination.[30] The lynch-victim, similar to Dionysus, is both a part of the community and an outsider.

Patterson convincingly shows that no observation of the historical journey of blacks in America is truly complete without gazing upon the black form of the lynch-victim, a fragment of the bodies transported from Africa in the Middle Passage across the Atlantic Ocean. Patterson could have pushed his analysis farther, however, by symbolically connecting American Dionysus (figures of desire like Willie Horton or Michael Jordan) to his social and cultural past. That is, the hypersexual and violent black male, the rap star who "spits" disturbing lyrics (to borrow a metaphor from rap), and the demigod athlete, is each Dionysiac symbol, and yet each is a part (albeit a repressed and feared aspect) of a broader American history and imagination. Lynching is the abysmal reality that Ulysses in black journeys through, his *katabasis* experience with the past, his ancestry, and his legacy.

As Patterson sees, the unselfconscious appropriation of Dionysian symbolism—here specifically of *desire*—such as that found among black youth (namely in hip-hop) is detrimental to black culture. Although it is a fact that the racial subject must find a self-emanating, moral response to degradation, it is curious that a sociologist would fail to emphasize American Dionysus's connection to his sociocultural origins. Put otherwise, ritual violence and dismemberment (of a physical, moral, and social nature) shape American Dionysus's esthetic and his imagination. For young black men throughout the late nineteenth and early twentieth century, the threat of violence through lynching amounted to a rite of passage.[31] This violence, moreover, was ritualistic, based on the controlled impulse in communities to direct disorder (violence) into galvanizing and productive social habits (rituals), such as war or the brutalization of marginal members. At least until the late 1960s (by Patterson's estimation) and primarily in the South, this ritual violence was directed at (predominantly) black males. From the 1960s on, police brutality or the threat thereof in many ways replaced the ritual violence of lynching.[32]

What effects did the practice of lynching have on the African American (on American Dionysus's) psyche? What I proffer here is the idea that violence through lynching, American ritual *sparagma*, amounts to an unofficial rite of passage for Americans—specifically *black* Americans but, as Ellison suggests, whites also, and every hue in between.[33] The biographical testimonies of blacks corroborate a fear of the fragmentation of the self—or its dismemberment at the hands of others—present in the African American mind. Prominent black men like James Baldwin, Shelby Steele, and Muhammad Ali, all of whom were in their adolescence at the time of Emmett Till's lynching, attest to how pivotal such incidents were to their own coming-of-age stories. In *Black Male: Representations of Masculinity in Contemporary Art,* Elizabeth Alexander astutely describes the Till case as

> a touchstone, a rite of passage that indoctrinated these young people into understanding the vulnerability of their own black bodies, coming of age, and the way in which their fate was interchangeable with that of Till. (104)

Indeed through the words of black males contemporary to the event we come to an understanding of "how storytelling works to create a collective memory of trauma" (104). The repeated violence and violation of African Americans delineate a social matrix within which blacks traverse the American terrain. African Americans "are contained when these images are made public" (106).

My analysis of American Dionysus as a lynch victim should not remove agency from the African American subject. Rather, it should be clear that ritual violence would inform black agency. The need for a black esthetic—for a revolution, as it were—derives from such experiences, experiences that shape the African American imagination. Black men and women historically have had "to witness their own murder and defilement in order to survive and then to pass along the epic tale of violation" (106). (Here we might read Alexander's words not only in terms of lynching, but also of slavery and, more recently, practices such as police brutality.) Yet the black esthetic idea imagines an audience composed primarily—if not exclusively—of black subjects. As I argue later of Ellison's treatment of lynching both in the motif of dismemberment in his Parker essay and in *Juneteenth,* imagining a broader audience of Americans—to which even Morrison is resistant—does not exclude a strong, black sensibility. Ulysses in black can build on broader esthetic realities while speaking radically for African Americans.

The larger, mythological context of Patterson's idea of American Dionysus amounts to a deft integration of classical mythology with local cultural realities, and this mixing is, in and of itself, revolutionary. Ellison's extraordinary view on American culture, moreover, is the basis of this connection, as Patterson himself sees. Ellison's idea of lynching as human sacrifice was part and parcel of his ritual understanding of myth and his efforts to reuse tradition in a way that was relevant for his sociocultural and political concerns. Ellison's prose and fiction amount to a blueprint for Patterson's study of lynching, human sacrifice, and the Bacchic symbolism around the African American body. The theme of taboo rites is present throughout Ellison's body of work, as the examples of "A Coupla Scalped Indians," Ellison's treatment of Charlie Parker's life, and the lynching motif in *Juneteenth* reveal. These writings give us a view into Ellison's esthetics, his classicism, and his response to the question of the integrity of American identity.

### Rites of Initiation in America: Taboo Rituals, Lynching, and Violence against Blacks in Ellison's Prose and Fiction

#### "A Coupla Scalped Indians"

The reading I offer here of Ellison's prose and fiction demonstrates the extent to which he absorbed a ritual approach myth (see chapter 5) and integrated it into his sociocultural, political, and literary realities. Patterson's offering of American Dionysus testifies to the lasting significance of Ellison's classical orientation. As is demonstrated in his character-construction around the motif of Ulysses and the Cyclops, Ellison's ritual approach to myth informs his treatment of initiation rites in America. Ellison saw that rituals, including rites of passage, shape the lives of individuals within society. The improvisational nature of rites in modern society in no way detracted from their significance. In Ellison's words,

> primitive societies are much more efficient and consistent; they are much more concerned with guiding the young through each stage of their social development, while we leave much of this to chance, perhaps as part of the responsibility of freedom. (1986b, 51)

Similar to the artist, the individual's improvisational range depends on his or her surroundings, inclinations, and willingness to experience new things. Yet the unstructured nature of modern society would not obscure the responsibility that comes with individual and artistic growth. For Ellison, the "responsibility of freedom" requires the individual to account not only for his or her immediate concerns but also for the broader society in which he or she participates. For the American, race is as much a part of the historical and cultural landscape as classicism.

Ellison's early short story "A Coupla Scalped Indians," originally published in 1956, could be read as a blueprint for the author's view of the universality of rites, the reality of initiation (the rite of passage) in America as improvisational, and the role of desire in these rites.[34] The story provides a prototype of the themes that are also present in *Invisible Man* and later developed for Ellison's second novel, the posthumous *Juneteenth*. In particular, the notions of sexuality, taboo, and initiation play out masterfully in this story. Ellison would later develop the themes of race and violence, particularly the sacrificial violence implied in lynching, in later works.

In "Scalped Indians," two boys who frequent Ellison's early stories, Buster and an unnamed protagonist, pass the time together somewhat aimlessly. Their meandering takes the definite shape of a Boy Scouts' initiation, despite the fact that "we didn't even have a troop, only the *Boy Scout's Handbook* that Buster had found" (Ellison 1996, 65). Race and class to some extent localize the free-floating nature of their adventure. These boys do not officially belong to the Boy Scouts (despite toting a manual), and they see themselves as somehow different from the "white boys" who do. Their social obstacles, however, do not block the inevitability of rituals, and the boys are clever enough to realize that, as it pertains to issues of personal style, their deficits can become advantages. As Buster asserts, "who wants to be like them? Me, *I'm* gon be a scout and play the twelves too" (71). The boys pretend to be "Indian" scouts, as the title of the story intimates. The reader comes to find that the boys underwent a scarring ritual a short time before the story begins, and the theme of "scalped Indians" becomes the link between the tropes of initiation and desire throughout the story.

It is suggested by a number of references that both boys were scarred, likely circumcised, shortly before the narrative starts. For example, Buster and the protagonist begin their improvisational play "even though we were both still sore and wearing bandages." The connection between circumcision and initiation into manhood becomes clear in the protagonist's preoccupation with the latter subject: "The doctor had said that it would make us men and Buster had said, hell, he was a man already—what he wanted was to be an Indian" (67). (It is fitting that the more precocious boy Buster is "a man already" because his feisty nature has likely led him through more experiences.) Later in the story, when sexually aroused, the protagonist feels "a warm pain grew beneath [his] bandage," which also forges the link between sexual desire (through an erection) and initiation rites. That is, rites of passage contain desire within society, so that through initiation (of various sorts) men and women assume their socially acceptable roles. Here again, within this context the potentially damaging nature of rites such as lynching should come to mind. The characters in "Scalped Indians," similar to their counterparts, who rely on handbooks to guide them, are part of a broader society in which individuals improvise climatic moments in their lives. For the boys in "Scalped Indians," circumcision, the makeshift Boy Scout rituals, and, later, sexuality shape their consciousness as social beings.

Initiation sets socially acceptable parameters around desire, and as such any uncontrolled desire, sexual or otherwise, could lead to taboo transgressions across social boundaries. While sexual desire might be fitting and fruitful when properly expressed, societies mark such desire as taboo when it is directed toward an illicit object. Yet, as our scalped Indians discover, taboos are sometimes learned by breaking them. Unsupervised, the boys are free to wander and roam across boundaries. As they do, they happen upon the "old shack" (a place for shacking up?) of Aunt Mackie, a mysterious woman who is mentioned from early in the story and is "nobody's sister but still Aunt Mackie to us all" (68). Mackie is an adult, whom the protagonist had seen "about town" all of his life. For the people in the town, the reclusive Aunt Mackie is the subject of folkloric play: "Even some of the grown folks, both black and white, were afraid of Aunt Mackie, and all the kids except Buster" (68). The legendary Mackie becomes a reality for the protagonist when he stumbles into her shack while running from a dog. Mackie is a conjurer of sorts and is "like the moon" to the protagonist: "Ho' Aunt Mackie, talker-with-spirits, prophetess-of-disaster, old-dweller-alone in a riverside shack surrounded by sunflowers, morning-glories, and strange magical weeds" (68). Mackie's mysterious, moonlike nature, her "magical weeds," and the dog that guards her shack (Cerberus, the watchdog of the Underworld?) announce a mythical figure suggestive of the "Queen Goddess" of Joseph Campbell's *The Hero with a Thousand*

*Faces.* Indeed Mackie's sensuality and mystery will baffle the boys since, as Campbell puts it, "only geniuses capable of the highest realization can support the full revelation of the sublimity of this goddess" (Campbell 1973, 115).[35]

The reader immediately senses the sexual nature of the protagonist's encounter with Mackie, which is taboo because she is "Aunt" and an adult. The protagonist eyes Mackie's naked shape beneath a somewhat transparent garment. Although an adult, she has "a young, girlish body with slender, well-rounded hips." She plays an adult game with the protagonist. The seductress warns, "lips that touch wine shall never touch mine" despite her ability to intoxicate: "Her breath came to me, sweetly alcoholic." She notes that the protagonist is carrying an axe (clearly a phallic symbol) and teases him: "You're a hatchet man and you stopped to peep." The sexual overtones (along with the possibility of violence and penetration, or incision) advance as the woman, seeing the protagonist's bandage, taunts him for having been "pruned. Boy, you have been pruned." The encounter, the first of its kind for the boy, is both stimulating and unnerving: "And I was both ashamed and angry and now I stared at her out of a quick resentment and a defiant pride. *I'm a man,* I said within myself. *Just the same I am a man*" (Ellison 1996, 78)! Violation (the boy transgresses Mackie's boundaries by entering her home, and she in turn violates his dignity), the potential for (sexual) violence (he carries an axe/penis), and the containment of desire mark the coming of age ritual.

The boys of "Scalped Indians" prefigure both Invisible Man and *Juneteenth*'s Bliss in illuminating ways, and the keynotes of wandering, initiation, and desire create a triad that would be played and replayed throughout Ellison's compositions. While the story highlights one initiation in the life of the young protagonist, *Invisible Man* is a series of initiations that contribute to shaping the protagonist's worldview. In both cases, the rites of passage involve violence and the socially acceptable control of desire. Mackie might parallel Mary Rambo, the sexless, mammy figure who helps Invisible Man (and who also had magical herbs in earlier manuscripts of the novel), but the "brown" woman of the story is just as likely comparable to the white female figures of transgression in *Invisible Man,* such as Sybil.[36]

In *Invisible Man,* Ellison infuses the themes of initiation and sexual transgression with a deeper racial element; in America, race is an aspect of initiation and desire. In addition to the issue of desire, Ellison never left the theme of boyhood, as *Juneteenth* demonstrates. For the man-child

Bliss, misplaced desire interrupts initiation into manhood. Bliss is unable to master his desire and therefore remains a boy at heart—although an adult with a damaging (to himself and society) worldview. As we will see, the boy's "hatchet" in "Scalped Indians" morphs in *Juneteenth* into the "knife," a faux phallus with which boy Bliss plugs the ripe watermelon for his sexualized, black mammy. Bliss reflects on this incident later as he lies on a hospital bed on the brink (symbolically) of manhood. The improvisational nature of initiation in all of Ellison's writing suggests the "responsibility of freedom in America," a country in perpetual wandering, seemingly toward no particular goal.

As Robert J. Butler argues, through his characters Ellison "connects personal and cultural narratives to stress the integral connection between individual lives and the life of the nation" (2003, 299). If America is born out of the miscegenation taboo, as Ellison offers, then its maturation depends at least in part on an understanding of this origin. Individuals within the society work out what Ellison (1986e) calls their "personal culture" through improvisation, yet they draw from a common set of notes. This improvisation could just as easily include classical myth and literature as more native cultural forms.

The question of what makes a man, or a mature, adult person (within this particular society), might provide another point of entry into Ellison's writing, and clearly for him manhood (or personhood) amounts to anything but a "socially unsituated self" (Bellah in Butler, 309). The coming-of-age narrative is the backdrop to the ritual of dismemberment, namely lynching, because, as the narratives and biographical sketches from the time show, for many black Americans during the late twentieth century coming of age *was* concomitant with a time in their lives when they could experience ritual violence (a fact which the Emmett Till case crystallizes).

### "On Bird, Bird-Watching, and Jazz"

Ellison's essay "On Bird, Bird-Watching, and Jazz" was a review of Robert Reisner's biography *Bird: The Legend of Charlie Parker*. In it Ellison reads Parker as an orphic figure, dismembered through the broader society's consumption of his musical craft. The key to Parker's symbolic import is, of course, the bird. For Ellison, the name Bird itself was suggestive of myth and the creation of an icon because "nicknames are indicative of a change from a given to an achieved identity, whether by rise or fall, and they tell us something of the nicknamed individual's interaction with his fellows" (1966d, 219). Ellison offers several etiologies of Parker's nickname, and he speculates about exactly what kind of bird the jazz saxophonist would have been. Ellison's irreverent irony takes on nuances of religious mysticism when he associates the legend of Charlie Parker with "the story of a saint," and he notes that saints were also often identified with symbolic animals, including birds. He suggests that as a goldfinch, Parker would have a significant connection to Christ: "An apocryphal story has it that upon being given a clay bird for a toy, the infant Jesus brought it miraculously to life as a goldfinch" (219). Similar to Christ, Parker would undergo a ritual sacrifice for the benefit of his followers.

The darker motifs in Ellison's discussion of Parker prefigure Patterson's American Dionysus and foreshadow the link, present in the sociological work, between the "Dionysian ethos" and hip-hop culture. Ellison's reading of Parker as a victim of sacrificial dismemberment, moreover, suggests the tragic ritual of the lynching of African Americans. While Ellison's bird imagery helps him to amplify the legend over the man, Parker as legend becomes a significant cultural icon. Ellison claims that "when we read through the gossip of the accounts [of Parker's life] we recognize the presence of a modern American version of the ancient myth of the birth and death of the hero" (224). This heroic journey includes "his wandering and early defects," his "initiation into the mysteries revealed by his drug and the regions of terror to which it conveyed him," and his "obsessive identification with his art and his moment of revelation and metamorphosis" (225).[37] As with all heroic journeys, the hero, in this case Parker, returns with something novel to offer his society. Yet the offering of his beautiful, orphic ecstasy in music results, as was the case with Orpheus, in destruction and dismemberment.

Despite Parker's own role in his demise (i.e., his drug use), Ellison reads his life within the context a ritual sacrifice that transforms him into a legend. Ellison uses the symbolism of the bird to link Parker to the sacrificial figure of Christ. Parker, as an emblem of potency, ecstasy, and transformation, is

a sacrificial figure whose struggle against personal chaos, on stage and off, served as entertainment for a ravenous, sensation-starved, culturally disoriented public which has but the slightest notion of its real significance. While [Parker] slowly died (*like a man dismembering himself with a dull razor on a spotlighted stage*) from the ceaseless conflict from which issued both his art and his destruction, his public reacted as though he was doing much the same thing as those saxophonists who hoot and honk and roll on the floor. (my italics, 223)

Although Parker owed much of his suffering to the self-destructiveness of drug use, in Ellison's reading his dismemberment resulted in great part from a "ravenous, sensation-starved" public. Nor was Bird's destruction unique. Rather, an all-American pastime, a ritual of consumption, can be discerned in Parker's demise. Ellison describes an American popular culture in which "political power and entertainment alike are derived from the viewing and manipulation the human predicaments of others" (222). Although all public figures—perhaps all people—inevitably suffer a similar personal fragmentation, the problem is especially pronounced for black Americans, about whom the collective, psychological expectations so far exceed reality. These expectations have a profound impact both on African Americans and on the larger society. Interestingly, Ellison argued that Parker was a "'white' hero," since his appeal was primarily to "the educated white middle-class youth whose reactions to the inconsistencies of American life was the stance of casting off education, language, dress, manners, and moral standards" (224). He was writing about a jazz hero, but Ellison could just as easily have been pontificating about latter-day rap stars.

Certainly there is a tangible distance between the actual lynching of black men historically and the symbolism of dismemberment as it pertains to Charlie Parker, who some might argue caused his own destruction. Yet, as Ellison sees, the lynch victim and the Bird both emerge out of the same social condition. Both are consumed in an orgiastic rite that involves transgression across taboo boundaries. In the case of lynching, miscegenation—or the threat of it—points to a cultural longing for the prohibited object and creates the need for expiation. In Bird's case, the desire of "educated white middle-class youth" for ecstasy provides a market for the music of transgression, which was performed in uncommonly integrated spaces. (This is the common heritage of jazz and hip-hop.) In both cases, the black body becomes the site of desire—a desire so consuming that it threatens to destroy its host. External forces of otherness, and the transgression of desire, "overdetermine," to borrow again from Franz Fanon, the black body, at times depleting it of any self-generated meaning or volition.[38] Again, this is not to remove responsibility from the individual. Yet in Parker's case, his legendary status cannot be separated from the society within which he lived and worked. Given the inevitability of the terms of engagement for African Americans, it is no wonder that Ellison returned time and again to the themes of sacrificial violence and dismemberment throughout his prose and fiction.

### Lynching and Violation in Juneteenth

Before turning to the themes of lynching and orgiastic rites in *Juneteenth*, a brief encore from *Invisible Man* should recall the role of sacrificial violence in that novel. As has already been explored, the main character in *Invisible Man* undergoes the cruel ritual of the battle royal, which draws from the symbolism of cannibalism and consumption. The scene, as has been demonstrated, amounts to an equivalent of Ulysses' encounter with the cannibalistic Cyclops, with the protagonist in limbo between hero and ogre. By the end of the novel, he is transformed into an individual who speaks for all because of the way in which his experiences reflect that of human beings in general. Yet the specifics of being black in America are contained not only in the protagonist's life but also in that of other characters throughout the novel. Part of those specifics, Ellison offers, is the surrender to sacrificial violence and dismemberment. In the novel, Tod Clifton is the icon that "plunges outside of history" and thereby leaves a moment and image for contemplation. In *Invisible Criticism*, Alan Nadel argues that Tod Clifton, whose name announces the death of the black male in part because of social forces, is a "martyr-saint" (1986, 65). Although Tod, similar to Ellison's Charlie Parker, choreographs his own death, in this case by provoking a police officer to shoot him, the tragedy develops out of the character's sense of hopelessness. The Brotherhood to which Tod belonged would damn him to obscurity by ignoring his death, but the protagonist recognizes the extent to which Tod's life was bound up in the life of all black men and, by extension, all human beings. Invisible Man's public funeral for Tod in Harlem elevates his life to the level of a collective symbolism. Tod crystallizes the suffering and ecstasy of black men within a society that often dismisses their humanity.

While Ellison's allusions to lynching in *Invisible Man* rely on a broader symbolism, including ritual violence against black men, the subject of lynching in particular is broached explicitly in *Juneteenth*. This is significant because we see that as Ellison's writing progressed, and as he became more and more steeped in classical symbols, his interest in the contemporary problem of violence against blacks did not diminish. Rather, Ellison's classically trained understanding of ritual and myth, which we see not only in the Ulysses theme but also in his representation of coming of age and ritual violence, was pivotal to his interpretation of contemporary issues.

In the scene derived from the short story "Bliss's Birth," Daddy Hickman recalls how he became the father of the racially ambiguous child when the boy's mother abandoned him at birth.[39] For the black preacher, taking on this new responsibility involves an excruciating difficulty (beyond the change in his lifestyle that a child would normally entail). That is, Bliss's white mother had falsely attributed her unwanted pregnancy to a sexual violation at the hands of Hickman's brother, Robert. The innocent Robert was lynched as a result of the woman's claim. Ellison conveys the pain of this experience in Hickman's anger toward Bliss's mother:

> Oh, I was already feasting on revenge and sacrifice, telling myself: Those eyes for Bob's eyes; that skin or Bob's flayed skin; those teeth for Bob's knocked-out teeth; those fingers for his dismembered hands. And remembering what they had done with their knives I asked myself, But what can I take that can replace his wasted seed and all that's now a barbaric souvenir floating in a fruit jar of alcohol and being shown off in their barbershops and lodge halls and in the judge's chambers down at the courthouse. (*Juneteenth*, 296–97)

Hickman's repressed desire to kill Bliss's mother conveys the potentially sacrificial nature of life in general. In his mind, the woman's death would somehow compensate for Bob's. Yet Robert's death, like that of so many historical lynch victims, bears an inexpiable stain, that of his "wasted seed," the "barbaric souvenir" of his dismembered parts. Robert embodies the angst surrounding the miscegenation taboo in America, and as such he suffers despite his innocence.

Bliss's birth, the culmination of an event that caused Robert's lynching, is one of the centerpieces of *Juneteenth*, along with the emancipation ceremony from which the novel takes its name.[40] Bliss's birth is at once horrific and hopeful, similar to the individual and collective experiences out of which he is born. That is, through Bliss, Ellison offers the harsh truth that America is also born out of a violation of the miscegenation (or incest) taboo and its accompanying Dionysiac rite: the desire for and destruction of dark bodies. Bliss's later denial of his racial heritage is tantamount to America's ongoing repression of race as a cultural reality. ("I'll call him Bliss, because they say that's what ignorance is," 311.) Yet because of the significance of race, a legacy of miscegenation colors even Bliss's youthful experiences.[41] Ellison suggests that a violation of the incest taboo becomes a rite of passage not only for blacks but for others as well. Historically, violence against black bodies during slavery was inevitable, as the testimonies of beating and sexual violation throughout the slave narratives indicate. Yet the experience was also seminal for the perpetrators of violence. Juneteenth, the ceremony celebrating emancipation on June 19th, 1865, contains the memory of violation as well as the hope of the reconstruction of lives.

Harriet A. Jacobs's account from *Incidents in the Life of a Slave Girl* further illustrates the foundational nature of the ritual violence around miscegenation for both blacks and whites, at the time, slave and slave-owner:

> No pen can give an adequate description of the all-pervading corruption produced by slavery. The slave girl is reared in an atmosphere of licentiousness and fear. The lash and the foul talk of her master and his sons are her teachers. When she is fourteen or fifteen, her owner, and his sons, or the overseer, or perhaps all of them, begin to bribe her with presents. If these fail to accomplish their purpose, she is whipped or starved into submission to their will. (Jacobs 1987, 51)

Harriet Jacobs implies two initiations occasioned by slavery: that of the black slave, here the female who undergoes violation, and that of the white male(s) who violates her. While black males in the twentieth century suffered through lynching as a rite of passage, and while black women undergo sexual violence, white males in the context of the antebellum South gain their sense of self in part through ritual violence. Through the violation of the slave's humanity, whites in America learned the cultural modes for the expression of desire. This is not to say that whites suffered equally to blacks during slavery. Rather, I am suggesting that the violated slave girl's cries, which announce her coming of age (at "fourteen or fifteen"), reverberate throughout the culture. One of Ellison's ongoing literary projects, discernable throughout *Juneteenth*, was the representation of the violence around miscegenation and its lasting psychological effects on blacks and whites alike. For Ellison, blacks amounted to the Dionysus from which America (parallel to Thebes) would seek to "get shut," the term he uses so powerfully in the essay quoted in the epigraph.

Bliss's self-imposed, racial ignorance belies his own Dionysiac rite of passage, a scene that, along with Bliss's birth and the lynching of Robert, is one of *Juneteenth*'s most compelling. In other words, Bliss tries to repress his past, his birth within the context of race and the miscegenation taboo. Bliss's lifelong attempt to "get shut" of race amounts to a perpetual and prodigal wandering that Ellison associate with America. That is, Bliss is Pentheus to Robert's Dionysus.

Throughout the novel, it is suggested that the protagonist's dalliances with black women are numerous (despite his evasion of race), and they perhaps represent the return of his repressed childhood experiences. These experiences include not only his taboo birth but also his own unconscious desire to cross racial boundaries. In one incident, the boy Bliss is left in the care of a black woman from Hickman's congregation, Sister Georgia, who becomes the object of potentially incestuous sexual desire. The black woman "*know[s]* [her] way through these woods like a rabbit," a description that suggests both the cleverness of the animal and its fertility. Bliss admires her "*kinda funky*" smell, which he associates with her womanhood: "But this was a good smell although it wasn't supposed to be and the sister was good to be carrying him so gently and she was nice and soft" (*Juneteenth*, 177). As Sister Georgia teasingly flatters the boy-minister "Revern' Bliss" ("It's a mystery to me how you manage to remember so much," 182), Bliss endeavors to "plug" a "ripe" watermelon:

> And he took the knife and felt the point go in hard and deep to the width
> of the blade; then again, and again, and again, making a square in the rind.
> He felt the blade go deep and deep and then deep and deep again. Then he
> removed the blade . . . and struck the point in the middle of the square and
> lifted out the wedge-shape plug, offering it to her. (183)

The sexually suggestive encounter becomes actual violation during the night when Bliss goes to sleep with Sister Georgia after wetting his bed. His curiosity slowly emboldens him, and he lifts the woman's dress "stealthily, cunningly, as though he had done so many times before." The imagery of a social context marks Bliss's transgression. When he touches Georgia, he envisions "a troop of moldy Confederate cavalry galloping off into the sky with silent rebel yells bursting from their distorted faces" (193).

Along with the imagery of Confederate troops, Ellison's self-conscious allusions to the Trueblood episode in *Invisible Man* forge the link between

Bliss's boyhood transgression and the taboo against miscegenation, or crossing the "straight white line" in America (Stephens 1999). Like Trueblood, who, finding himself between his wife and his daughter in bed, has to find a way to "move without moving," Bliss is also caught between the proverbial rock and hard place before Sister Georgia awakens: "*I've got to get out of here,* he thought. *I got to move*" (*Juneteenth,* 192). I read this as a self-conscious allusion to the Trueblood scene. The allusion is repeated again in a moment of deft Ellisonian riffing: "You're It this time for sure but you must never be caught again. Not like this again—move. When they come toward you, move. Be somewhere else, move. Move!" (194)

The childhood game of tag plays in Bliss's mind during this serious and threatening experience. The connection between Bliss and Trueblood, moreover, situates Bliss's act within a broader context than that of a private, familial violation. While each character is on an opposite side of a racial polarity, each conveys a tragicomic dimension of the miscegenation taboo. Bliss, similar to Trueblood, goes unpunished; he acts on his desire with impunity. Certainly Bliss's violation of Georgia is, on one level, nothing more than a childhood indiscretion. Yet the reference to a "Confederate cavalry" points to a deeper symbolism, i.e., the social matrix within which he acts. Along with the allusions to Trueblood, Bliss's transgression reifies a racial reality (with the slave girl transformed into an otherwise sexless mammy) that will shape his future outlooks. Through Bliss, Ellison also reminds the reader that even a seemingly private act happens along a social grid imprinted on the individual's psychological landscape. While in *Invisible Man* the protagonist is left to reconcile the disparities embodied in (white) Mr. Norton and (black) Trueblood, Bliss recalls his encounters with Daddy Hickman and Sister Georgia later in life, years after his self-conscious rejection of his racial origins.

The Trueblood episode in *Invisible Man* and Bliss's encounter with Sister Georgia convey the tragicomic nature of miscegenation as a Bacchic rite. In the case of the former, the comic overtones of Ellison's portrayal of Trueblood—his blues-laden tale, his seemingly unselfconscious ignorance—belie the tragic potential of his transgression. Trueblood more than suggests that he has committed incest with his own daughter, yet the truth of the matter is that, within American society, his actual transgression would be less of a violation than if he had slept with a white woman. It is important to recall how the sharecropper tells his audience that, during that fateful night, he dreamt of a more ineffable desire. In his dream, the wife of a man named Broadnax tries to seduce him: "I tries to talk to her, and I tries to get away. But she's holdin' me and I'm scared to touch her 'cause she's white" (*Invisible Man,* 58).[42] Trueblood's dream suggests that either he sublimates the fear of incest as miscegenation, or his awareness of Norton's lily-white worldview informs the details of his story. In either case, Trueblood's narrative succeeds in providing his audience—both Invisible Man and Norton—with images that reinforce its own fears and desires. Proof of Trueblood's success is that, as Houston Baker (1984) argues, Mr. Norton in fact rewards him for having transgressed and yet feeling "no inner turmoil, no need to cast out the offending eye" (*Invisible Man,* 51). (We might also read an allusion here not only to biblical parables but also to Sophocles' *Oedipus the King.*) The blues-singing storyteller receives one hundred dollars from the man whose attachment to his own dead daughter is rather questionable. That is, the orgasmic details of Trueblood's performance provide release for his racially obsessed audience, which remains within the socially proscribed lines while experiencing catharsis through the satyr figure.

The crossing of taboo boundaries, however, must be punished somehow; otherwise the power of the taboo becomes questionable. In *Invisible Man,* the protagonist is expelled from school for taking Norton across the "straight white line" to the black slum. This is the tragic outcome of coming of age in a society in which sublimated fears of crossing the taboo line of segregation will eventually surface. While Trueblood maneuvers within this matrix with great facility, Invisible Man learns that, where race is concerned, things are never what they seem.

The outcome of Trueblood's encounter with Mr. Norton, at least for Trueblood, is comic for one central reason: Trueblood, unlike the protagonist of *Invisible Man,* acknowledges race. Trueblood does not evade the reality of race in America; he knows it is to be feared, feels that certain encounters should be avoided, and works other encounters to his advantage. While *Juneteenth* is left unresolved, Ellison more than suggests that Bliss's fate will reside in the degree to which he comes to terms with his racial heritage, even if he himself is not black.

Trueblood and Bliss are perfect foils because, while the former understands and therefore has to some extent reconciled himself to race, the latter's attempt to escape his racial past causes his demise and is detrimental to society. In *Juneteenth,* Bliss emerges from his Dionysiac rites not through a transformation of the past but through a constant and unresolved return to its darkest moments. There is no personal revolution for Bliss, who is born out of a ritual of dismemberment. His coming of age as a racial subject in America is interrupted because he refuses to integrate his past with his present. That is, Bliss is, psychologically, dis-integrated, dismembered. As is clear from the first pages of the novel, Bliss becomes a senator who uses race divisively, despite his biracial upbringing. As part of the community that nurtures Bliss after his mother abandons him, Georgia (as only one example) could just as well have been a surrogate mother to Bliss as the object of incestuous desire. Yet his search for his (white) biological mother, which amounts to a longing for a lily-white—and unreal—past of purity and innocence, causes him to reject the only family he knows.[43] Bliss is unable to understand, moreover, that his own past is steeped in the reality of race and its accompanying Dionysiac rites, including the Otherness of the black body, ecstatic desire across racial lines, and lynching. Even for the character who still danced in Ellison's mind during postsegregation times of the 1970s, 1980s, and early 1990s, the taboo of miscegenation has a primordial, unconscious significance.

To summarize, I have used Soyinka's notion of revolution because it neatly conveys the link between the classical god and modern uses of him, especially in a racially charged context. In Soyinka's essay, "Between Self and Society," revolution is an "idiom" (44), or a "metaphor." For the Nigerian playwright, as we have seen, Dionysus embodies revolution: "Revolution, as idiom *of* the theatre and explication of Nature itself is, in my opinion, at the heart of *The Bacchae* of Euripides" (45). Perhaps we might go as far as to say that *sparagmos* is an expression of a natural, though at times destructive, process in culture. Although he does not discuss ritual dismemberment in his essay, Soyinka saw that to connect with Bacchus was to reconnect with (revolutionary) nature, but not in the orgiastic manner of Nietzsche's interpretation. At the same time, cultures organize themselves differently around *sparagmos* (or the fear of disintegration/dismemberment), so that American Dionysus, the lynch victim, has a social context and subjective repercussions.

Revolution is the natural metaphor for *Bacchae* because to rend the subject to pieces is also to reconstitute it differently. Ellison's writings, to my mind, drew his readers, black and white Americans alike, to the ritual dismemberment of the black body, so as to assert that to witness this body is to be changed irrevocably, to undergo a transformation. Certainly this Bacchic revolution was not what proponents of political revolution and regime change have in mind. Nevertheless, as Harold Cruse saw, the revolutionary talk of the Black Power era, which resulted in not-so-subtle social and esthetic change, did not bring radical regime change. The critique against Ellison's literary and esthetic agenda, as we see in the next chapter, is, to my mind, ill-founded.

In his prose and fiction, Ellison does not make any clear, single allusion to Euripides' *Bacchae*. As I have shown here, he does demonstrate a deep knowledge of myth and ritual, especially Western narratives. Ellison's notion of ritual dismemberment, which is at core the story of Dionysus, is intricately woven into his poetic and esthetic expression, as we saw in his discussion of Charlie Parker. Thus the premise of *Ulysses in Black* not only signals the classicism found throughout Ellison's work (as well as that of other black authors), but the notion that blacks were steeped in the classics allows for deeper readings of their works along classical lines. In this case, I have used Ulysses in black, or black classicism, as a point of departure for reading the trope of ritual dismemberment throughout Ellison's work. Dismemberment, which is at core a Dionysiac ritual, is a symbol both of the taboo relationships within society *and* the possibility of *revolution,* or change, from the established taboos. This revolution can be as much social as sexual. Revolution, or, to return to another trope, the return from a black (w)hole, is also a symbol of the possibility of reading Greek Thebes alongside American Dionysus. Revolution can be the self-conscious shift in our social, esthetic, and literary orientation, as we have, through the reality of black classicism (and Ulysses in black) performed a ritual dismemberment of the status quo in reading classical and African American literature.

# Ulysses (Re)Journeying Home

## Bridging the Divide between
## Black Studies and the Classics

In the beginning was not the word, but its contradiction.

> —RALPH ELLISON, "Society, Morality, and the Novel," in
> *Going to the Territory*

Ah know another man wid a daughter.
The man sent his daughter off to school for seben years,
den she come home all finished up. So he said to her,
"Daughter, get yo' things and write me a letter to my brother!" So she did.
He says, "Head it up," and she done so.
"Now tell 'im, 'Dear Brother, our chile is done come
home from school and all finished up and we is very proud of her.'"
Then he ast de girl "Is you got dat?" She tole 'im "yeah." "Now tell him
    some mo'.
'Our mule is dead but Ah got another mule and when Ah say
    (clucking sound of tongue
and teeth) he moved from de word.'"
"Is you got dat?" he ast de girl. "Nah suh," she tole 'im.
He waited a while and he ast her again, "You got dat Down yet?"
"Nah suh, Ah ain't got it yet."
"How come you ain't got it?"
"Cause Ah can't spell (clucking sound)."
"You mean to tell me you been off to school seben years
And can't spell (clucking sound)? Why Ah could spell dat
Myself and Ah ain't been to school a day in mah life. Well
Jes' say (clucking sound) he'll know what yo' mean and go on wid de letter."

> —ZORA NEALE HURSTON, *Mules and Men*

The folkloric tale here hits upon the limits of the written word, the difficulty that comes in expressing certain cultural experiences in text. In chapter 3, I touched on the limits of classicism for twentieth-century black literary and sociopolitical thought, a limit that forced radicalism proscribed.[1] The tale suggests that, aside from forced radicalism, it is possible that literacy cannot govern every experience, particularly those on the periphery of canons and norms of expression. The "clucking sound" that the father asks his literate daughter to write is reminiscent of certain African languages, such as the Khoisan languages of the Bushmen, which is comprised in part by certain clicking sounds. The man in the tale cannot understand why seven years of school is insufficient to afford his daughter the ability to transcribe something that is basic to him. The exchange between the father and daughter recalls the chasm between Choc Charlie, the black storyteller of Brer Rabbit tales in Ralph Ellison's *Juneteenth,* and Donaldson, the literate man who sees that the wily rabbit is comparable to Ulysses. "You drinkin' too fast," suggests Choc. "Don't nobody name of Polly mess with Brer Bear" (*Juneteenth* 1999, 324). Choc Charlie to some extent offers that Ulysses might not be a vehicle for all of his experiences after all, at least not until Ulysses comes to bear witness to who Choc Charlie is, on the higher frequencies.[2]

The negative critical reception of Ralph Ellison's opus, among the forced radicals of the Black Power movement and later, to a great extent has to do with how Ellison approached those realities to which some blacks thought the novelist had perhaps closed his eyes, such as violence against blacks or urban poverty. As Irving Howe put it in 1963, "what astonishes one most about *Invisible Man* is the apparent freedom it displays from the ideological and emotional penalties suffered by Negroes in this country."[3] Jerry Gafio Watts (1994) complicates Howe's criticism somewhat, noting that Ellison *does* display the "ideological and emotional" sphere of Negro life, but he does it through folklore rather than through sociopolitical means. Watts's complaint is that Ellison valorizes Negro folklore positively because it validates his authenticity, not because of any concern for the broader cause of social and political uplift for blacks in America.[4] Watts argued that Ellison idealized Negro folklore, which he mixed with the written word, to the exclusion of a broader black experience. Watts, to my mind, reads Ellison through the prism of Houston Baker, who frames the discussion in terms of an antithesis between the vernacular and the classical, with the former always implicated as a low cultural form in contrast to the "high art" of the Greek hydrias.[5] Watts ultimately sees Ellison as an elitist and a "dogmatic individualist" (109). Certainly Ellison's approach to the hero as an individual, which itself stems from classical ideals, raises questions about the relationship between politics, as it pertains to a group with pressing social issues, and the desirability of Western myth to address their concern.

Prior to *Ulysses in Black,* no one has directly addressed the issue of the relationship between Ellison's politics and his myth analysis. At the same time, it was clear that his broader literary approach, such as his celebration of such authors of Homer, Vergil, and James Joyce alongside his deliberate silence in the political arena, alienated those blacks who saw the need for a more transparent tie between writing and politics.[6] I will return to this issue, but it might first be instructive to draw a parallel between Ellison and others who privileged myth over the political, such as Joseph Campbell. In *The Politics of Myth,* Robert Ellwood suggests that Campbell's approach to mythology was concomitant with a political withdrawal that, despite the author's scholarly pronouncements, inevitably privileged West over East, the individual over the collective.[7] Ellwood attunes the reader to the shrill outcome of Campbell's "heroic individualism," to borrow from Watts's critique of Ellison, namely his noncommittal to the struggle of Jews in Germany under the Nazi regime.[8] In times that, as most would concede, called for even the artist to take sides, Campbell saw himself as "an Olympian above the fray" (Ellwood 1999, 141). Campbell, as one of Ellison's intellectual influences, provides a telling parallel.[9] In dangerous times for blacks, with the violence of the pre–, inter–, and post–Civil Rights eras and the urgency that other black intellectuals expressed, Ellison was, similar to Campbell, concerned with the separation of art (in this case myth) and politics. Yet, to Ellison's credit, his silence in the political arena belied his head-on approach to race in his writings, as I have shown in chapter 6. It has been my contention that critics have not looked deeply enough into Ellison's corpus of work, where we find that he was in fact transforming a Western esthetic to address the concerns, political and otherwise, of blacks in America.

While Ellison thought that the classics—and myth specifically—was for anyone who could "dig it," and that black folklore, conversely, had something to offer the broader Western mythology, it might be conceded that certain experiences call for more radical responses, as was also the case with Campbell's approach to the politics of his time.[10] It has been suggested, particularly with the Black Arts movement, that certain experiences are beyond the scope of literature—or at least literature that is overly inflected with Western emblems, in its current shape—to express. At the same time, even the Black Power movement was itself inadequate to the task of radical revolution, as Harold Cruse suggests. Whether because of the absence of a truly radical political agenda, or because of the underlying interconnections across American literature and society, Black Power, Cruse offers, was not ultimately viable. At the same time, acquiescence to a broader Western esthetic—a heroic individualism—in areas of politics or literary expression does not necessarily mean the eradication of alternate sociocultural realities. One such reality, as a case in point, is that of the black body of slavery, to which Ellison bore witness in his prose.

In his response to the debate over literary canons in American education, Houston Baker offered that the esthetic value of the classics notwithstanding, America had its own, classic corpus for which to account.[11] Baker was referring to the brutalized *body* of the black figure, which is a feature of American literature from at least the eighteenth century. Baker calls readers—black and white—to the narratives of slaves and their brutalization, their "battery" (1988, 351), a reality from which "one cannot merely turn one's eyes" (352). Put otherwise, John F. Callahan asserts that black literature as a whole, moving forward from the slave past to diverse experiences in the twentieth century, asks the mixed audience of readers, "Who you for?"[12] Could a sympathetic reader encounter the local, vernacular experience of blacks in America and turn away? Baker calls readers to view the vernacular of American esthetics, initially "situated outside *written* language" (348). Just as the modern reader, whether literary artist or critic, encounters the classics as a broader *literary* and cultural heritage, so the classicist, if we apply Baker's argument, should account for the vernacular experiences that shape a nation.

With the thirty years or so that have passed since Black Studies became a part of the American academy, we have gained a perspective that adds to our understanding of theories regarding African American literature, such as Baker's idea of *vernacular*. Baker addressed those experiences peripheral to literature in the main, namely the experiences of blacks, through the notion of the vernacular. By contrast, Henry Louis Gates Jr., in his earlier writings applied Yale Criticism to black literature, arguing that literature was a closed system of texts and that, as such, black literature amounted to a discourse unto itself (Brenkman 1994). Baker's vernacular theory acknowledged a broader literary horizon. John Brenkman proffers that Gates eventually conceded Houston Baker's central argument of a black vernacular through *The Signifying Monkey*, which "explores the relation of the black vernacular tradition to the Afro-American literary tradition" (Gates 1988, xix). For Gates, this "literary tradition" clearly now included "the curious tension between the black vernacular and the literate white text, between the spoken and the written word, between the oral and the printed forms of literary discourse" (131). Baker, somewhat gloatingly, thanked Gates for this concession: "I wish to thank [Henry Louis Gates Jr.] not only for providing a detailed and thorough reading of my manuscript . . . but also for paying me the supreme compliment of altering his critical vocabulary to accord with mine" (Baker 1984, x).

Brenkman phrases the tension about which Gates spoke, a tension apparent in Baker's writing, as a question: "How is a minority cultural tradition transformed when forced to assert itself within a context, typically a national context, it does not control?" (Brenkman, 62). While others rejected the national context, Ellison saw that the answer to the question of cultural transformation had to come within a workable paradigm.

The Black Power approach to this question of cultural transformation was to reimagine the national context in terms of a radical revolution. Cruse (1967) conceded that even here revolution never added up politically; revolution in black thought never amounted to anything other than metaphor. At the same time, there is meaning in metaphors. (The notion of a "mere" metaphor is deceiving.) Ellison's failure to embrace the metaphor of revolution, the metaphor of the collective, black cause that Morrison mastered, was the basis of his undoing among some critics (such as Watts) and in Black Power circles.

To some extent, both Gates and Baker use metaphors to account for reality. For Baker, the black reality—and by extension American reality—could be embodied, literally. In whatever way the circumstances of slavery, freedom, and the vernacular expression of the blues came to be arranged in literature, these circumstances were real and part of an American literary corpus. Baker used the ontology of the blues (which I read as metaphor, which is *not* to say *unreal*) to speak to the broader, vernacular experience. For Gates, who in Baker's mind had adapted his critique toward a theory of vernacular, the figure was that of the signifying monkey (Gates 1988). Gates argued that the Yoruba trickster Esu-Elegbara, in his manifestation as the signifying monkey, was the cultural reality that underpinned the

oral, black vernacular transformed into texts. More recent criticism has
helped readers to see the metaphors behind what Gates and Baker might
pass off as essential reality. Sandra Adell (1994), for example, argues that
Gates, on the one hand, is still steeped in an idea of hermeneutics that is
essentially Western, while Baker, on the other hand, borrows from notions
of Being found in the works of European philosophers. For Adell, even
W. E. B. DuBois, who so eloquently expressed the Negro dilemma in terms
of a double consciousness, is as Hegelian as he is Afrocentric in thought.
The point here is that, to my mind, Ellison takes unfair criticism for his
recognition, before Adell, of the innately Western—though not *exclusively*
Western—context of black esthetics.

As their ideas pertain to Ellison, it is worth taking a brief look at how
Gates and Baker interpret an emblematic figure from Ellison's essays,
namely the Little Man at Chehaw Station himself. This figure is worth
discussing because he is a literary critical trope, an idea that brings us back
to Ellison's notion of craft, which I ultimately read in a favorable light vis-
à-vis the classics. In the essay "The Little Man at Chehaw Station" (1986a),
Ellison relates some advice that his college music teacher, Hazel Harrison,
gave him. "Baby," she said, "in this country you must always prepare your-
self to play your very best wherever you are, and on all occasions" (4).
The advice takes on a strange, oracular quality as Harrison's words flow:
"You must *always* play your best, even if it's only in the waiting room at
Chehaw Station because in this country there'll always be a little man hid-
den behind the stove" (4).

Ellison's Little Man is a connoisseur of craft ("connoisseur, critic, trickster," 11), and in the essay Ellison goes on to assert (as I have pointed to
at various points in this book) that craft *completes* the person. In Gates's
interpretation, the Little Man is, of course, the African trickster "surfac-
ing when we least expect him, at a crossroads of destiny. This particular
little man evokes Esu, the little man whose earthly dwelling place is the
crossroads" (1989, 64). Baker, on the other hand, interprets the Little Man
as the vernacular, which "always *absorbs* 'classical' elements of American
life and art. Indeed, Ellison seems to imply that expressive performers in
America who ignore the judgments of the vernacular are destined to failure" (1984, 12–13). Certainly each interpretation of Ellison's Little Man is
equally viable, and Gates's and Baker's ideas are not necessarily mutually
exclusive. Put otherwise, if the Little Man is a *protean* trickster, he might
be white, black, or both at the same time, but he always judges mastery

of craft, whether language, music, or the plastic arts. Ellison hits at the protean nature of the Little Man in *Invisible Man,* through the figure of *Proteus* Bliss Rinehart. He returns to the idea of changeability through Bliss, the racially ambiguous protagonist in *Juneteenth.*

Yet Ellison's Little Man at Chehaw Station is not *only* a hermeneutic symbol. Rather, he represents a call to the mastery of craft:

> Well, if you ask me, artistic talent might have something to do with race, but you do *not* inherit culture and artistic skill through genes. No, sir. These come as a result of personal conquest, of the individual's applying himself to that art, that music—whether jazz, classical, or folk—which helps him to realize and *complete himself.* (31, my italics)

If, for Ellison, craft completes the individual, he himself would be whole as a novelist. (This again explains Ellison's withdrawal from politics; he saw writing as enough activism.) For Morrison, this completing attribute, the refining fire, to borrow from Albert Murray, was travel.[13] Ellison's call to the mastery of craft, as he suggests, could apply to any field, from art and music, to literature and its criticism. Here classicists might read the painstaking process of learning Greek and Latin, itself an aspect of the broader craft of criticism and interpretation. At the same time, Ellison also locates the education, or acculturation, of the individual in "culture," not only in personal, "artistic skill." In doing so, he complicates his own paradigm by conceding the necessity of a favorable cultural context for individual, artistic growth. (It is worth recalling here again the abysmal minority presence in such rarified academic fields as the Classics.[14])

Again, it is easy with hindsight to recognize the limitations of this self-imposed proscription on Ellison's life—a stifling limitation that might to some extent explain his reduced literary output. At the same time, it is surprising that a work such as Watts's *Heroism and the Black Intellectual,* which claims to be a study of Ellison's "intellectual life" (as suggested in the title and in much of the book) does not account for such major influences on Ellisonian thought as Kenneth Burke. Indeed through Burke's idea of language as symbolic action, Ellison conceived of a method of changing the world around him—the revolution *in other terms* that Cruse sees as the only viable one—through a mastery of the craft (which might be translated to *technē* in Greek) of language and writing.

Burke (1945, 1969) saw that each person (the *agent* of an act) could in subtle ways change his environment (the *scene*). (This is Burke's *scene–act ratio*.) It is worthwhile here to evoke the revolutionary, Burkean idea of language as the decisive means of creation and change:

> If an agent acts in keeping with his nature as an agent (act–agent ratio), he may change the nature of the scene accordingly (scene–act ratio), and thereby establish a state of unity between himself and his world (scene–agent ratio). . . . In reality, we are capable of but partial acts, acts that but partially represent us and that produce but partial transformations. Indeed, if all the ratios were adjusted to one another with perfect Edenic symmetry, they would be immutable in one unending "moment."
>
> Theological notions of creation and re-creation bring us nearest to the concept of total acts. (19)

Ellison perhaps read Burke in terms of the possibility of revolution through the written word: "In the beginning was not the word, but its contradiction."

The influence of Burke on *Invisible Man* is overt, and it is surprising that this association does not factor into black esthetic interpretations of the novel. A couple of brief examples should suffice. In *A Grammar of Motives*, Burke is at one point interested in what motivates action, collective and individual, and he claims that a motive "becomes 'pure' motive when matched against some individual locus of motivation. . . . A soldier may be *nationally* motivated to kill the enemy of his country, whereas *individually* he is motivated by a horror of killing his own enemies" (Burke 37). Ellison seems to be interpreting Burke in *Invisible Man* when the protagonist meets Mr. Emerson, the son of an addressee of the letter meant to prevent him from returning to college. Emerson wants to help the protagonist, and he, along with the reader, wonders about his own purpose, because "all of our motives are impure" (*Invisible Man* 1995, 186). James Saunders (1997), who argues for the homosexuality of Emerson given signs he notes in the passage, points to one of several motives (namely attraction) that might have prompted the character toward apparent "sincerity" (*Invisible Man* 1995, 186).

Later in the novel, the protagonist's observations about P. B. Rinehart (Proteus Bliss) once again recall Burke. Rinehart, who is numbers-runner and preacher, pimp and politician, all at once, prompts Invisible Man to wonder about the appropriate theory and method to understanding him:

"I should search out the proper political classification, label Rinehart and his situation and quickly forget him" (498). This recalls Burke's citation of the "scientific method (*met-hodos*)," which he sees "not as a way of life, or *act* of *being*, but as a *means* of *doing*" (15). Rinehart defies the political method of classification through which Invisible Man has come to organize his world. Ellison points here again to a "method" that is at the periphery of the literate, or that is "invisible" to most of the outside world.

Burke's idea of language as symbolic action is, more importantly here, evident in "The Little Man at Chehaw Station." In the essay, Ellison cites the promise of American democracy no less than twenty times, and a superficial reading of the essay might lead to the conclusion that Ellison blindly accepted a status quo, bourgeoisie idealism regarding his nation. A deeper reading, however, reveals Burkean influence, as Ellison asserts the philosopher's contention that "man uses language to moralize both nature and himself" (Ellison 1986a, 18). Ellison sees, for example, that democracy is an ideal, a principle, and his notion of "democratic faith" (9, 18) announces a willful choice to believe. Yet just as God creates man in his image, Ellison chooses to *re*create American democracy in his image, through language:

> In our national beginnings, all redolent with Edenic promises, was the word *democratic,* and since we vowed in a war rite of blood and sacrifice to keep its commandments, we act in the name of a word made sacred. Yes, but since we are, as Burke holds, language-using, language-misusing animals—beings who are by nature vulnerable to both the negative *and* the positive promptings of language as symbolic action—we Americans are given to eating, regurgitating, and, alas, re-eating our most sacred words. (19)

Although the notion that all *men* were created equally did not initially include blacks (or women), Ellison, similar to the writers of slave narratives from a prior generation, reuses language, "misusing" it, as it were, in expansive ways so as to include black men, and women. Ellison's "Edenic promises" not only recalls Burke's "Edenic symmetry," but the locus also transforms the secular into the sacred, as language—here the notion of American democracy—becomes the host, to be broken in remembrance and feasted upon. This reuse of language is, for Ellison, the ultimate political act. Ellison's notion of revolution is the turbulence of language, the

"Adamic wordplay" (29) that is, in essence, the "democratic ideal" (a notion that recurs several times in the essay).

In Ellison's evaluation, both Baker and Gates might be viewed as equally abusive—and this is *good*—of language in the framework they provide for viewing black literature. This is not to say that Esu Elegbara, or the signifying monkey, is not a feature of African American life, thought, and cultural expression. There is no science (which is not to say no method) in reconstituting the cultural fragments transported to America during the Middle Passage and across centuries.[15] At the same time, the signifying monkey, as Adell suggests, is a metaphor, one no less viable, radical, and no more authentic, than Ulysses. Baker, through his evocation of the black body, articulates an at-times ineffable cultural reality, but the broader blues ontology is as much metaphor as it is historical fact. It was Baker, after all, and not Ellison (contrary to Baker's suggestion) who explicitly juxtaposed black vernacular to classical motifs and evaluated the former as *low* and the latter as *high:* "The shift from Greek hydrias to ancestral faces is a shift from high art to vernacular expression" (Baker 1984, 2).

The aim of this book was to bring the relationship between the classics and black thought (particularly black literature) out in the open, as it were, to shift the nature of a conversation that was already taking place between the Classical Studies and Black Studies—to violently reconstitute our critical language. As I have stated, the contact between blacks and the classics has been, for the most part, clandestine because, on the surface, black classicism, in the context of twentieth-century developments in African American literary and sociopolitical theory, seemed old hat. Yet the contact between broader literary tropes and black literature continued, even in such seemingly radical Black Aesthetic works as Toni Morrison's *Song of Solomon.* In this context, Ralph Ellison, as an author who unabashedly claimed Western influence, is a template for viewing the corpus and reception of black classicism. Hopefully, the reading I provided of such Ellisonian passages as the lynching scene in *Juneteenth* begins a radical reconstitution. What Black Studies or the Classical Studies will do with a transformed paradigm I will leave for future works. Black esthetics will continue to face the challenge of minority cultural expression in a national context, while the Classics, if the field reaches out for further diversity, might take stock of the transformation our discipline has already undergone in the black Underworld of the postmodern mind.

# NOTES
# REFERENCES CITED
# INDEX

# Notes

Prologue

1. For the essay, see Ellison 1986a.

2. As the September 8, 2004, *Los Angeles Times* article by John H. McWhorter shows, these categories are not at all seamless. McWhorter posits "black" as more preferable than "African American" because the latter suggests a connection to a location that is distant ideologically, geographically, historically. He sees himself as wholly American, but for him this America has nothing to do with a slave past or any mythic, "homeland" connection known to a Diaspora.

3. See Paul Cartledge's 1993 discussion of slavery in the Greek context for more. In particular, he argues that the Greek notion of polarity, what Cartledge calls "heterology," made slavery inevitable in the ancient world and led to Aristotle's "uninspiring views of the nature of man (or some men)" (169).

4. The reader could go in several directions to learn more about the rise of the concept of Europe postantiquity, and the centrality of Africa, or the Other, to this concept. On the former subject, see Amin 1989, Leyser 1992, and West 1999. On what Edward Said would call Europe's "textual attitude," see Johnston 1918 (still relevant despite the date), and Johnson 1998.

5. On the construction of the Other, i.e., the origins of race, in the New World, see Todorov 1999.

6. On whiteness, see Allen 1994; Malcolmson, especially 263ff; and Roediger 1999.

7. On education, see Tatum 1999 and Wilson 1990; on employment, see Roediger 1999; on housing, see Hirsch 1998, Palm 1985, and Sugrue 1998.

8. An example of this is the ongoing controversy over the immigration policy toward Haiti. See Dawkins 2000.

9. Among countless discussion on the representations of blacks (and particularly men) in the media, see Patterson 1990.

10. See Haley 1975, the autobiography in which Malcolm X discusses their terms and their impact on his formation.

11. On the New Negro, see Locke 1925. On the Black Aesthetic, see Gayle 1971.

12. Despite McWhorter's emphasis on the *dis*connection between Africa (with its countless cultures) and America, within the scholarly community stronger culture connections have been made in anthropology, art history, and sociology. See, for example, Thompson 1984.

13. Here I am paraphrasing from the *Merriam-Webster's Collegiate Dictionary, Deluxe Edition*, 1998.

14. For her arguments pertaining to the Black Athena debate and to Afrocentrism, see Lefkowitz 1992, 1996, and 1997. That the last word on Black Athena is yet to be uttered is clear in Bernal's latest volume, *Black Athena Writes Back* (2001).

15. I became aware of Sanders 1970, Stark 1973, and Scruggs 1974 in 1998. While the first two treat Ellison's Homeric allusions, the last looks at a Vergilian reference in *Invisible Man*. I discuss Ellison's relationship to the Ulysses theme from Homer in chapter 5 of this book.

16. The only biography of Ellison to date is Jackson 2002.

17. For the comparative mythology in general, see Penglase 1994.

18. On Bernal's own discussion of his choice for a title and the desire to create a "black" Egypt, see Berlinerblau 1999.

19. The criticism of Ellison, which I see as an imposition of a somewhat artificial choice—either be African or be European, was recently expressed in Vernon Williams's 2003 "Black Thought" graduate seminar, which I visited at Purdue University for the class's discussion of Ellison's collection of essays, *Shadow and Act*. Students objected to Ellison's self-identification as simply a writer and not necessarily a *Negro* writer. Without a deeper understanding of Ellison's broader literary imagination, such a claim might seem, to some, objectionable.

20. See The American Philological Association newsletter, report from the Committee on the Status of Women and Minorities, 2002. As the book goes to press, the 2004 statistics from the same committee shows only a slight fractional increase in these numbers, which were up to 3 percent.

21. His discussion of this appears in a letter to Albert Murray; see Ellison 2000.

22. See Ronnick's various works on Scarborough and others in the bibliography.

23. For a cursory overview of the presence of the classics in black intellectual life, see Fikes 2002.

24. For the exact quote, see Ellison 1986, 3.

25. For a brief description of the cases and, in some cases, the newspaper reports on them, see Ginzburg 1998. On the sociological data, see also Patterson 1998.

26. Similar constraints are placed on Wheatley's work and that of Toni Morrison. I discuss the issue of the reception of black classicism in chapter 4 of this book.

27. For work directly on Williams, see Becker 1999. Ronnick recently toured a photographic exhibit titled "Twelve Black Classicists." These photos included some of the first African American practitioners of Greek and Latin. They also

represent some of the first PhDs awarded to African Americans in the country. Robert Bruce Slater (1994) gives an overview of the blacks who preceded them in earning some of the first degrees of higher education among African Americans.

28. This was Ellison's argument in "Twentieth-Century Fiction and the Black Mask of Humanity" (1966a), where he offered that Mark Twain and William Faulkner were great authors in part because they refused to ignore the vital principle in America's racial dichotomy.

## 1. *Classica Africana*

1. I am speaking here of the Hellenistic period, when, as one of many examples of the beginning of classicism, scholars like Aristarchus and Zenodotus undertook to edit and systematize the texts of Homer's epics. This was a highly significant act during a period that saw the birth of literary criticism and the rise of the major disciplines, which would later constitute a university education. Although there was a great sense of community for Greeks during the classical period, the third century BCE, it might be argued, marks the beginning of a classical heritage. For a general history of ancient historical periods to Hellenistic times, see Martin 2000.

2. In her article, Margaret A. Burcia (2002, 515) offers Jupiter Hammon, with a poem dating to 1760, as the first black poet published. His work would antedate Phillis Wheatley's by thirteen years and the American Revolution by sixteen. See also Baker 1988.

3. On the relationship between the classics and notions of citizenship, nobility, and identity in America, see Reinhold 1984. On classicism and specific personalities, such as Thomas Jefferson, see also G. Chinard 1932, E. Miles 1974, and Carl J. Richard 1994. For more on the relationship between the classics and race in early American debates see S. F. Wiltshire 1977 and Ronnick 1998.

4. I am not referring here to the Afrocentric claim that Greece "stole" civilization from Africa, but rather to the simple, imaginative contact between ancient Greece and Africa, such as the banquets between the Olympian gods and Ethiopians made iconic in Homer's *Iliad,* book 1. See Snowdon 1970. Even if this relationship should be more mythological than historical, the myth would speak to the unconscious, though natural, creative interaction in which I am interested. For a survey of this contact, see Fikes 2002. I am of course playing on the first lines of Ralph Ellison's *Invisible Man:* "I am an invisible man. No, I am not a spook like those who haunted Edgar Allan Poe; nor am I one of your Hollywood-movie ectoplasms. I am a man of substance, of flesh and bone, fiber and liquids— and I might even be said to possess a mind" (1952; 1995, 3).

5. On King, see, for example, Becker 2000 and West 2000.

6. The interest seems to have begun with a 1996 American Philological Association panel, titled "Classica Africana: The Graeco-Roman Heritage and People of African American Descent." See Ronnick 2001.

7. As I make clearer later in this chapter, race was already, in a manner of speaking, on the table in classics circles at least since Frank Snowden's 1970 publication, but the Black Athena debate became a benchmark for how the issue would be treated.

8. This particular quote is from one of Ronnick's essays, "Classica Africana," http://department.monm.edu/classics/CPL/PromotionalMaterials/Africana.htm (accessed June 16, 2008). Similar assertions can be found throughout her writing (e.g., Ronnick 2000a and 2000b).

9. See Lefkowitz 1992, 1996a, and 1996b; see Howe 1998.

10. In his work of 2001, Bernal makes the point that many of the issues raised throughout the Black Athena debate remain fundamentally unresolved, despite the classical establishment's dismantling of Bernal's methodology.

11. Berlinerblau (1999) cites this claim of legal scholar Patricia Williams, although the truism is known and felt by scores of Americans on either side of the racial divide.

12. The statistics in such areas as American higher education reflect disparities in opportunities for blacks. See Wilson 1990. By "higher frequencies," I am again riffing on *Invisible Man:* "Who knows but that on the higher frequencies I speak for you."

13. On later treatments, now of blacks and Romans, see also Lloyd A. Thompson 1999.

14. See Snowden 1996 for the publication within Lefkowitz's volume; Snowden's essay directly takes on the idea of Afrocentrism.

15. See Ronnick 2000b for her essay on Scarborough; 2001 for early black membership in the American Philological Association; and 2002a for Scarborough's relationship to the Classical Association of the Middle West and South. Ronnick published an edition of Scarborough's autobiography in 2005.

16. King's claim might well be the case within the classics. The University of Colorado, however, lists Flowers as the *second* black female graduate. See http://www.cualum.org/heritage/virtual_tour/hall_alumni.html.

17. On Jupiter Hammon, see Margaret Brucia 2002; on Wheatley, see John Shields 1988, Robert Kendrick 1996, and Herbert Renfro 1998.

18. See especially Ronnick 2000a on Booker T. Washington.

19. For the debate in writers concerned with black classicism, see Becker 2001 and Ronnick 2000a.

20. On classicism and both issues (of citizenship and nobility) see Meyer 1984 and Richard 1994.

21. On whiteness as a new social category in America, see Malcolmson 2000. Malcolmson argues that "within premodern written record of, globally speaking, light-skinned people, references to white people as white people, as a race, are remarkably scarce" (277). Yet regarding Europeans in early American history, "slowly and reluctantly whites accepted their skin color as their distinguishing characteristic" (281). New laws and social practices accompanied the birth of race. Bernard

Knox's *Oldest Dead White European Males* (1993) attests to the imposition of this seemingly natural, unconsciously accepted racial category onto the ancient world: "It is clear, from their artistic representations of their own and other races, that they were undoubtedly *white* or, to be exact, a sort of Mediterranean olive color" (26, my italics).

22. On nobility and white manhood in the South, see Nadel 1988, 1–26.

23. Again, on the relationship to black classicism, see Becker 2001 and Ronnick 2000a.

24. Classics did remain a feature of the oft-quoted Morrill Land-Grant act of 1862, which called for teaching "agriculture and the mechanic arts," but schools were called to do so "without excluding other scientific and classical studies." See Becker 2001, 317.

25. See Washington 1967, 62.

26. Washington 1967, 62.

27. See Du Bois [1903] 2003. This quote is from the 1989 Bantam edition, p. 68.

28. The idea is already well articulated in Du Bois [1903] 2003. See also Ronnick 2000a.

29. Discussion in recent publications shows that the debate about education and the proper use of knowledge for blacks continues into the twenty-first century. See, for example, Davis 2002, 28–34.

30. Scarborough argued that classical education was not wasted on blacks and that "higher education is, after all, to be the most powerful lever in the Negro's development and in the ultimate perfection of humanity at large." See Ronnick 2000b.

31. For Washington's relationship to the Negro community, see Cruse 1984, 11–63.

32. See particularly his enthusiasm at attending Hampton, 1967, 37–48.

33. The issue of audience has recently entered the discussion of black classicism with the work of Steven Mailloux. In the fall of 2002, he delivered the Leonora Woodman Lecture at Purdue University, where he investigated the "rhetorical paths" particularly in the oratory of Frederick Douglass and William Scarborough. The talk was titled "Rhetorical Paths of Thought: Visual Rhetoric, Classical Traditions and Performing Identity in Nineteenth-Century America." With respect to the Washington–Du Bois debate, we find that the reception of these authors also changes over time. See Alilunas 1973, 176–86.

34. See Du Bois [1903] 2003. Du Bois claimed that blacks were always of two minds, at once American and at the same time other, and that life is often lived in the space of otherness, behind the veil of race.

35. In contrast to this, Washington, who argued that Negroes and whites in America could be as separate as the fingers on a hand yet united in a common cause, was himself a product of the American education system. That is, the sharp dichotomies—between education and training, integration or segregation—belie the true nature of America and the American imagination.

36. For a full discussion of Black Nationalism vis-à-vis black identity within America, see Cruse 1984.

37. Flowers is quoted in King 1996, 60. Flowers's words echo the earlier explanation of Phillis Wheatley's classicism. For a context, see Gates 1987, 61–79. Black classicists were also noted as exemplary citizens of their intellectual community. See Ronnick 2002b. The broader context for these comments has to do not only with race, but also with notions of citizenship within an American community, such as the work ethic. Becker quotes a description of Daniel Williams as "a hard-working student, devout Christian, and the possessor of a well stored mind" (1999, 95).

38. In his talk, Steven Mailloux discussed these rhetorical paths in the oratory of Frederick Douglass and William Scarborough.

39. I catalogue what has been done in chapter 5.

40. See Irving Howe 1963 on the criticism of Ellison. On biographical notes, see Jackson 2002.

41. Orlando Patterson (1990) uses the term "social death" to refer to the cultural, linguistic, and political isolation that the slave, in any context, whether ancient or modern, experiences in the environment of his or her captivity.

42. Shelley Fisher Fishkin (1995) argues that a "remapping" of American culture, in which Ellison's notion of America as an integral whole (in terms of race and the divide between black and white) became more prevalent, began to take place in the 1990s. If the booming interest in black classicists (and even white rappers) is any testimony, Fishkin's claim is worth considering.

43. Certainly identity politics become a factor, and it might at times be more expedient for an African American to identify more with the ethnic group than with the broader culture. Indeed this can cause confusion and feelings of betrayal, as the nation's reaction to the O. J. Simpson verdict in 1995 revealed. In the world of literature, John Duvall (2000) explores how these identity politics play a role, as one example, in Toni Morrison's fictive- and self-constructions.

## 2. Birth of a Hero

1. Stanford's understanding of Ulysses as a folkloric figure who existed even before Homer is an important consideration here. See *The Ulysses Theme*, 8–24. This understanding was based on the studies of myth and folklore popular during Stanford's time, such as Hyman 1955 and 1963. I trace this strand of the study of myth, as opposed to structuralist approaches or Jungian approaches, as two viable alternatives, because more than any other the ritual approach to myth underpinned Ellison's technique, as we see in his own essays. Ulysses as folklore, moreover, to some extent destabilizes readings of classical myth as hegemonic, making the classics, as we saw in Ellison's own words, for anyone who could "dig it."

2. On the variations of the name, see Stanford, 8. I use Odysseus when talking about Greek texts and Ulysses when talking about the Roman and later contexts.

3. Stanford in fact argues that, after Homer, we must wait until the modern novel for the "re-integration" of Ulysses as subject. See Stanford, 211–40.

4. I cannot, in this book, expand on the social, political, and historical reasons for the dominance of Homeric epic over, for example, the older and equally noteworthy traditions of the Sanskrit epics (the Mahabharata and the Rāmāyana) or the Babylonian epic of Gilgamesh. For a discussion of the Rāmāyana, see Blank 1992 (for an attempt at understanding the work within its cultural contexts, ancient and modern) and Richman 1991; on Gilgamesh, see Kramer 1981.

5. Although Rosalind Thomas (1992) does not discuss Homer in the context of the Near Eastern traditions, the following quote should suffice to convey the gist of the argument: "The overall coherence must surely indicate that, however traditional the language and basic story, the *Iliad* bears the mark of a master poet at the end of a long line, a so-called 'monumental poet'" (35). This "monumental poet" would outstrip not only the poets of his own society, but his genius would also extend beyond Greece.

6. In the case of the Rāmāyana, the oral tradition travels far and wide, reaching such places as Bali, as Therese de Vet (1996) demonstrates.

7. See, for example, Romila Thapar (1989), who argues for the Rāmāyana playing a role in the shaping of ideas about kingship, and religious outlooks.

8. On literacy and oral tradition in Greece, see Thomas 1992 and 2003; for the role of writing in shaping cultural values, such as notions of justice, see also Havelock 1988 for a synopsis of that same scholar's important body of work.

9. For the dynamic and changing nature of oral epic in relation to its written form, see Thomas 1992 and de Vet 1996.

10. The subject of literary "criticism" in margins of text is covered in Meijering 1987.

11. The following is a summary of Dupont, 1–17.

12. Dupont certainly does not go nearly as far as the deconstruction theory that Jacques Derrida laid out in 1967, including "On Grammatology" and "Writing and Difference." (I have not listed either of these works in the bibliography; the reader can find various translations into English of the 1967 French originals.)

13. One of the fundaments of Thomas's (1992) theory of orality in Greece is in fact the simultaneity and coexistence of writing and oral culture. See also de Vet 1996.

14. On literature as a hazard in the expression of cultural values in the context of the numerous cultures of modern Africa, see Reckord, et al. 1997.

15. The objection becomes especially polemical when we consider Harold Bloom's pronouncement that much of African American literature would fall under the category of period pieces, as opposed to timeless contributions to the canon. See Bloom 1994.

16. There are legitimate esthetic and ethical reasons to resist the idea of a canon. For sophisticated discussion, see Gates 1992, and Baker 1998 and 1990.

17. Knox (1979), for example, finds traces of a Cyclops tradition outside of Greece and earlier than Homer.

18. Stanford argues the following of Ulysses: "Undoubtedly some of Odysseus's ruses, especially as described in the *Odyssey* and in the Epic Cycle, deviate from the normal conventions of heroic conduct, suggesting, rather, the more plebeian atmosphere of folk-tales. At times, too, especially in the *Iliad,* one finds traces of something like a conflict between the diverse genres of epic poetry and folk-tales in Homer's characterization of Odysseus" (10).

19. See Baker 1984, 113–99.

20. I am referring here to the 2004 blockbuster movie *Troy.* For all of the film's shortcomings, which are too numerous to discuss here, it at least conveys the magnitude, the larger-than-life persona, of this hero.

21. For a discussion of these and other heroic terms, see Nagy 1999.

22. For issues of audience and storytelling—put otherwise, why Odysseus is telling *this* story to *this* audience with *these* particular emphases—see Ahl and Roisman 1996. Ahl and Roisman argue that the implicit message of Odysseus's well-crafted tale is that the Phaeacians would do well to aid the hero, or they might suffer similar consequences.

23. Ann Astell (1994) summarizes a view of Odysseus received in the Middle Ages: "The ancient philosophers gave three answers to the question 'What is a human being?' Each of these found its confirmation in the inspired poetry of Homer. The first answer recalls our mortality, our necessary subjection to death and to fortune as bodily creatures existing in time, exposed to temporal change, and fated to die. . . . The second answer to the question 'Quid est homo?' recalls human rationality, the power of a person's higher nature over his passions, his body, and his external situation. . . . The third response to the call for self-knowledge requires a person to recall the immortality of his soul, its divine origin and end" (6–8).

24. I have already quoted in the epigraph Ellison's statement on Ulysses from the essay "Change the Joke and Slip the Yoke," which I discuss in detail in chapter 5. He also refers to the Ulysses theme, as I have noted, in his *Letters.* In fiction, I argue in chapter 5 that the motif of Ulysses and the Cyclops impacts *Invisible Man* to a much greater extent than has been noted by critics. In addition to this, *Juneteenth* returns to the motif.

25. For the problems of acquisitiveness as a heroic quality, see Rainer Friedrich 1987 and 1991, which ultimately concludes that the trait is in keeping with classical heroism.

26. As Stanford concurs, the word *polytropos* simply means "of many turns," so Odysseus is the man of many turns or many wiles, yet the fifth-century BCE response to this was that Odysseus was "'unstable, unprincipled, unscrupulous'" (Stanford, 99), as the genre of tragedy begins to represent him. The modern term corresponding to this might be "shifty."

27. For a discussion of the centrality of the idea of *xenia,* to the epic, see Reece 1993.

28. Stanford sees acquisitiveness as "a normal part of the heroic etiquette" (76).

29. See Clark 1989.

30. Ahl argues that Odysseus might be emphasizing the wine and his rouse to warn the Phaeacians of the danger that could come to them if they do not help him.

31. And yet the wine, in Ahl and Roisman's interpretation, might evidence on Maron's part a failed attempt to intoxicate Odysseus and his men. See Ahl and Roisman 1996, 106–9. As a whole, therefore, *xenia* might not be as innocent and straightforward an institution as we think.

32. For support of this argument, see Rutherford 1986.

33. Given the subject matter here, it is interesting that Lambropoulos (1993) reads Auerbach in terms of Eurocentric textual criticism. He questions Auerbach's authority as critic within a hermeneutics that is presented as ostensibly but falsely objective.

34. Erwin Cook (1999) speaks of Odysseus's suffering in terms of "passive," as opposed to "active," heroics, although he does not go as far as to assert learning through suffering.

35. K. Reinhardt sees the curse that befalls Odysseus, which is really Zeus' curse and not Poseidon's, as punishment for the hero's hubris. For the argument and some overview of its reception, see Rainer Friedrich 1991.

36. On the issue of playing the clown in the context of minstrelsy, see Patterson 1998.

37. See Bernard Williams 1994 for the role of shame (i.e., an "ethical" disposition stemming from one's relationship to others in society) over guilt (a moral response from internalized superstructures—narratives, superegos, etc.) in Homeric society.

38. On the adaptation of folklore into the Homeric passage, see Podlecki 1961, Schein 1970, and Mondi 1983. Schein directly discusses the variation of "Nobody" instead of "Myself."

39. See Brown 1966 and Friedrich 1991.

40. On the folkloric tradition of the Cyclopes outside of Homer and then within the epic, see Mondi 1983.

41. For a bit of the psychological interpretation, see Schein 1970.

42. Sophocles' *Ajax* would be an exception to this rule in Stanford's reading. See Stanford 102–17.

43. Although it comes within the context of a discussion of *Oedipus Tyrannus,* Charles Segal's (2001, 7–14) brief introduction to the period is worth citing here.

44. For an overview of the myth and details of the key characters, see Gantz 1993.

45. For a general discussion of the role of women as Other (especially as slave) in the play, see Segal 1990.

46. For a general discussion of unity and plot, see Conacher 1961 and Michelini 1987, 131–80.

47. On *Hecuba* and heroic honor, see King 1985.

48. If at all neutral, the valence of the term would be pushed in the context of Thucydides, given the general philosophy of leadership not only in his evaluation of Pericles but also in his treatment of such popular leaders as Alcibiades.

49. I am here teasing out a more ambivalent view of Odysseus in the rhetorical tradition—though there is no question about his demagoguery. See Buxton 1982, 172, and Michelini 1987, 144.

50. On the problem of textual attitudes that can even create the idea of a barbarian in the first place, see Said 1979.

51. For Michelini, even the treatment of Polyxena is ambivalent. I wonder about her reading, given the valorization of Polyxena's sacrifice in the play.

52. See, for example, Segal 1990.

53. See most recently Mossman 1995.

54. To some extent, Nussbaum moves the focus back from Hecuba's desperate attempt to persuade, to the ethical framework that has failed her. For the background to *nomos* as opposed to *peitho*, or persuasion, see Kirkwood 1947.

55. See a discussion of Hecuba's debate with Odysseus in the context of the argument for justice, see Mossman 1995.

56. Michelini (1987, 142–57) denies any moral dismissal of sophistic rhetoric in the play. Hecuba's and Odysseus's attempts to persuade are juxtaposed but not expressly judged. Sophistry certainly seems to be the case, by Scodel's (1998) argument, of Hecuba's appeal to Agamemnon to help her given his sexual relationship with her daughter, which she calls *charis,* a reciprocal exchange (as opposed to one-sided, sexual exploitation).

57. On the relationship between this style of patriotic death (as opposed to what we see in Homer) and the institution of the funeral oration, see Loraux 1986.

58. Kirkwood (1947) sees that the argument for sacrifice is based also on *nomos*— it benefits the Greek community of the army. I wonder, however, whether these two presentations of beautiful deaths cancel each other out, or if perhaps one is given priority over the other. If we are to feel Aristotelian pity and fear for Hecuba, then I would argue for a priority of Polyxena's sacrifice.

59. This latter antithesis is certainly important to the Greek setting and might be simply phrased as the question of whether Hecuba's corruption *results from* her barbarian character. The question is certainly a factor in the play, and it is one that Nussbaum's reading (and mine) directly counters. In other words, in the *nomos/physis* antithesis, *nomos* wins out in shaping Hecuba. A fuller inversion might ask what this means to *Greek* inborn nobility (*physis*). For the antithesis, see Guthrie 1983, who builds on Heinemann 1945.

60. As the reader will see in comments below, it is unclear when Seneca wrote the *Troades,* so that by attributing it to "Nero's court" I am asserting what I

consider to be an attractive possibility for the dating of the play, i.e., between 54 and 65 CE.

61. On the negative criticism of Ellison, see especially Watts 1994.

62. For the relative dating of the plays, see Fitch 1981. On the dating of *Troades* in particular, see Fantham 1982a.

63. The most comprehensive study in English of Stoicism in the tragedies is Rosenmeyer 1989. For the intrinsic problem—and potentialities—of political readings for literature of this period, see Bartsch 1994 and Schiesaro 2003.

64. It should be noted that Seneca makes only passing references to Ulysses in his prose, and these references, perhaps as with any other "idea" in Seneca, offer an at times contradictory impression of what Seneca thinks of the character in the end.

65. For the expansion in the meaning of *imperium* from the right of command to "empire" proper, see Richardson 1991.

66. For post-Rosenmeyer readings beyond Stoicism see first Braden 1985 on power, Boyle 1997, and more recently Schiesaro 2003.

67. For a discussion of the plays as a whole, see Boyle 1997 and Schiesaro 2003. Seneca's relationship to the tripartite self in Plato's *Republic* has not been fully explored.

68. For introductory comments on *Medea*, see Costa 1973; for a reading of the play, see Boyle 1997.

69. I have already mentioned Bartsch 1994 and Schiesaro 2003 on the issue of readings along political lines.

70. Escapism and withdrawal are the key ideas of Williams 1978 on literature of this period.

71. Again, see for example Bartsch 1994.

72. See Bartsch 1994.

73. For more recent views of Otto Zwierlein's (1966) reading of Senecan drama as plays for recitation, see Harrison 2000.

74. It should suffice here to cite Fitch 1974 and Fantham 1982a for the favorable dating of such a reading. How exactly to read Seneca's essay to Nero in the context of Neronian "doublespeak" (Bartsch 1994) and innuendo is another matter entirely. Rudich's (1997) argument that Seneca holds a favorable view of moderate monarchy throughout his writing merits strong consideration.

75. For the myth, see Gantz 1993.

76. Rosenmeyer (1974) does not trust Agamemnon and finds him unpersuasive.

77. On the problems with the scene, see Calder 1970.

## 3. Ulysses Lost on Racial Frontiers

1. Most remarkable in the current wave of scholarship is Benjamin Isaac 2004. See also Keita 1994 and Thompson 1999.

2. See Snowden 1970, 1983.

3. Black Studies of course constitutes another component of this. See Gates 1992.

4. On the reception of the classics in Victorian England, for example, see Jenkyns 1980 and Turner 1981; in eighteenth-century America and beyond, see Reinhold 1984 and Richard 1994; in France, see Gumpert 2001. More generally, the bibliography would be too broad for my purposes here. See in particular Knox 1994.

5. On the rise of "Orientalism" in the West, see Said 1979; Amin 1989 is an offshoot of Said's ideology. For a classical theory on the origins of the opposition of Europe and Asia, or the East, in Greek tragedy, see Hall 1989.

6. Even Bernal's detractors concede some degree of anti-Semitism and racism in the mentalities of Bernal's subjects. See, for example, Marchand and Grafton 1997.

7. I quote Samir Amin's term because it eloquently conveys the iconic and ideological significance of a "Western heritage" or "European heritage." See Amin 1989, 89.

8. For a history, see Martin 2000. For a more impressionistic look at the continuity between ancient and modern, Hellas (or Greece) and Hellenism, see Thomson 1971.

9. Any number of ancient sources, from Cato the Elder to Cicero, could be cited to corroborate this claim, so basic is it to an understanding of the Roman Republic. For a modern discussion, see Gruen 1992.

10. For the history of Greeks in early Italy, see Lomas 1993; for a perspective that emphasizes the visual culture, see Carratellia 1996.

11. Cicero's letters to Atticus reveal the tensions firsthand. See Bailey 1999.

12. For a general overview of the representation of Ulysses in Vergil, see Stanford, 128–37.

13. Much could also be said here on the repression of anger in Stoic ethics. See, for example, Seneca's essay "On Anger," written within a generation after Vergil's death, in Cooper et al. 1995.

14. For Ulysses in Dante, see Stanford, 175–210.

15. See the history of the reception of Euripides in Michelini 1987. Regarding the primacy of Greek over Roman, see Wilhelm Schlegel on Seneca in Lefèvre 1972. I believe that some of the harsh treatment of Senecan drama, including Eliot 1927, up to the tide change in Herrington 1966, had to do with Romantic esthetics more than any other single factor (such as Seneca's proclivity to bombast or his lack of skill as a poet). On Seneca more recently, see Schiesaro 2003.

16. See Clark 1989, who speaks of Odysseus in terms of "bourgeois imperialism."

17. On Eurocentrism, see, again, Amin 1989. See also Lambropoulos 1993. For an overview of Bernal and the pros and cons of his method and arguments, see Rankine 2005. Some of what is contained here is influenced by the discussion of myth and, more specifically, of Berlinerblau in the Rankine publication.

18. On classical myth, and especially Odysseus as hero, for what she calls "epic truth" in such authors as Boethius, see Astell 1994.

19. Stanford discusses this on pp. 159 and 294.

20. I have already mentioned this schism in terms of Euripides (Michelini 1987) and Seneca (Schlegel in Lefèvre 1972).

21. Berlinerblau 1999, in fact, sees the exploration of these factors in the sociology of knowledge as the real contribution of Bernal's work, not the restoration of the Ancient model, which Bernal asserts as his goal.

22. The Greeks, according to the Aryan Model, which Bernal further divides between an initial "Broad" and a later "Extreme" one leading into the Jewish Holocaust of the twentieth century, were not significantly influenced by Egypt, Phoenicia, or any of the major civilizations of the ancient world. In this modern ideological reception of the classics, Greece was the birthplace of Europe, and as such it gave the culture its *raison d'être* and a wellspring for its values. See Bernal 1987.

23. For the most comprehensive refutation of Bernal's thesis from a classical standpoint, see Lefkowitz and Rogers 1996.

24. The argument that Greece did to a great extent see itself through the eyes of Africa is supported, more recently, in Keita 1994.

25. On the problems with this approach, see Hall 1996.

26. For the myth and its representation throughout classical literature and art, see Gantz 1993, ad hoc. The myth is also discussed in Rankine 2005.

27. An overview of this recent trend in classical scholarship is presented here in chapter 1 of this book.

28. For more balanced studies of Afrocentrism, see Berlinerblau 1999, 133–46; Howe 1998; and Moses 1998.

29. It is telling the extent to which Lefkowitz's rhetoric relies on a Eurocentric worldview. As Howe puts it, "her main purpose is, quite simply, to defend the 'integrity' of ancient Greece and of traditional classical scholarship against what she regards as Afrocentric calumnies. In this respect, she regularly slips into the kind of ethnocentric arguments which she protests elsewhere" (9–10).

30. Leonard Jeffries, as one example, was among the most caustic of scholars, Afrocentric or otherwise. See Dinnerstein 1995.

31. The simple search for early African parallels to black American realities, or the search for an objective correlative in the past, is evident in the Wheatley epigraph with which I open chapter 1. Even this kind of appropriation has been labeled by some as Afrocentric. See, for example, Smith 1989 and Kendrick 1996.

32. For a discussion of these "flashes" of the spirit of West Africans in America through slavery, see Thompson 1984.

33. By these "counterparts" I mean Eurocentrism, which is discussed in Amin 1990. Again, Orientalism, by Said's definition, is also an offshoot of Eurocentrism. See Said 1979.

34. Berlinerblau's discussion of orthodoxy in the American academy provides a broader framework for the politics of ideas in institutions of higher learning, of which the classics has been representative of the pinnacle. See Berlinerblau, 1–20; 110–29.

35. Lefkowitz extended this analysis in her 1997 book of the same title. It is worth noting that the original book cover featured a well-known, white marble bust of Aristotle donning a black baseball cap with the letter $X$ in white. The cover, which was later changed, was incendiary, to say the least. It is also worth putting the cap in context. The black cap with the white letter $X$ was part of a fundraiser to save Spike Lee's film *Malcolm X*. The filmmaker discusses this grassroots fundraising in Poussaint 1999.

36. Lefkowitz misses the historical context for Garvey's movement, which was one in a long line of repatriation attempts extending back to at least the eighteenth century. As I have stated, blacks and whites alike were proponents of the back-to-Africa idea. See Cruse (1984) and Berlinerblau (1999) for more balanced treatments.

37. At issue is the question of orthodoxy within the academy as Berlinerblau formulates it. It is curious, for example, that in American universities Black (or Africana, or African American) Studies programs, which might be called Afrocentric in their focus on the history, literature, and experiences of peoples of African descent, escapes the critique of Lefkowitz. My point is that these programs have gained orthodox status, while "Afrocentrism" per se has not. Needless to say, it also would not have been politically expedient for Lefkowitz to attack these programs, although the opposition between older disciplines like classics and newer ones is certainly an unstated reality.

38. See, for example, Hanson and Heath 2001, who urge that the classics should "nudge out sociology, make self-esteem give way to mythology, *La Raza* studies to Latin; become, in other words, a part of contemporary American life" (209). More broadly and hearkening back to the culture wars, see Bloom 1988. Knox 1993 is also topical, although his approach is much more pro-European than antiethnic.

39. The page numbers here are from Locke [1925] 1997. The text is also available online at http://us.history.wisc.edu/hist/02/pdocs/locke_new.pdf (accessed June 16, 2008).

40. For a biography of Hughes and a discussion of his white patrons, see Rampersad 1986.

41. On the historical basis of *Native Son*, see Wright [1940] 1998a.

42. See Walling 1973.

## 4. The New Negro Ulysses

1. Mr. Wheatley's full statement of Wheatley was that "she has a great Inclination to learn the Latin Tongue, and has made some Progress in it." See Shields

Notes to pages 84–86

1980, 98; and 1988. Refer to my first chapter and introduction for a full treatment of the broader context of responses to black classicism.

2. On Wheatley criticism, see in particular Gates 1987.

3. For a comprehensive analysis, see Gates 1987, 61–79. Gates sums up the Wheatley controversy best at the end of his chapter, which is titled "Phillis Wheatley and the 'Nature of the Negro,'" by stating that "the criticism of Wheatley's poetry has been a matter centered primarily around exactly what the existence of the poiesis faculty signifies about a far more problematic inquiry" (79).

4. For discussion, see Gates 1987, 61–79 and Shields 1988.

5. See Jefferson 1984. The direct quote is from Kendrick 1996, 75.

6. On the slave narrative, see Andrews 1993.

7. For more biographical information on Wheatley, see Shields 1988 and Renfro 1988.

8. To my mind, Wheatley makes at least two statements that have been the object of discussion regarding her view on being black. One is the statement that the Muses gave "partial grace" to one "alone of *Afric*'s fabled race." These statements, discussed below, are from her poem "To Maecenas." For a discussion of the poem that treats these lines, see Smith 1989. A second verse, found in "On Being Brought From Africa to America," tells the (white) reader to "Remember, *Christians, Negroes,* black as *Cain* / May be refin'd, and join th' angelic train." The convergence of race and moral judgment (with the villainous Cain) is disturbing and can be explained, to my mind, only as an unfortunate characteristic of the symbolism of Wheatley's day. For a more radical reading, see Kendrick 1996.

9. Not only did Horace, as an Augustan poet, evoke Maecenas in his writings, but Catullus's dedication also reveals his self-consciousness (whether sincere or as a trope) about the reception of his poems. Catullus begins his book of poems with a dedicatory inscription: "To whom inscribe my charming new book—just out and with ashen pumice polished? Cornelius, to you" (translation: Lee 1990). In the poem, Catullus positions himself as a suppliant asking for the favor of his addressee, citing precedent for the relationship. The poem ends with a concern for the writer's longevity—indeed his immortality: "May it [the book of poems] outlive generations more than one."

10. For analysis, see Smith 1989.

11. Kendrick's radical reading (1996) is of course more conscious of rhetoric than of any direct or subversive (read nationalistic) message in Wheatley's poems.

12. The main interpretation of Cullen's play that I use here is Corti 1998; the critical reception is discussed to some extent there.

13. For a brief literary and social biography of Cullen, see Early 1991, 3–73.

14. The January 12, 1936, review speaks about the play's "characteristic Negro sentiment and rhythm."

15. As it pertains to black authors, see, for example, Wright 1989.

16. See Kramer 1987, 220.

17. Toni Morrison's approach to this problem is revealed in her claim to write for herself first, which is her essential black audience. From there, whoever likes the product can read also, and whoever does not like it can leave it alone. For a discussion and critique of this position, see Duvall 2000.

18. While many exciting critical theories exist for approaching African American literature, including Gates's signifying monkey (discussed briefly in chapter 3), I have chosen Baker's theory because it contains the themes I am concerned with here somewhat neatly. In addition to this, the notion of a black (w)hole is a trope that is quite compatible with the idea of the quest, or the heroic journey. The black journeyman might think he has arrived to his destination (i.e., a whole), but my argument is that within American society the black hole is one point on a longer journey, albeit the most important juncture, the *katabasis*. The black (w)hole, as we will see, pulls in black and white travelers alike.

19. Most recently, see Jimoh 2002.

20. See, for example, Cose 1994.

21. Baker's analysis of this episode is among the most powerful. See Baker 1984, 172–99.

22. The term "bad nigger" was used to describe the fearless slave who would revolt and act out without regard for punishment or authority. His bravery to some extent makes him a figure of great esteem. The term is still in use. See Kennedy 2002.

23. For more on Bob Marley and sociopolitical analyses of such songs as "Concrete Jungle," see Stephens 1999.

24. On black wholes, see Overbye 2004.

25. See "American Literature and the Black Mask of Humanity," in *Shadow and Act* 1966a.

26. Fishkin 1995, as we have seen, traces the popularity of notions of a racial integrity to the 1990s.

27. See Eliot 1992.

28. On the latter, see Richard 1994.

29. James Baldwin's 1949 essay "Everybody's Protest Novel" was originally published in the *Partisan Review*. See Baldwin 1998.

30. The biographical information here can primarily be found in Early 1991. Early's edition is the collected works of Cullen and includes expert historical and biographical information. See also Early's biographical sketch at http://www. english.uiuc.edu/maps/poets/a_f/cullen/life.htm.

31. The quote is from Early's sketch at http://www.english.uiuc.edu/maps/poets/ a_f/cullen/life.htm.

32. The quote is from Early at http://www.english.uiuc.edu/maps/poets/a_f/ cullen/life.htm.

33. The common take is that Cullen simply burned out at a relatively young age. See Early 1991, 3–73.

34. Among those discussed here, see also Gates 1987.

35. His poem "Scottsboro, Too, Is Worth Its Song," printed in the same volume as *Medea* in 1935, eulogizes the nine black men caught up in a typically American witch hunt for falsely accused sexual offenders. Although *Medea*, as I argue, cannot appropriately be called nationalistic or politically radical, the play might be read as Cullen's attempt to engage in the modernistic literary project of defamiliarizing the classical heritage through folklore.

36. Early (1991, 76) says that the additions were intended for publication in *On These I Stand*, the volume that was published in 1947, posthumously. Cullen died in 1946, at the age of forty-two. Corti 1998 mentions "Byword," but the additions, to her mind, only strengthen her reading, which is that *Medea* is a black nationalist text and the character a symbol of radical resistance. My objections to this reading are contained in this analysis.

37. For the dichotomy in tragedy, see Hall 1989. As the Persian Wars and the developing conflict between Greek city-states pertain to *Medea* (the beginning of the Peloponnesian War and the production of the play both occur in 431 BCE), see Page 1964. Master and slave is another dichotomy present.

38. For an overview of the myth throughout classical art and literature, see Gantz 1993.

39. In Euripides' *Herakles,* for example, the hero Herakles, who has murdered his own family members (albeit in error) incurs a blood pollution (*miasma*), but Theseus, the Athenian king, promises him safe harbor in Athens.

40. On the mythological tradition of Medea leading up to Euripides, see Gantz 1993.

41. For more on McClendon in the context of the Federal Negro Theater, see Fraden 1994. See also Ross 1974 for the theater and its period (1935–39).

42. For the argument that early Greek tragedy is dependent on the invention of the other while later plays invert that other, making the Greeks the subject of criticism, see Hall 1989.

43. Jennifer William, a colleague at Purdue University, has pointed out that Hans Henny Jahnn's 1926 *Medea*, which uses a black Medea in the context of colonialism and German culture, might be an interesting precedent for Cullen's adaptation. I know of no scholarship or reference connecting the two works. On Jahnn, see Freeman 2001.

44. This is even truer if, as I am arguing, Cullen was closely considering Euripides' play. As Pucci argues, there are implicit contradictions in reading Medea either as victim or as a vehicle for justice. She arrogates the language of justice, but the audience could never condone the action she takes. See Pucci 1980, 61–77.

45. This is an important distinction since in Euripides' play, the Nurse is one of the characters who is most sympathetic with Medea's plight. See Pucci 1980, 32–58.

46. For the notion of overdeterminism and blackness, see Fanon 1967.

47. Aegeus is already weak in Euripides' plays, as it is characteristic of Greek tragedy to portray older men as somewhat emasculated, fallen heroes. *Herakles'* Amphitryon is another example of this kind of aged hero. On Aegeus, see Page 1964.

48. In the Greek play, Medea's role as magician is salient here, since she will concoct a way for Aegeus to have children (11.709–30). In Cullen's version, Medea's magic is her sexuality.

49. As Pucci argues, Euripides' Medea sees herself as victim, and this victim status justifies, to her mind, the murder/sacrifice of her children.

50. In Nussbaum's words, "any person who loves is opening in the walls of self a hole through which the world may penetrate. Seneca's tragedies are full of images of the loss of bodily integrity—images in which, through an agent's loves and needs, pieces of the external world get taken into the self" (455).

51. Richard Heyman (1995) clearly builds on this motif in his essay.

52. The (w)holy black text is Powell's response to Baker's idea that the black (w)hole is primarily ignored by white authors and critics. As Powell puts it, "Houston Baker's phrase captures the experience of a generation of Afro-American novelists who have struggled to overcome the dilemma of how to inscribe the black self on the white page" (748). According to Powell, Morrison resolves this struggle in *Song of Solomon.* Milkman, whose teachers "erase the last vestiges of the white logos" for him, achieves black logos in his return to his own ancestors. He has "escaped the linguistic prison into which the drunken Yankee soldier wantonly threw his grandfather" (759). The Yankee soldier mistakenly circumscribed Milkman's family with the name Dead, but by discovering his true lineage the character has thrown off this "white logos," becoming alive to his own unique black heritage. The problem with this, however, is that it is based on the idea of an authentic—or essential—black identity. Put otherwise, negative experiences shape who we are as well. As we will see, Morrison is critical even of the seemingly authentic story of a man (Solomon) who, like Ulysses, picked up and left his children.

53. In book 10 of Homer's *Odyssey,* Circe transforms Odysseus's men into pigs. Odysseus is able to avoid a similar transformation through an herb given to him by Hermes. This same Circe will help Odysseus to journey to the underworld in book 11 and learn what the obstacles to his homecoming might be. Thus she is the ambivalent female figure referred to in Campbell's study (1973) as a staple of the heroic quest.

54. Morrison's discussion as a whole is relevant, but for the interpretation of Ulysses' travels as abandonment, which is as much playful as it is a serious critique, see Taylor-Guthrie 1994, 65.

55. Other studies of the Ulysses theme in the novel, though few, are covered in Awkward 1990 (a reference to an unpublished essay of Kimberly Benston) and Harris 1991 (whose essay on the novel is subtitled "An Anti-Classical Hero"). I

discuss Awkward below; in Harris's case, I find that the title itself, much like one of the essays regarding the Ulysses theme in *Invisible Man* (treated in chapter 5), says it all. Harris is dismissive of the classical frame; her understanding of classical myth is reductive. The following quote should convey the point: "The Greek and Roman world views are ones in which the dichotomies between good and evil are usually fairly clearly delineated—Odysseus is good; the Sirens are bad" (87). Anyone with even a cursory understanding of Homer's epic knows that this is too reductive. See, for example, Cook 1999 on the degree to which Odysseus develops and grows throughout the epic. His moral impropriety is at times exactly what causes some of his suffering.

56. For more on the Great Goddess concept, see Baring and Cashford 1993.

57. Heyman's argument is that "moving 'history' into 'memory' . . . is an individual and identity-building act that internalizes the objective, transforming it into the subjective" (385). He applies this to Milkman, but I would argue that the same analysis could be applied to Morrison's reception of the classics as an objective correlative in her novel. In other words, she takes ownership over this tradition.

58. See Amin 1989 again for the idea.

59. The archetype of the witch does not fully capture any of Morrison's characters. In the case of Pilate, it is interesting that Morrison casts her as having been born without a navel. As James Joyce craftily suggests, a woman born without a navel (i.e., without the mark of birth from a mother) is Eve: "Spouse and helpmate of Adam Kadmon: Heva, naked Eve. She had no navel" (*Ulysses* 38). (We might also place Athena, born from Zeus' head, in this category.)

60. I am suggesting here that desire and societal expectations are troublesome for every individual, especially as folklore and collective narratives impose an order on those desires. For a study of how these narratives shape the lives of individuals (especially women) in American society at large, see Dégh 1994.

61. See, for example, Jones 1995.

62. Again, Dégh 1994 discusses the problems American women experience because of fairytale expectations, which in modern society comes through the mass media. Dégh sees the media as generating variations of standard story patterns in folklore.

63. See Clark 1989 on the Homeric Cyclops and what seems to be the narrator's (Odysseus's) distortion.

## 5. "Ulysses alone in Polly-what's-his-name's cave"

1. Small portions of this analysis, particularly from the section on *Invisible Man*, appear in Rankine 2004. There is a sometime subtle (other times not-so-subtle) distinction throughout this chapter—as throughout Ellison's writing—between myth and folklore. For the sake of clarity, we might define myth as a narrative that "represents a collective expression of society, an expression that society itself deems to be true and valid. From the standpoint of the given society that it

articulates, myth *is* the primary reality" (Nagy 1990, 8). John T. Kirby (2001) refers to myth as the collective values of an interpretive community. Folklore, on the other hand, is often described as a subset of myth, including fairy tales and fables (Dorson 1973). A hierarchical distinction is often applied, with folklore being of lesser universal or archetypal value (e.g., African American *folklore* as opposed to classical *mythology*), but it is one that I do not believe Ellison ultimately held.

2. The significance that the mythological hero Ulysses (Odysseus in Greek literature) holds in Ralph Ellison's work has been hinted at for decades but never fully explored. In a 1963 article on Ellison's improvisation on the Brer Rabbit character from Uncle Remus lore, Floyd R. Horowitz writes of *Invisible Man*'s protagonist: "Like a continually endangered Odysseus under the polyphemal white eye of society he is Noman" (Horowitz 1970, 32). Horowitz alludes to the hero's encounter with the one-eyed giant Polyphemus, a classical commonplace found in literature from Greek tragedy to James Joyce's *Ulysses*. The episode, in which Ulysses causes the cannibalistic ogre's drunkenness and blinds him (and thus saves himself and many of his companions), is itself one of the more popular tales in Homer's *Odyssey*. (It is featured in book 9 of the epic.) As has been examined in a number of studies, the hero's conflict with a drunken ogre is a staple of folklore across cultures (Mondi 1983, Schein 1970).

3. See also Hyman 1955.

4. On the folkloric drunken ogre motif and its connection to Ulysses and the Cyclops, see Mondi 1983 and Schein 1970. In general it is agreed that in casting the episode, the oral poet is dependent upon a preexisting motif, which is found in folkloric traditions of many cultures.

5. The only biography of Ellison that exists to date is Lawrence Jackson's *Emergence of Genius* (2002). For my discussion of this work, see Rankine 2003.

6. For the period, see Woodward 1974.

7. Hyman, Ellison's opponent in this particular debate, offers a clear survey of scholarship on the ritual approach to myth and its relationship to Darwinian social theory in *The Promised End* (1963).

8. For an overview of these stories, see Gantz 1993.

9. For an overview of an alternative approach to mythology, one that runs counter to Campbell and the Jungian school, see Csapo 2005.

10. His formal training in classical literature stopped with high-school Latin. He completed three years of college at Tuskegee Normal School and Industrial Institute, which Booker T. Washington founded in 1881 as a vocational school for African Americans. Although he had some college training, Ellison was primarily an autodidact. On Ellison's exhaustive reading, see Jackson 2002.

11. This critical distance allows us, in Martin Luther King Jr.'s theory, to love our enemy, that is, love is not necessarily a natural response to suffering. Rather, love is a critical choice, and from it we are able to build, rhetorically and through action, the "beloved community." See Calloway-Thomas and Lucaites 1993.

12. This search for a transcultural solution to the race problem is what led Wright and others to the Communist Party. For full discussion of Ellison's relationship to communism (which was ideological—as opposed to actively political—and short-lived), see Lawrence Jackson 2002.

13. In general, episodes from Homer's *Odyssey,* fragmented and craftily interwoven into the narrative—as opposed to straightforward, literary allusions—structure *Invisible Man.* The imagery of Invisible Man being "shot forward with sudden acceleration into a wet blast of black emptiness" (230) echoes the blasts of Aeolus's misused winds, which throw Odysseus off-course.

14. Patterson's (1998) main source is Eric Lott, *Love and Theft* (1993), who sees that blacks were able to profit financially from the enterprise.

15. For an analysis of the notion of cunning intelligence in classical texts, see Detienne 1978.

16. Franz Fanon (1967, 109–40) discusses overdetermination as the expectations of others regarding blacks: "'Look, a Negro!' It was an external stimulus that flicked over me as I passed by. I made a tight smile. 'Look, a Negro!' It was true. It amused me. 'Look, a Negro!' The circle was drawing a bit tighter, I made no secret of my amusement" (112). In *Invisible Man,* the protagonist expresses this overdetermination in terms of confinement. Early in the chapter the protagonist states that "a flash of cold-edged heat enclosed me" (177). This idea is figured again a few lines later in the protagonist's "encircled" head, and the feeling causes the protagonist a great deal of irritation: "'But I need more room,' I insisted. 'I'm cramped'" (179). Here the external gaze is fixed so intently as to leave the agent little escape. See Per Winther (1983). Or as the chorus repeats in one 2Pac song, "They got me trapped!"

17. This portrait is the first image the reader has of Odysseus in *Odyssey* 5, since he is absent from the first four books of the epic, which focus on the quest of his son Telemachus.

18. On minstrelsy, see also Lott 1974.

19. See Du Bois [1903] 2003, for "double consciousness," and see also Adell's 1994 critique of it.

20. Throughout the Homeric epic, Odysseus depends upon the hospitality of the strangers that he encounters throughout his wandering. This guest–host relationship is expressed in the Greek noun *xenia.* The behavior of Polyphemus the Cyclops, and to an extent Odysseus's own unlawful entry into the Cyclops's cave, is a violation of this sacred code. See Ahl 1996.

21. This is the year of Rutherford B. Hayes's compromise, the year that ended radical reconstruction throughout the South. See Woodward 1974.

22. Lucius (Lucifer) is the protagonist's cynical and suspicious supervisor at the paint factory in New York where he is able to land a job after being expelled from school. Lucius, similar to the black school superintendent who expels Invisible Man earlier in the novel, is for him another example of an older, self-interested

approach to the relationship of blacks to whites in American society. Invisible Man is certainly more harmed by Lucius than helped. Lucius deliberately tries to electrocute Invisible Man.

23. It is well worth mentioning that there is little of the Ulysses theme in the original version of the chapter, "Out of the Hospital and Under the Bar." In terms of the motif of sight and blindness, the Oedipus myth is more present in the short story. As the book moved toward the market, Ellison would shorten the passage and point up the Ulysses theme. For a discussion of the story (although he does not discuss the classical motifs) see O'Meally 1980. The short story is noteworthy as an avant-text for *Invisible Man*.

24. For an analysis of the assertion of being in "I yam what I am," see Benton 1982.

25. On the autobiographical relationship between this cold image and the death of Ralph Ellison's father, when young Ralph was only three or four years old, see Rankine 2003.

26. On the dozens, see Gates 1988, 99–103.

27. Tod (Death) Clifton is a young black man, a counterpart to the protagonist, who, upon becoming disillusioned with the Brotherhood, orchestrates his own suicide/murder at the hands of police officers. Prior to this, he left the organization to sell black figurines, in keeping with his own philosophy that sometimes a person has to "plunge outside of history." The plunge outside of history for him is death, but it is also memory, reflection, and the pause that allows alternative perspective on reality.

28. The funeral is narrated in chapter 21 of *Invisible Man*. Nadel 1988, 63–84, has the best analysis I have read.

29. As Alan Nadel (1988) concludes of allusions in *Invisible Man*, each reading of a given myth or story changes something about it, since the reader emphasizes different aspects so that it speaks for him or her. Ellison's deployment of the Ulysses motif in *Juneteenth* is even more daring than that of *Invisible Man*, since in *Juneteenth* Ellison directly rewrites the Ulysses story through Choc Charlie, as we will see.

30. On homecoming as a spiritual quest, see Astell 1994.

31. On bourgeoisie materialism, see Clark 1989. I also touched on the idea in chapter 2 of this book.

32. As Gregory Stephens sees it, the frontier carries "a sense of the unknown, the unsettled, the partially unexplored" (1999, 14). The frontier represents a place of material and cultural exchange (Ellison 1986e) and is a fitting metaphor for American society at large.

33. The tales are part of the longer story the hero tells of his return home in *Odyssey* 9–12.

34. On the sermon, see Rankine 2001.

35. As a reminder to the reader, the character is "Bliss" to his surrogate father

Daddy Hickman, but he also transforms himself when he runs away from home. His transformation is conveyed in his renaming himself Adam Sunraider.

36. On the call-and-response theme, the idea of antiphony in African American literature and oratory, see Callahan 1990.

37. Meili Steele (2000) argues that perspective encourages agency, i.e., it is only through reflection on oneself and others that one is informed enough to act. The first person narrating an event in his life as if it were a third person is significant to the process of reflection.

## 6. Ulysses in Black

1. For the essay "Everybody's Protest Fiction," see Baldwin 1998.

2. I have discussed this position throughout the book, but see specifically Walling 1973, Cruse 1984, and Watts 1994.

3. See specifically the *sparagmos* associated with Dionysiac rites in Dodds 1951, which to some extent still owes something to Frazer (reprinted 1996). See also Seaford 1981.

4. See Amin 1989, 89.

5. See the notion of the white Negro in Mailer 1957.

6. Ritual dismemberment is discussed in Dodds 1951 and Seaford 1981.

7. Or see, for example, the 1955 essay of Ellison's rival in criticism, Stanley Edgar Hyman, who directly mentions the importance of *sparagmos* to the monomythic idea. The reader interested in tracing Ellison's intellectual roots should consult Ellison 2000 and Jackson 2002.

8. The essay on art and protest is printed in Soyinka 1988, 40–61.

9. For a general overview of the myth of Actaeon, see Gantz 1993, 478–81.

10. For a discussion of the myth, see Gantz 1993, 721–25; see also Dodds 1951, 147–49; and Heath 1994.

11. See Seaford 1981, who makes the direct association between ritual dismemberment in Dionysiac rites and the *sparagmos* of Dionysus himself; see Soyinka 1988.

12. For an overview of the myth and representations in classical literature and art, see Gantz 1993, 44–48.

13. The quote is from Cruse 1984, 507.

14. This chapter could have included a reading of Tod Clifton in *Invisible Man*, a character whose death the protagonist ritualizes as a result of violence against blacks. I do not believe it is necessary here, however, to take on Alan Nadel's expert analysis of Tod (Death) Clifton as a Christ figure.

15. See Toni Morrison and Brodsky Lacour 1997. In her introduction, Morrison draws from American literature to frame her discussion of the Simpson trial. Separate from the issue of guilt or innocence, Simpson was depicted in the media as "feral" (ix). In her own words, "The symbolic language that emanates from unforeseen events supplies media with the raw material from which a narrative emerges—already scripted, fully spectacularized and riveting in its gazeability" (xvi).

16. On blackface performance and its social context, see Lott 1974 and Lhamon 1998. Spike Lee's recent film *Bamboozled* (2000) dramatizes Lhamon's association of blackface performance and modern cultural forms, such as hip-hop.

17. I am referring here to Dionysus's association to the satyr. See Gantz 1993, 135–39.

18. Patterson puts it in the following way: "Each group may have influenced the other, but the terms of the trade were brutally asymmetric and amounted in most respects to outright social, economic, and cultural parasitism" (241). See also Lelyveld 2001.

19. In his book, Stephens discusses Ellison's work alongside Frederick Douglass and Bob Marley. See Stephens 1999, 114–47.

20. For the idea of race as a frontier, a place that "carries a sense of the unknown, the unsettled, the partially unexplored," see Stephens, 12–53. The idea is resonant with the Ellisonian notion of a frontier. See, for example, the essay "Going to the Territory" (1986, 120–44).

21. This is, again, part of the issue at stake in Euripides' *Bacchae,* where Pentheus sees Dionysus as a foreign import. Yet in myth Dionysus is also Greek, a son of Zeus. See Gantz, 112–19.

22. Dionysus is similar to the figure of Christ, whom Patterson does associate with the victim of lynching, in his ritual dismemberment. In his chapter on lynching, titled "Feast of Blood," Patterson raises the question of the relationship between the particular Christian worldview of white Southerners during segregation and such practices as lynching. Each practice involves a sort of feast of the gods, the former through communion and the latter through the celebration of the lynching ceremony. See Patterson 1998, 169–232.

23. On lynching, see Klotman 1985.

24. See also Patterson's chart of justifications (1998, 175), which includes homicide, robbery, and assault.

25. See Klotman 1985.

26. For a catalogue of lynching through one hundred years, including the Till case, see Ginzburg 1988, 240–43.

27. On the connection between the incest taboo and initiation, and particularly on the moveable nature of incest, see the following sources (I mention Raglan, though an old source, because of his especial influence on Ellison): Raglan 1931; Wagner 1972; Brain 1977; and Willner 1983.

28. The symbolism of this practice is still contained in the ancient sacrifices of animals such as lambs or goats (Dionysus in animal form), or in the Christian ritual of communion.

29. For the general occurrences within the ritual, see Klotman 1985 and Ginzburg 1988.

30. Patterson goes as far as to link the lynching of American Dionysus to essential aspects of the Christian worldview of twentieth-century Southerners. The

sacrificial ritual, similar to Christ's sacrifice ("Behold the lamb that was slain!"), is aimed at creating and sustaining a social order. In America, the social order was that of a racially segregated civility.

31. It would not be extreme to assert that few African American males growing up in America (up to the latter half of the twentieth century) are ignorant of the possibility of violence directly emanating from their racial identity.

32. See, for example, Carlyle Thompson (1999, 159–85) on the "sodomizing" of Abner Louima in Brooklyn, New York, in 1997, by white police officers.

33. In Klotman's words, "it [lynching] was an initiation ritual in reverse, a warning that white society would not allow, in fact forbade, the passage of the Afro-American from boy to man" (1985, 56).

34. Citations here are from John F. Callahan's 1996 edition of Ellison's short stories in *Flying Home*.

35. Although Ellison uses the symbol of Indian initiation in the story, his understanding of ritual has a distinctly Western (and classical) underpinning, as we have seen throughout this book.

36. See O'Meally 1980. Ellison's use of these symbols in the original version of chapter 11 of *Invisible Man* was in some ways more deeply suggestive of classical epic than the overt motifs. Campbell covers the general narrative, but one might consider, as an example, Odysseus's consultation with Hermes, from which he himself gains a magical herb, before his encounter with Circe.

37. Here Ellison is of course playing on the theme of the quest from Joseph Campbell's *The Hero with a Thousand Faces*. In the recently published correspondences between Ellison and Albert Murray, we find that, during his years at the American Academy at Rome, Ellison delved even deeper into classical myth and approaches to it. He read on the Roman emperor Hadrian, ordered a copy of W. B. Stanford's *The Ulysses Theme*, and read and discussed Campbell's work with Murray. That is, if the classics were a concern for Ellison in *Invisible Man*, that interest only grew in subsequent years. This reality is evident in his writing, where the classical themes are better integrated into the work, not always as apparent, but in some ways more deeply felt.

38. For the notion that society at large (read "white" society) overdetermines, see Fanon 1967, 109–40.

39. For a discussion of the story, see O'Meally 1980.

40. For a discussion of the Juneteenth ceremony in the novel, see Rankine 2001.

41. This is true even of Ellison's own childhood, as Lawrence Jackson's recent biography (2002) brings to light.

42. Interestingly, the motif in Trueblood's dream follows the motif evident in the biblical narrative of Joseph and Potifer's wife. Rene Girard relates this to aspects of the Oedipus myth.

43. On the link between the Juneteenth ceremony and Bliss's racial consciousness, see Rankine 2001.

## 7. Ulysses (Re)Journeying Home

1. On "forced radicalism," see chapter 3. The reference is from Alain Locke's "The New Negro."

2. The reference here again is to the last line of *Invisible Man:* "Who knows but that, on the lower frequencies, I speak for you?" (581).

3. The *Dissent* article is also available online at http://www.writing.upenn.edu/~afilreis/50s/howe-blackboys.html.

4. For the critique of Ellison, see particularly Watts 1994, 99–120.

5. For the context, see Baker 1984, 2.

6. The sparse reference to contemporaries Martin Luther King Jr. and Malcolm X is glaring in comparison to chats about T. S. Eliot, Joyce, or Homer. See Graham and Singh 1995.

7. See Ellwood 1999. Carl Jung's curious politics, incidentally, is also a topic covered in Ellwood's book.

8. See Watts 1994 on Ellison, 99–120. For the discussion of the "politics of myth," see Ellwood 1999, 127–69.

9. The author discusses Campbell and others intermittently in his letters to Albert Murray. See Ellison 2000.

10. Ellison 2000, 99.

11. See Baker 1988.

12. See Callahan 1988. The question frames his study, as the title of the first chapter of Callahan's book on call-and-response in black discourse. The retort, in the last chapter of his book, is "Who We For?: The Extended Call of African American Fiction."

13. See chapter 4 of this book.

14. See the prologue and chapter 1 of this book.

15. For more on this, see Thompson 1984.

# References Cited

Adell, Sandra. 1994. *Double Consciousness/Double Bind: Theoretical Issues in Twentieth-Century Black Literature.* Champaign: University of Illinois Press.

Ahl, Frederick, and Hanna M. Roisman. 1996. *The Odyssey Re-Formed.* Ithaca, N.Y.: Cornell University Press.

Alexander, Elizabeth. 1995. In *Black Male: Representations of Masculinity in Contemporary American Art,* ed. Thelma Golden. New York: Whitney Museum of Art.

Alilunas, Leo J. 1973. "What Our Schools Teach About Booker T. Washington and W. E. B. Du Bois." *Journal of Negro Education* 42:176–86.

Allen, Theodore W. 1994. *Invention of the White Race: Racial Oppression and Social Control.* Vol. 1. New York: Verso.

Amin, Samir. 1989. *Eurocentrism.* Translated by Russell Moore. New York: Monthly Review Press.

Anderson, Benedict. 1991. *Imagined Communities.* Rev. ed. London: Verso.

Andrews, William. 1993. "The Representation of Slavery and Afro-American Literary Realism." In *African American Autobiography: A Collection of Critical Essays,* ed. William L. Andrews. Englewood Cliffs, N.J.: Prentice Hall.

Asante, Molefi Kete. 1998. *The Afrocentric Idea.* Rev. ed. Philadelphia: Temple University Press.

Astell, Ann W. 1994. *Job, Boethius, and Epic Truth.* Ithaca, N.Y.: Cornell University Press.

Auerbach, Erich. 1953. *Mimesis: The Representation of Reality in Western Literature.* Trans. Willard R. Trask. Princeton, N.J.: Princeton University Press.

Awkward, Michael. 1990. "'Unruly and Let Loose': Myth, Ideology, and Gender in *Song of Solomon.*" *Callaloo* 13:482–98.

Bailey, Shakleton, trans. 1999. *Cicero: Letters to Atticus (Loeb Classical Library).* Cambridge, Mass.: Harvard University Press.

Baker, Houston A., Jr. 1984. *Blues, Ideology, and Afro-American Literature: A Vernacular Theory.* Chicago: University of Chicago Press.

————. 1987. *Modernism and the Harlem Renaissance.* Chicago: University of Chicago Press.

————. 1988. "The Promised Body: Reflections on Canon in an Afro-American Context." *Poetics Today* 9:339–55.

————. 1990. "Handling 'Crisis': Great Books, Rap Music, and the End of Western Homogeneity (Reflections on the Humanities in America)." *Callaloo* 13:173–94.

Baldwin, James. 1964. *Blues for Mister Charlie.* New York: Vintage Books.

————. 1998. *Collected Essays: Notes of a Native Son, Nobody Knows My Name, The Fire Next Time, No Name in the Street, The Devil Finds Work, Other Essays.* New York: Library of America.

Baring, Ann, and Jules Cashford. 1993. *The Myth of the Goddess: Evolution of an Image.* London: Penguin Books.

Barthes, Roland. *S/Z.* 1970. Paris: Éditions du Seuil.

Bartsch, Shadi. 1994. *Actors in the Audience: Theatricality and Doublespeak from Nero to Hadrian.* Cambridge, Mass.: Harvard University Press.

Becker, Trudy Harrington. 1999. "Daniel B. Williams." *Classical Outlook* 76:94–95.

————. 2000. "A Source for Ideology: The Classical Education of Martin Luther King." *Classical Bulletin* 76:181–89.

————. 2001. "Broadening Access to a Classical Education: State Universities in Virginia in the Nineteenth Century." *Classical Journal* 96:309–22.

Benton, Kimberly W. 1975. "Tragic Aspects of the Blues." *Phylon* 36:164–76.

————. 1978. "Ellison, Baraka, and the Faces of Tradition." *Boundary* 2:333–54.

————. 1982. "'I Yam what I Yam': Naming and Unnaming in Afro-American Literature." *Black American Literature Forum* 16:3–11.

Berlin, Ira. 2000. *Many Thousands Gone: The First Two Centuries of Slavery in North America.* Cambridge, Mass.: Harvard University Press.

Berlinerblau, Jacques. 1999. *Heresy in the University: The Black Athena Controversy and the Responsibilities of American Intellectuals.* New Brunswick, N.J.: Rutgers University Press.

Bernal, Martin. 1987. *Black Athena: The Afroasiatic Roots of Classical Civilization.* Vol. 1, *The Fabrication of Ancient Greece 1785–1985.* New Brunswick, N.J.: Rutgers University Press.

————. 1991. *Black Athena: The Afroasiatic Roots of Classical Civilization.* Vol. 2, *Archaeological and Documentary Evidence.* New Brunswick, N.J.: Rutgers University Press.

————. 1996. "The Afrocentric Interpretation of History: Bernal Replies to Lefkowitz." *Journal of Blacks in Higher Education* 11:86–94.

————. 2001. *Black Athena Writes Back: Martin Bernal Responds to his Critics.* Ed. David Chioni Moore. Durham, N.C.: Duke University Press.

Black, Ray. 1999. "Book Reviews (*Juneteenth*)." *Black Scholar* 29:54–56.

Blank, Jonah. 1992. *Arrow of the Blue-Skinned God: Retracing the Ramayana through India.* Boston: Houghton Mifflin.

Bloom, Allan. 1988. *The Closing of the American Mind: How Higher Education Has Failed Democracy and Impoverished the Souls of Today's Students.* New York: Simon and Schuster.

Bloom, Harold. 1990. *Modern Critical Views: Toni Morrison.* New York: Chelsea House Publishing.

———. 1994. *The Western Canon: The Books and School of the Ages.* New York: Harcourt Brace.

Boas, Franz. 1928–1962. *Anthropology and Modern Life.* New York: Dover.

Boyle, A. J. 1986. "Senecan Tragedy: Twelve Propositions." In *The Imperial Muse: To Juvenal through Ovid.* Victoria, Australia: Aureal Publications.

———. 1997. *Tragic Seneca: An Essay in the Theatrical Tradition.* New York: Routledge.

Brain, James L. "Sex, Incest, and Death: Initiation Rites Reconsidered." *Current Anthropology* 18:191–208.

Brenkman, John. 1994. "Politics and Form in Song of Solomon." *Social Texts* 39:57–82.

Brown, C. S. 1966. "Odysseus and Polyphemus: The Name and the Curse." *Comparative Literature* 18:193–202.

Brucia, Margaret. 2002. "The African-American Poet, Jupiter Hammon: A Home-Born Slave and his Classical Name." *International Journal of the Classical Tradition* 7:515–22.

Burke, Kenneth. 1945, 1969. *A Grammar of Motives.* Berkeley: University of California Press.

Burkert, Walter. 1966. "Greek Tragedy and Sacrificial Ritual." *Greek, Roman, and Byzantine Studies* 7:87–121.

———. 1987. *Ancient Mystery Cults.* Cambridge, Mass.: Harvard University Press.

Butler, Robert J. 2003. "The Structure of Ralph Ellison's *Juneteenth.*" *CLA Journal* 47:291–311.

Buxton, R. G. A. 1982. *Persuasion in Greek Tragedy: A Study of Peitho.* Cambridge: Cambridge University Press.

Calder, William III. 1970. "Originality in Seneca's *Troades.*" *Classical Philology* 65:75–82.

———. 1976. "Seneca's Agamemnon." *Classical Philology* 71:27–36.

Callahan, John F. 1990. *In the African-American Grain: Call-and-Response in Twentieth-Century Black Fiction.* 2nd ed. Middletown, C.T.: Wesleyan University Press.

Calloway-Thomas, Carolyn, and John L. Lucaites. 1994. *Martin Luther King, Jr., and the Sermonic Power of Public Discourse.* Tuscaloosa: University of Alabama Press.

Campbell, Joseph. 1973. *The Hero with a Thousand Faces.* Princeton, N. J.: Princeton University Press.

Csapo, Eric. 2005. *Theories of Mythology (Ancient Cultures).* Oxford: Blackwell.

Caratellia, G. Pugliese. 1996. *The Greek World: Art and Civilization in Magna Grae-cia and Sicily.* Milan: Rizzoli International Publications.

Cartledge, Paul. 1993. "Like a Worm i' the Bud? A Heterology of Classical Greek Slavery." *Greece and Rome* 40:163–80.

Chevannes, Barry. 1995. *Rastafari: Roots and Ideology.* Mona, Jamaica: University of West Indies Press.

Chinard, G. 1932. "Thomas Jefferson as a Classical Scholar." *American Scholar* 1:133–43.

Clark, Michael. 1989. "Adorno, Derrida, and the Odyssey: A Critique of Center and Periphery." *Boundary* 2:109–28.

Conacher, D. J. 1961. "Euripides' *Hecuba*." *American Journal of Philology* 82:1–26.

Cook, Erwin. 1995. *The Odyssey in Athens: Myths of Cultural Origins (Myth and Poetics).* Ithaca, N.Y.: Cornell University Press.

———. 1999. "'Active' and 'Passive' Heroics in the *Odyssey*." *Classical World* 93:149–68.

Cooper, Ana Julia. 1998. *A Voice from the South.* Oxford: Oxford University Press.

Cooper, John M., et al., eds. 1995. *Seneca: Moral and Political Essays (Cambridge Texts in the History of Political Thought).* Cambridge: Cambridge University Press.

Corti, Lillian. 1998. "Countee Cullen's *Medea*." *African American Review* 32: 621–34.

Cose, Ellis. 1994. *The Rage of a Privileged Class.* New York: HarperCollins.

Costa, C. D. N. 1973. *Seneca: Medea.* Oxford: Oxford University Press.

Crouch, Stanley. 1990. *Notes of a Hanging Judge: Essays and Reviews, 1979–1989.* New York: Oxford University Press.

———. 1995. *The All-American Skin Game, or, The Decoy of Race: The Long and Short of It, 1990–1994.* New York: Pantheon Books.

———. 1995/6. "The Afrocentric Hustle." *Journal of Blacks in Higher Education* 10:77–82.

Cruse, Harold. [1967] 1984. *The Crisis of the Negro Intellectual.* New York: Quill.

Curtis, Nancy. 1998. "Classics and Our African American Students." *American Classical League Newsletter* 20.1:6–9.

D'Souza, Dinesh. 1996. *The End of Racism: Principles for a Multiracial Society.* New York: Simon and Schuster.

———. 1998. *Illiberal Education: The Politics of Race and Sex on Campus.* New York: Free Press.

Datcher, Michael, and Kwame Alexander. 1997. *Tough Love: The Life and Death of Tupac Shakur.* Philadelphia: Alexander Publishing.

Dawkins, Marvin. 2000. "Rethinking U.S. Immigration Policy." *Black Issues in Higher Education* (April 27): 120.

De Luce, Judith. 1999. "Classics in Historically Black Colleges and Universities." *American Classical League Newsletter* 21.2:10–12.

Dégh, Linda. 1994. *American Folklore and the Mass Media.* Bloomington: Indiana University Press.

Detienne, Marcel, and Jean-Pierre Vernant. 1978. *Cunning Intelligence in Greek Culture and Society.* Trans. J. Lloyd. Leiden: E. J. Brill.

———. 1989. *Cuisine of Sacrifice among the Greeks.* Trans. Paula Wissing. Chicago: University of Chicago Press.

Dinnerstein, Leonard. 1995. *Anti-Semitism in America.* Oxford: Oxford University Press.

Dodds, E. R. 1951. *The Greeks and the Irrational.* Berkeley: University of California Press.

Dominik, William J. 1997. "The Style is the Man: Seneca, Tacitus, and Quintilian's Canon." In *Roman Eloquence: Rhetoric in Society and Literature.* New York: Routledge.

Dray, Philip. 2003. *At the Hands of Persons Unknown: The Lynching of Black America.* New York: Random House.

Du Bois, W. E. B. [1903] 2003. *The Souls of Black Folk.* New York: Random House.

———. 1911. *The Quest of the Silver Fleece.* New York: Negro University Press.

Dupont, Florence. 1999. *The Invention of Literature: From Greek Intoxication to the Latin Book.* Trans. Janet Lloyd. Baltimore: Johns Hopkins University Press.

Duvall, John N. 2000. *The Identifying Fictions of Toni Morrison.* New York: Palgrave.

Dyson, Michael Eric. 1996. *Between God and Gangsta Rap: Bearing Witness to Black Culture.* New York: Oxford University Press.

———. 2001. *Holler If You Hear Me: Searching for Tupac Shakur.* New York: Basic Books.

Early, Gerald, ed. 1991. *My Soul's High Song: The Collected Writings of Countee Cullen, Voice of Harlem Renaissance.* New York: Doubleday.

Eliot, T. S. 1920. *The Sacred Wood.* London: Methuen.

———. [1932] 1950. "Seneca in Elizabethan Translation" In *Selected Essays, 1917–1932.* Rev. ed. New York: Harcourt Brace.

———. 1965. *To Criticize the Critic and Other Writings.* Lincoln: University of Nebraska Press.

———. 1997. *The Sacred Wood and Major Early Essays.* New York: Dover.

Ellison, Ralph. [1952] 1995. *Invisible Man.* 2nd ed. New York: Vintage Books.

——— 1966a. "Twentieth-Century Fiction and the Black Mask of Humanity." In *Shadow and Act,* 42–60. New York: Signet.

———. 1966b. "Change the Joke and Slip the Yoke." In *Shadow and Act,* 61–73. New York: Signet.

———. 1966c. "Harlem is Nowhere." In *Shadow and Act,* 282–89. New York: Signet.

———. 1966d. "On Bird, Bird-Watching, and Jazz." In *Shadow and Act,* 218. New York: Signet.

———. 1986a. "The Little Man at Chehaw Station." In *Going to the Territory,* 3–38. New York: Random House.

———. 1986b. "On Initiation Rites and Power: Ralph Ellison Speaks at West Point." In *Going to the Territory*, 39–63. New York: Random House.

———. 1986c. "What These Children Are Like." In *Going to the Territory*, 64–75. New York: Random House.

———. 1986d. "What America Would Be Like without Blacks." In *Going to the Territory*, 104–19. New York: Random House.

———. 1986e. "Going to the Territory." In *Going to the Territory*, 120–44. New York: Random House.

———. 1995. *The Collected Essays of Ralph Ellison*. Ed. John F. Callahan. New York: Modern Library.

———. 1996. *Flying Home*. Ed. John F. Callahan. New York: Vintage Books.

———. 1999. *Juneteenth*. Ed. John F. Callahan. New York: Vintage Books.

Ellison, Ralph, and Albert Murray. 2000. *Trading Twelves: The Selected Letters of Ralph Ellison and Albert Murray*. New York: Vintage Books.

Ellwood, Robert. 1999. *The Politics of Myth: A Study of C. G. Jung, Mircea Eliade, and Joseph Campbell*. Albany: State University of New York Press.

Evans, Elizabeth C. 1950. "A Stoic Aspect of Senecan Drama, Portraiture." *TAPA* 81:169–84.

Fanon, Franz. 1967. *Black Skin, White Masks*. New York: Grove Press.

Fantham, Elaine. 1982a. "Seneca's 'Troades' and Agamemnon: Continuity and Sequence," *Classical Journal* 77:118–29.

———. 1982b. *Seneca's Troades: A Literary Introduction with Text, Translation, and Commentary*. Princeton, N.J.: Princeton University Press.

Fikes, Robert, Jr. 2002a. "It Was Never Greek to Them: Black Affinity for Ancient Greek and Roman Culture." *Negro Educational Review* 53:3–12.

———. 2002b. "African-American Scholars of Greco-Roman Culture." *Journal of Blacks in Higher Education* 35:120–24.

Fishkin, Shelley Fisher. 1995. "Interrogating 'Whiteness,' Complicating 'Blackness': Remapping American Culture." *American Quarterly* 47:428–66.

Fitch, John G. 1981. "Sense-Pause and Relative Dating in Seneca, Sophocles, and Shakespeare." *AJP* 102:289–307.

Forman, Murray. 2002a. "No Sleep 'Til Brooklyn." *American Quarterly* 54:101–27.

———. 2002b. *The 'Hood Comes First: Race, Space, and Place in Rap and Hip-hop*. Middletown, C.T.: Wesleyan University Press.

Foucault, Michel. 1990. *The History of Sexuality*. New York: Knopf.

Fraden, Rena. 1994. *Blueprints for a Black Federal Theatre, 1935–1939*. Cambridge: Cambridge University Press.

Franklin, John Hope, and Alfred A. Moss, Jr. 2000. *From Slavery to Freedom: A History of African Americans*. 8th ed. New York: Knopf.

Frazer, James George. 1996. *The Golden Bough: A Study in Magic and Religion*. New York: Simon and Schuster.

Freeman, Thomas. 2001. *The Case of Hans Henny Jahnn Criticism and the Literary Outsider*. Rochester, N.Y.: Camden House.

Friedrich, Rainer. 1987. "Heroic Man and *Polymetis:* Odysseus in the *Cyclopeia.*" *Greek, Roman, and Byzantine Studies* 28:121–33.

———. 1991. "The *Hybris* of Odysseus." *Journal of Hellenic Studies* 111:16–28.

Futrell, Alison. 1997. *Blood in the Arena: The Spectacle of Roman Power*. Austin: University of Texas Press.

Gantz, Timothy. 1993. *Early Greek Myth: A Guide to Literary and Artistic Sources*. Baltimore: Johns Hopkins University Press.

Gates, Henry Louis, Jr. 1986. *"Race," Writing, and Difference*. Chicago: University of Chicago Press.

———. 1987. *Figures in Black: Words, Signs, and the "Racial" Self*. New York: Oxford University Press.

———. 1988. *The Signifying Monkey: A Theory of African-American Literary Criticism*. New York: Oxford University Press.

———. 1992. *Loose Canons: Notes on the Culture Wars*. New York: Oxford University Press.

Gayle, Addison Jr., ed. 1971. *The Black Aesthetic*. New York: Doubleday and Company.

Gentili, Bruno. 1988. *Poetry and its Public in Ancient Greece: From Homer to the Fifth Century*. Trans. A. Thomas Cole. Baltimore: Johns Hopkins University.

Ginzburg, Ralph. 1988. *100 Years of Lynching*. Baltimore: Black Classic Press.

Glicksberg, Charles I. 1970. "The Symbolism of Vision." In *Twentieth Century Interpretations of Invisible Man*, ed. John M. Reilly. Englewood Cliffs, N.J.: Prentice Hall.

Goldberg, Sander M. 1996. "The Fall and Rise of Roman Tragedy." *TAPA* 126:265–86.

Gonzalez-Wippler, Migene. 1994. *Santeria: The Religion: Faith, Rites, Magic*. 2nd ed. St. Paul, MN: Llewellyn Publications.

Graham, Maryemma, and Amritjit Singh. 1995. *Conversations with Ralph Ellison*. Jackson: University Press of Mississippi.

Graham, Lawrence Otis. 2000. *Our Kind of People: Inside America's Black Upper Class*. New York: HarperCollins.

Grant, Michael. 1989. *Cicero: Selected Political Speeches*. New York: Penguin.

Griffin, M. T. 1976. *Seneca: A Philosopher in Politics*. Oxford: Oxford University Press.

Grube, G. M. A., trans. 1975. *Plato: The Trial and Death of Socrates*. Indianapolis: Hackett.

Gruen, E. S. 1992. *Culture and National Identity in Republican Rome*. Ithaca, N.Y.: Cornell University Press.

Gumpert, Matthew. 2001. *Grafting Helen: The Abduction of the Classical Past*. Madison: University of Wisconsin Press.

Guthrie, W. K. 1983. *History of Greek Philosophy: The Fifth-Century Enlightenment: The Sophists.* Vol. 3. Cambridge: Cambridge University Press.

Haley, Alex. 1975. *The Autobiography of Malcolm X.* New York: Random House.

Hall, Edith. 1989. *Inventing the Barbarian: Greek Self-Definition through Tragedy.* Cambridge: Cambridge University Press.

———. 1996. "When is a Myth Not a Myth?: Bernal's 'Ancient Model.'" In *Black Athena Revisited*, ed. Mary Lefkowitz and Guy Rogers. Chapel Hill: University of North Carolina Press.

Hallett, Judith P. 1984. *Fathers and Daughters in Roman Society and the Elite Family.* Princeton, N.J.: Princeton University Press.

Hallett, Judith P., and Marilyn B. Skinner. 1997. *Roman Sexualities.* Princeton, N.J.: Princeton University Press.

Halliburton, R., Jr. 1972. "The Tulsa Race War of 1921." *Journal of Black Studies* 2:333–57.

Halperin, David. 1989. *One Hundred Years of Homosexuality: And Other Essays on Greek Love.* New York: Routledge.

Halperin, David, John J. Winkler, and Froma Zeitlin. 1990. *Before Sexuality: The Construction of Erotic Experience in the Ancient Greek World.* Princeton, N.J.: Princeton University Press.

Hanson, Victor Davis, and John Heath. 2001. *Who Killed Homer? The Demise of Classical Education and the Recovery of Greek Wisdom.* San Francisco: Encounter Books.

Harris, Joel Chandler. 2002. *The Complete Tales of Uncle Remus.* New York: Houghton Mifflin Company.

Harris, Trudier. 1984. *Exorcising Blackness: Historical and Literary Lynching and Burning Rituals.* Bloomington: Indiana University Press.

———. 1991. *Fiction and Folklore: The Novels of Toni Morrison.* Knoxville: University of Tennessee Press.

Harrison, George W. M. 2000. *Seneca in Performance.* London: Duckworth.

Havelock, Eric A. 1988. *The Muse Learns to Write: Reflections on Orality and Literacy from Antiquity to the Present.* New Haven, C.T.: Yale University Press.

Heath, John. 1994. "The Failure of Orpheus." *Transactions of the American Philological Association* 124:163–96.

Heinemann, Felix. 1945. *Nomos und Physis: Herkunft und Bedeutung einer Antithese im griechischen Denken des 5. Jahrhunderts.* Basel: Reinhardt.

Henrichs, Albert. 1995. "Graecia Capta: Roman Views of Greek Culture." *Harvard Studies in Classical Philology* 97:243–61.

Herrington, John C. 1966. "Senecan Tragedy." *Arion* 5:422–71.

Heyman, Richard. 1995. "Universalization and its Discontents: Morrison's Song of Solomon—A (W)hol(e)y Black Text." *African American Review* 29:381–92.

Hirsch, Arnold R. 1998. *Making the Second Ghetto: Race and Housing in Chicago, 1940–1960.* Chicago: University of Chicago Press.

Homer. 2000. *Odyssey*. Trans. Stanley Lombardo. Indianapolis: Hackett Publishing Company.

Horowitz, Floyd R. 1970. "Ralph Ellison's Modern Version of Brer Bear and Brer Rabbit in *Invisible Man*." In *Twentieth Century Interpretations of Invisible Man*, ed. John M. Reilly, 32–37. Englewood Cliffs, N.J.: Prentice Hall.

Howe, Irving. 1963. "Black Boys and Native Sons." *Dissent* (Autumn): 353–68.

Howe, Stephen. 1998. *Afrocentrism: Mythical Pasts and Imagined Homes*. New York: Verso.

Hurston, Zora Neale. 1935. *Mules and Men*. New York: HarperPerennial.

Hyman, Stanley Edgar. 1955. "The Ritual View of Myth and the Mythic." *Journal of American Folklore* 68:462–72.

———. 1963. "American Negro Literature and the Folk Tradition." In *The Promised End*, 295–315. New York: World Publishing.

Isaac, Benjamin. 2004. *The Invention of Racism in Classical Antiquity*. Princeton, N.J.: Princeton University Press.

Jackson, Lawrence. 2002. *Emergence of Genius*. New York: John Wiley and Sons.

Jacobs, Harriet. 1987. *Incidents in the Life of a Slave Girl*. Cambridge, Mass.: Harvard University Press.

Jefferson, Thomas. 1984. *Notes on the State of Virginia*. New York: Viking.

Jenkyns, Richard. 1980. *The Victorians and Ancient Greece*. Cambridge, Mass.: Harvard University Press.

Jimoh, Yemisi A. 2002. *Spiritual, Blues, and Jazz People in African American Fiction*. Knoxville: Tennessee University Press.

Johnson, Lemuel A. 1998. *Shakespeare in Africa (and Other Venues)*. Trenton, N.J.: African World Press.

Johnston, Harry H. 1918. "The Importance of Africa." *Journal of the Royal African Society* 17:177–98.

Jones, Leroi. 1963. *Blues People: The Negro Experience in White America and the Music that Developed from It*. New York: Morrow Quill.

Jones, Lisa. 1995. *Bulletproof Diva: Tales of Race, Sex and Hair*. New York: Doubleday and Company, Inc.

Joyce, James. [1934] 1990. *Ulysses*. New York: Vintage Books.

Jung, Carl, and Kark Kerenyi. 1972. *Essays on a Science of Mythology: The Myth of the Divine Child and the Mysteries of Eleusis*. Princeton, N.J.: Princeton University Press.

Keita, Maghan. 1994. "Deconstructing the Classical Age: Africa and the Unity of the Mediterranean World." *Journal of Negro History* 79:147–66.

Kendrick, Robert. 1996. "Re-membering America: Phillis Wheatley's Intertextual Epic." *African American Review* 30:71–88.

Kennedy, Randall. 2002. *Nigger: The Strange Career of a Troublesome Word*. New York: Pantheon Books.

King, Joy. 1996. "Ruth Cave Flowers." *Classical Outlook* 74:59–60.

King, K. 1985. "The Politics of Imitation: Euripides' *Hecuba* and the Homeric Achilles," *Arethusa* 18:47–66.

Kirby, John T. 2001. *Secret of the Muses Retold: Classical Influences on Italian Authors of the Twentieth Century.* Chicago: University of Chicago Press.

Kirkwood, Gordon M. 1947. "Hecuba and Nomos." *Transactions of the American Philological Association* 78:61–68.

Kitwana, Bakari. 2002. *The Hip Hop Generation: Young Blacks and the Crisis in African-American Culture.* New York: Basic Books.

Klotman, Phyllis R. 1985. "'Tearing a Hole in History': Lynching as Theme and Motif." *Black American Literature Forum* 19:55–63.

Knox, Mary. 1979. "Polyphemus and his near Eastern Relatives." *Journal of Hellenic Studies* 99:164–65.

Knox, Bernard M. 1993. *The Oldest Dead White European Males: And Other Reflections on the Classics.* New York: W. W. Norton.

———. 1994. *Backing into the Future: The Classical Tradition and its Renewal.* New York: W. W. Norton.

Korfmacher, William Charles. 1946. "Stoic Apatheia and Seneca's *De Clementia*." *TAPA* 77:44–52.

Kramer, Samuel Noah. 1981. *History Begins at Sumer.* Philadelphia: University of Pennsylvania Press.

Kramer, Victor A. 1987. *The Harlem Renaissance Re-examined.* New York: AMS Press.

Lambropoulos, Vassilis. 1993. *The Rise of Eurocentrism: Anatomy of Interpretation.* Princeton, N.J.: Princeton University Press.

Larson, Victoria Tietze. 1994. *The Role of Description in Senecan Tragedy.* Frankfurt: Peter Lang.

Lattimore, Steven. 1998. *Thucydides: The Peloponnesian War.* Indianapolis: Hackett Press.

Laureys, Marc. 1991. "Quintilian's Judgment of Seneca and the Scope and Purpose of *Inst.*, 10, 1." *Antike und Abendland* 37:100–25.

Lee, Guy, trans. 1990. *Catullus: The Complete Poems.* Oxford: Oxford University Press.

Lefèvre, Eckard. 1972. *Senecas Tragödien.* Darmstadt: Wissenschaftliche Buchgesellschaft.

Lefkowitz, M. R. 1992. "Not Out of Africa: The Origins of Greece and the Illusions of Afrocentrists." *New Republic* (10 February): 29–36.

———. 1996. "The Afrocentric Interpretation of Western History: Lefkowitz Replies to Bernal." *Journal of Blacks in Higher Education* 12:88–91.

———. 1997. *Not Out of Africa: How Afrocentrism Became an Excuse to Teach Myth as History.* New York: New Republic Books.

Lefkowitz, M. R., and Guy Rogers. 1996. *Black Athena Revisited.* Chapel Hill: University of North Carolina Press.

Lelyvald, Joseph. 2001. *How Race is Lived in America: Pulling Together, Pulling Apart.* New York: Times Books.

Lepper, F. A. 1957. "Some Reflections on the 'Quinquennium Neronis.'" *JRS* 47: 95–103.

Lévi-Strauss, Claude. 1971. *Totemism.* Trans. Rodney Needham. Boston: Beacon Press.

Lewis, John, Leon F. Litwack, and Hilton Als. 1999. *Without Sanctuary: Lynching Photography in America.* Santa Fe, N.Mex.: Twin Palms Publishers.

Leyser, Karl J. 1992. "Concepts of Europe in the Early and High Middle Ages." *Past and Present* 137:25–47.

Lhamon, W. T., Jr. 1997. *Raising Cain: Blackface Performance from Jim Crow to Hip Hop.* Cambridge, Mass.: Harvard University Press.

Livy. 2002. *The Early History of Rome.* Books 1–5 of *The History of Rome from its Foundations.* Trans. Aubrey de Sélincourt. New York: Penguin.

Locke, Alain, ed. [1925] 1997. *The New Negro: Voices of the Harlem Renaissance.* New York: Simon & Schuster.

Lomas, Kathryn. 1993. *Rome and the Western Greeks, 350 B.C.—A.D. 200: Conquest and Acculturation in Southern Italy.* London: Routledge.

Loraux, Nicole. 1986. *The Invention of Athens: The Funeral Oration in the Classical City.* Cambridge, Mass.: Harvard University Press.

Lott, Eric. 1974. *Love and Theft: Blackface Minstrelsy and the American Working Class.* New York: Oxford University Press.

Mailer, Norman. 1957. "The White Negro: Superficial Reflections on the Hipster." *Advertisements for Myself.* New York: Andre Deutsch.

Mailloux, Steven. 2002. "Rhetorical Paths of Thought: Visual Rhetoric, Classical Traditions and Performing Identity in Nineteenth-Century America." Leonora Woodman Lecture, Purdue University.

Malcolmson, Scott L. 2000. *One Drop of Blood: The American Misadventure of Race.* New York: Farrar, Straus and Giroux.

Marchand, Suzanne, and Anthony Grafton. 1997. "Martin Bernal and His Critics." *Arion* 5:1–35.

Martin, Thomas. 2000. *Ancient Greece: From Prehistoric to Hellenistic Times.* New Haven, C.T.: Yale University Press.

McDowell, Deborah E., and Arnold Rampersad. 1989. *Slavery and the Literary Imagination.* Baltimore: Johns Hopkins University Press.

McWhorter, John H. 2004. "Why I'm Black, Not African American." *Los Angeles Times,* September 8. http://www.manhattan-institute.org/html/_latimes-why_im_black.htm.

Meijering, R. 1987. *Literary and Rhetorical Theories in Greek Scholia.* Groningen: John Benjamins Publishing Company.

Mendell, Clarence W. 1941. *Our Seneca.* New Haven, C.T.: Yale University Press.

Meridor, Ra'anana. 1978. "Hecuba's Revenge: Some Observations on Euripides' *Hecuba.*" *American Journal of Philology* 99:28–35.

————. 1984. "Plot and Myth in Euripides' *Hecuba* and *Troades.*" *Phoenix* 38: 205–15.

Michelini, Ann Norris. 1987. *Euripides and the Tragic Tradition.* Madison: University of Wisconsin Press.

Middleton, Joyce Irene. 1993. "Orality, Literacy, and Memory in Toni Morrison's *Song of Solomon.*" *College English* 55:64–75.

Miller, Allen, and Charles Platter. 2005. *History in Dispute.* New York: Scribner's/Gale.

Miles, E. "The Young American Nation and the Classical World." *Journal of the History of Ideas* 35:259–74.

Mondi, Robert. 1983. "The Homeric Cyclopes: Folktale, Tradition and Theme." *Transactions of the American Philological Association* 113:17–38.

Morgan, Edmund Sears. 1995. *American Slavery, American Freedom: The Ordeal of Colonial Virginia.* New York: W. W. Norton.

Morrison, Toni. 1977. *Song of Solomon.* New York: Penguin Books.

————. 1993. *Playing in the Dark: Whiteness and the Literary Imagination.* New York: Knopf.

Morrison, Toni, and Claudia Brodsky Lacour. 1997. *Birth of a Nation'hood: Gaze, Script and Spectacle in the O. J. Simpson Trial.* New York: Knopf.

Moses, Wilson Jeremiah. 1998. *Afrotopia: The Roots of African American Popular History.* Cambridge: Cambridge University Press.

Mossman, Judith. 1995. *Wild Justice: A Study of Euripides' Hecuba.* Oxford: Clarendon Press.

Murray, Albert. [1973] 1995. *The Hero and the Blues.* Columbia: University of Missouri Press. New ed: New York: Vintage.

Nadel, Alan. 1988. *Invisible Criticism: Ralph Ellison and the American Canon.* Iowa City: University of Iowa Press.

Nagy, Gregory. 1990. *Greek Mythology and Poetics.* Ithaca, N.Y.: Cornell University Press.

————. 1999. *The Best of the Achaeans: Concepts of the Hero in Archaic Greek Poetry.* Rev. ed. Baltimore: Johns Hopkins University Press.

Nietzsche, Friedrich. 1976. *The Birth of Tragedy* and *The Genealogy of Morals.* Trans. Francis Golffing. New York: Doubleday.

Nussbaum, Martha C. 1986. *The Fragility of Goodness: Luck and Ethics in Greek Tragedy and Philosophy.* Cambridge: Cambridge University Press.

————. 1993. "Poetry and the Passions: Two Stoic Views." In *Passions and Perceptions: Studies in Hellenistic Philosophy of Mind,* ed. Jacques Brunschwig and Martha C. Nussbaum. Cambridge: Cambridge University Press.

————. 1996. *The Therapy of Desire: Theory and Practice in Hellenistic Ethics.* Princeton, N.J.: Princeton University Press.

O'Meally, Robert G. 1980. *The Craft of Ralph Ellison.* Cambridge, Mass.: Harvard University Press.

Ong, Walter. 1982. *Orality and Literacy: The Technologizing of the Word.* London: Routledge.

Overbye, Dennis. 2004. "About Those Fearsome Black Holes? Never Mind." Science and Technology, *New York Times,* July 22.

Owen, William H. 1968. "Commonplace and Dramatic Symbol in Seneca's *Troades.*" *TAPA* 99:219–313.

Page, Denys L., ed. 1964. *Euripides Medea.* Oxford: Clarendon Press.

Page, T. E., ed. 1957. *The Aeneid of Virgil.* London: Macmillan and Co. Ltd.

Palm, Risa. 1985. "Ethnic Segmentation of Real Estate Agent Practice in the Urban Housing Market." *Annals of the Association of American Geographers* 75:58–68.

Patterson, Orlando. 1990. *Slavery and Social Death.* Cambridge, Mass.: Harvard University Press.

———. 1991. *Freedom in the Making of Western Culture.* New York: Basic Books.

———. 1998. *Rituals of Blood: Consequences of Slavery in two American Centuries.* New York: Basic Books.

Penglase, Charles. 1994. *Greek Myths and Mesopotamia: Parallels and Influences in the Homeric Hymns and Hesiod.* New York: Routledge.

Podlecki, A. J. 1961. "Guest-Gifts and Nobodies in *Odyssey 9.*" *Phoenix* 15:125–33.

Poussaint, Alvin F., and Ellen Hodgson Brown. 1999. *Black Genius.* New York: Carroll and Graf Publishers.

Powell, Kevin. 1998. *Keepin' it Real: Post-MTV Reflections on Race, Sex, and Politics.* New York: Random House.

Powell, Timothy B. 1990. "Toni Morrison: The Struggle to Depict the Black Figure on the White Page." *Black American Literature Forum* 24:747–60.

Pucci, Pietro. 1980. *The Violence of Pity in Euripides' Medea.* Ithaca, N.Y.: Cornell University Press.

Raglan, Lord (Fitzroy Richard). 1931. "Incest and Exogamy." *Journal of the Royal Anthropological Institute of Great Britain and Ireland* 61:167–80.

———. 2003. *The Hero.* London: Dover.

Rampersad, Arnold. 1986. *The Life of Langston Hughes: Volume 1: 1902–1941.* New York: Oxford University Press.

Rankine, Patrice D. 1998. *Facing Power: Moral Agency in Seneca's Tragedies.* PhD diss., Yale University.

———. 2001. "Epic, the Oral Community, and the Memory of Emancipation in Ralph Ellison's *Juneteenth.*" *Profils Américains* 13:103–13.

———. 2003. "American Ulysses: Lawrence Jackson's *Emergence of Genius* and the Legend of Ralph Ellison." *Florida Atlantic University Comparative Studies.*

———. 2004. "Ralph Ellison, Ulysses, and Invisible Man." *Amphora* 2.2.

———. 2005. "Does Black Athena Make a Critical Contribution to Our Understanding of the Ancient World?" In *History in Dispute: Classical Antiquity and Classical Studies,* ed. Paul Allen Miller. Farmington Hills, Mich.: St. James Press.

————. Unpublished. "Passing as Tragedy: Philip Roth's *The Human Stain* and the Oedipus Myth (The Myth of the Self-Made Man)."

Rath, Richard Cullen. 1997. "Echo and Narcissus: The Afrocentric Pragmatism of W. E. B. Du Bois." *Journal of American History* 84:461–95.

Reckford, Kenneth. 1985. "Concepts of Demoralization in the *Hecuba*." In *Directions in Euripidean Criticism*, ed. Peter Burian. Durham, N.C.: Duke University Press.

Reckord, Barry, et al. 1997. "Polemics: The Dead End of African Literature." *Transitions* 75/76:335–41.

Reece, Steve. 1993. *The Stranger's Welcome: Oral Theory and the Aesthetics of the Homeric Hospitality Scene.* Ann Arbor: University of Michigan Press.

Reesor, M. 1951. *The Political Theory of the Old and Middle Stoa.* New York: J. J. Augustine.

Reilly, John M., ed. 1970. *Twentieth Century Interpretations of Invisible Man.* Englewood Cliffs, N.J.: Prentice Hall.

Reinhold, Meyer. 1984. *Classica Americana: The Greek and Roman Heritage in the United States.* Detroit, Mich.: Wayne State University Press.

Renfro, G. Herbert. 1998. *Life and Works of Phillis Wheatley.* North Stratford, N.H.: Ayer Company.

Richard, Carl J. 1994. *The Founders and the Classics: Greece, Rome, and the American Enlightenment.* Cambridge, Mass.: Harvard University Press.

Richardson, J. S. 1991. "Imperium Romanum: Empire and the Language of Power." *Journal of Roman Studies* 81:1–9.

Richman, Paula, ed. 1991. *Many Ramayanas: The Diversity of a Narrative Tradition in South Asia.* Berkeley: University of California Press.

Roediger, David R. 1999. *The Wages of Whiteness: Race and the Making of the American Working Class.* New York: Verso.

Roller, Matthew Benedict. 1994. *Early Imperial Literature and the Crisis of Aristocratic Authority.* PhD diss., University of California, Berkeley.

Romero, Patricia W. 1976. "W. E. B. Du Bois, Pan-Africanists, and Africa, 1963–1973." *Journal of Black Studies* 6:321–36.

Ronnick, Michele Valerie. 1997a. "William Sanders Scarborough: The First Professional Classicist of African-American Descent." *Negro Educational Review* 47:162–68.

————. 1997b. "William Sanders Scarborough (1852–1926)." *Classical Outlook* 74:139–40.

————. 1998. "Virgil's *Aeneid* and John Quincy Adams' Speech on Behalf of the Amistad Africans." *New England Quarterly* 71:473–77.

————. 2000a. "Racial Ideology and the Classics in the African-American University Experience." *Classical Bulletin* 76:169–80.

————. 2000b. "William Sanders Scarborough: The First African American Member of the Modern Language Association." *Publications of the Modern Language Association, Special Millennium Edition* 115:1787–93.

————. 2001. *The First Three African American Members of the American Philological Association*. Philadelphia: American Philological Association. Pamphlet.

————. 2002a. "The African American Classicist William Sanders Scarborough (1852–1926) and the Early Days of CAMWS." *Classical Journal* 97:263–66.

————. 2002b. "A Look at Booker T. Washington's Attitude Toward the Study of Greek and Latin by People of African Ancestry." *Negro Educational Review* 53:59–70.

————. 2005. *The Autobiography of William Sanders Scarborough: An American Journey from Slavery to Scholarship*. Detroit, Mich.: Wayne State University Press.

Rose, Tricia. 1994. *Black Noise: Rap Music and Black Culture in Contemporary America*. Hanover, N.H.: Wesleyan University Press.

Rosen, Ralph, and Victoria Baines. 2002. "'I Am Whatever you Say I Am . . .': Satiric Program in Juvenal and Eminem." *Classical and Modern Literature* 22: 103–27.

Rosenmeyer, T. G. 1989. *Senecan Drama and Stoic Cosmology*. Berkeley: University of California Press.

Ross, Ronald. 1974. "The Role of Blacks in the Federal Theatre, 1935–1939." *Journal of Negro History* 59:38–50.

Roth, Philip. 2001. *The Human Stain*. New York: Vintage Books.

Rudich, Vasily. 1993. *Political Dissidence under Nero: The Price of Dissimulation*. London: Routledge.

————. 1997. *Dissidence and Literature under Nero: The Price of Rhetoricization*. London: Routledge.

Rutherford, R. B. 1986. "The Philosophy of the Odyssey." *Journal of Hellenic Studies* 106:145–62.

Said, Edward W. 1979. *Orientalism*. New York: Knopf.

Sanders, Archie D. 1970. "Odysseus in Black: An Analysis of the Structure of *Invisible Man*." *CLA Journal* 13:217–28.

Saunders, James Robert. 1997. *Tightrope Walk: Identity, Survival and the Corporate World in African American Literature*. Jefferson, N.C.: McFarland.

Schafer, William J. 1970. "Irony from Underground—Satiric Elements in *Invisible Man*." In *Twentieth Century Interpretations of Invisible Man*, ed. John M. Reilly. Englewood Cliffs, N.J.: Prentice Hall.

Schein, S. L. 1970. "Odysseus and Polyphemus in the *Odyssey*." *Greek, Roman, and Byzantine Studies* 11:73–83.

Schiesaro, Alessandro. 2003. *The Passions in Play: Thyestes and the Dynamics of Senecan Drama*. Cambridge: Cambridge University Press.

Scott, A. O. 2004. "Greeks Bearing Immortality." *New York Times Film Review*, May 12, 2004.

Scruggs, Charles W. 1974. "Ralph Ellison's use of *The Aeneid* in *Invisible Man*." *CLA Journal* 17:368–78.

Schlegel, August Wilhelm. [1809] 1966. *Vorlesungen über dramatische Kunst und Litteratur,* 1. Stuttgart: Wilhelm Kohlhammer.

Schrager, Cynthia D. 1996. "Both Sides of the Veil: Race, Science, and Mysticism in W. E. B. Du Bois." *American Quarterly* 48:551–86.

Scodel, Ruth. 1998. "The Captive's Dilemma: Sexual Acquiescence in Euripides' *Hecuba* and *Troades.*" *Harvard Studies in Classical Philology* 98:137–54.

Seaford, Richard. 1981. "Dionysiac Drama and the Dionysiac Mysteries." *Classical Quarterly* 31:252–75.

Segal, Charles. 1990. "Violence and the Other: Greek, Female, and Barbarian in Euripides' *Hecuba.*" *Transactions of the American Philological Association* 120: 109–31.

———. 2001. *Oedipus Tyrannus: Tragic Heroism and the Limits of Knowledge.* 2nd ed. Oxford: Oxford University Press.

Shakur, Tupac. 1999. *The Rose that Grew From Concrete.* Ed. Karolyn Ali. New York: Pocket Books.

Shelton, Jo-Ann. 2000. "The Spectacle of Death in Seneca's *Troades.*" In *Seneca in Performance,* ed. George W. M. Harrison. London: Gerald Duckworth.

Shields, John C. 1980. "Phillis Wheatley's Use of Classicism." *American Literature* 52:97–111.

———, ed. 1988. *The Collected Works of Phillis Wheatley.* New York: Oxford University Press.

Silk, M. S. 1996. *Tragedy and the Tragic: Greek Theater and Beyond.* Oxford: Clarendon Press.

Singleton, Gregory Holmes. 1982. "Birth, Rebirth, and the "'New Negro'" of the 1920s." *Phylon* 43:29–45.

Slater, Robert Bruce. 1994. "The Blacks who First Entered the World of White Higher Education." *Journal of Blacks in Higher Education* 4:47–56.

Smethurst, James. 2005. *The Black Arts Movement: Literary Nationalism in the 1960s and 1970s.* Chapel Hill: University of North Carolina Press.

Smith, Cynthia. 1989. "'To Maecenas': Phillis Wheatley's Invocation of an Idealized Reader." *Black American Literature Forum* 23:579–92.

Smith, G. 1984. "The Black Protest Sonnet." *American Poetry* 1:2–12.

Snowden, Frank M., Jr. 1970. *Blacks in Antiquity: Ethiopians in the Greco-Roman Experience.* Cambridge, Mass.: Harvard University Press.

———. 1983. *Before Color Prejudice: The Ancient View of Blacks.* Cambridge, Mass.: Harvard University Press.

———. 1996. "Bernal's 'Blacks' and the Afrocentrists." In *Black Athena Revisited,* eds. Mary R. Lefkowitz and Guy MacLean Rogers, 112–28. Chapel Hill: University of North Carolina Press.

Soyinka, Wole. 1988. *Art, Dialogue, and Outrage: Essays on Literature and Culture.* New York: Pantheon Books.

———. 1991. *Myth, Literature, and the African World.* Cambridge: Cambridge University Press.

Stanford, W. B. [1963] 1992. *The Ulysses Theme.* Ann Arbor: University of Michigan Press.

Stark, John. 1973. "*Invisible Man:* Ellison's Black Odyssey." *Negro American Literature Forum* 7:60–63.

Starr, Chester G. Jr. 1949. "Epictetus and the Tyrant." *Classical Philology* 44:20–29.

Steele, Meili. 2000. *Theorizing Textual Subjects: Agency and Oppression.* Cambridge: Cambridge University Press.

Stephens, Gregory. 1999. *On Racial Frontiers: The New Culture of Frederick Douglass, Ralph Ellison, and Bob Marley.* Cambridge: Cambridge University Press.

Stone, Robert. 1999. "Ellison's Promised Land." *New York Review of Books,* August 12.

Stovall, Tyler. 1998. *Paris Noir: African Americans in the City of Light.* New York: Houghton Mifflin.

Sugrue, Thomas J. *The Origins of the Urban Crisis.* Princeton, N.J.: Princeton University Press.

Syme, Sir Ronald. 1939–1992. *The Roman Revolution.* Oxford: Oxford University Press.

Tatum, Beverly Daniel. 1999. *Why Are All the Black Kids Sitting Together in the Cafeteria? And Other Conversations About Race.* New York: Basic Books.

Taylor-Guthrie, Danille K. 1994. *Conversations with Toni Morrison.* Jackson: University of Mississippi Press.

Thapar, Romila. 1989. "Epic and History: Tradition, Dissent and Politics in India." *Past and Present* 125:3–26.

Thomas, Rosalind. 1992. *Literacy and Orality in Ancient Greece.* Cambridge: Cambridge University Press.

———. 2003. *Oral Tradition and Written Record in Classical Athens.* Cambridge: Cambridge University Press.

Thompson, Carlyle. 1999. "White Police Penetrating, Probing, and Playing in the Black Man's Ass: The Sadistic Sodomizing of Abner Louima." *Warpland* 5:159–85.

Thompson, Lloyd A. 1999. *Blacks and Romans.* Norman: University of Oklahoma Press.

Thompson, Robert Farris. 1984. *Flash of the Spirit: African and Afro-American Art and Philosophy.* New York: Vintage Books.

Thomson, George. 1971. "The Continuity of Hellenism." *Greece and Rome* 18:18–29.

Todorov, Tzvetan. 1999. *The Conquest of America: The Question of the Other.* Trans. Richard Howard. Norman: University of Oklahoma Press.

Trimmer, Joseph F. 1978. "The Grandfather's Riddle in Ralph Ellison's *Invisible Man.*" *Black American Literature Forum* 12:46–50.

Turner, Frank. 1981. *The Greek Heritage in Victorian Britain.* New Haven, C.T.: Yale University Press.

de Unamuno, Miguel. 1954. *Tragic Sense of Life.* Trans. J. E. Crawford Flitch. New York: Dover.

de Vet, Therese. 1996. "The Joint Role of Orality and Literacy in Composition,

Transmission, and Performance of the Homeric Texts: A Comparative View." *Transactions of the American Philological Association* 126:43–76.

Wagner, Roy. 1972. "Incest and Identity: A Critique and Theory on the Subject of Exogamy and Incest Prohibition." *Man* 7:601–13.

Walden, Daniel. 1974. "Du Bois' Pan-Africanism, a Reconsideration." *Negro American Literature Forum* 8: 260–62.

Walling, William. 1973. "'Art' and 'Protest': Ralph Ellison's Invisible Man Twenty Years After." *Phylon* 34:120–34.

Washington, Booker T. 1967. *Up from Slavery.* New York: Airmont Publishing Company.

Watts, Jerry Gafio. 1994. *Heroism and the Black Intellectual: Ralph Ellison, Politics, and Afro-American Intellectual Life.* Chapel Hill: University of North Carolina Press.

West, Cornel. 1999. *The Cornel West Reader.* New York: Basic Books.

West, William C. 2000. "Socrates as a Model of Civil Disobedience in the Writings of Martin Luther King, Jr." *Classical Bulletin* 76:191–200.

Wexler, Laura. 2003. *Fire in a Canebrake: The Last Mass Lynching in America.* New York: Scribner.

Williams, Bernard. 1994. *Shame and Necessity.* Berkeley: University of California Press.

Williams, Gordon. 1978. *Change and Decline: Roman Literature in the Early Empire.* Berkeley: University of California Press.

Willner, Dorothy. 1983. "Definition and Violation: Incest and the Incest Taboos." *Man* 18:134–59.

Wilson, William Julius. 1990. *The Truly Disadvantaged: The Inner City, the Underclass, and Public Policy.* Chicago: University of Chicago Press.

Wiltshire, S. F. 1977. "Jefferson, Calhoun, and the Slavery Debate: The Classics and the Two Minds of the South." *Southern Humanities Review* 11:33–40.

Winther, Per. 1983. "Imagery of Imprisonment in Ralph Ellison's *Invisible Man*." *Black American Literature Forum* 17:115–19.

Wong, Alex. 2001. "Back to the 'Classics': Old Shoes Give Reebok New Life." *Wall Street Journal,* August 9, B4.

Woodruff, Paul. trans. 1998. *Euripides: Bacchae.* Indianapolis: Hackett Publishing.

Woodward, C. Vann. 1974. *The Strange Career of Jim Crow.* 3rd ed. New York: Oxford University Press.

Wright, John S. 1989. "The New Negro Poet and the Nachal Man: Sterling Brown's Folk Odyssey." *Black American Literature Forum* 23:95–105.

Wright, Richard. [1940] 1998a. *Native Son.* New York: HarperCollins.

———. 1998b. *Black Boy: (American Hunger).* New York: HarperCollins.

Zeitlin, F. I. 1996. *Playing the Other: Gender and Society in Classical Greek Literature.* Chicago: University of Chicago Press.

Zwierlein, Otto. 1966. *Die Rezitationsdramen Senecas. Mit einem kritisch-exegetischen Anhang.* Meisenheim a. Glan, Hain. [Abridgement of the author's thesis, Freie Universität, Berlin.]

# Index

abyss: black (w)hole, 18–19; in Frazer's *The Golden Bough*, 125–26; hero's journey through, 16–17; in *Juneteenth*, 148; lynching as, 163; Orpheus's dismemberment in, 157; in *Song of Solomon*, 116–18

Achilles, 38, 42, 43, 47

acquisitiveness of Ulysses, 44–46, 52, 57

Actaeon, 156–57

adaptability of Ulysses, 44

Adell, Sandra, 185, 189

Aegeus (Cullen's *Medea*), 97–99

Aeneas, 69–70, 125

*Aeneid* (Vergil), 58, 125

African American, as term, 5, 7, 193n2. *See also* "blackness"

Afrocentrism, 17, 24, 28–29, 30, 75–77, 117–18

*Afrotopia* (Moses), 4

Agamemnon (classical figure), 54, 62–64

*Agamemnon* (Seneca), 60, 62–64

agency: America as hostile to black, 55; Burke's scene-act ratio and individual, 186–87; classical concepts of individual agency, 55; collective *vs.* individual, 187; in Cullen's *Medea*, 90, 101; in Euripides' *Hecuba*, 54–55; and gender, 54–55, 115–16; individual struggle and Ellison's works, 129, 133–34, 140–41, 148; personal responsibility in *Juneteenth*, 148; ritual violence and African American, 164; self-awareness and, 140–41, 215n37; in *Song of Solomon*, 112, 115–16

Ahl, Frederick, 47

Alexander, Elizabeth, 88, 164

alienation: of audience, 31, 61, 99–100, 153; Patterson on alienation of black body in American culture, 159–61

ambivalence: and Euripides' characterization of Hecuba, 53–54; reception of African American classicism and, 11; representation of black men in American culture and, 128, 160; in *Song of Solomon*, 106; toward Greek cultural influence in Rome, 70

America: African Americans as integral to culture of, 75–76, 90–91, 152, 153, 198n42; ambivalent representation of black men in, 128, 160; as antagonist to black hero, 2, 55; Christianity in, 130; classicism in, 7–8, 25, 166; democracy in, 188–89; Ellison's perception of, 31–33, 50–51, 89, 152, 165, 188–89; ethnic and cultural distinctions within, 5;

America (*continued*)
  evasion of race and, 152–53, 157–58,
  173–74; frontier and, 93, 145–47; as
  homeland, 50–51; improvisational
  nature of ritual in, 165–66, 169;
  pluralism in, 32, 145, 147; race and,
  5–6, 29–30, 90–91, 128, 166 (*See also*
  evasion of race *under this heading*);
  vernacular models and, 11, 90–91
American Book Award for Fiction, 93
American identity, 16, 91–92, 108, 118;
  Ellison's concept of, 31–33, 89, 126,
  152, 165, 188–89
American Philological Association
  (APA), 3, 24
Amin, Samir, 41
animals: in African American folklore,
  134, 137–38, 144, 149–50; dogs, 54, 55,
  156–57, 167; sacrifice of, 162; totemism, 162, 170
antagonists: American homeland as
  antagonist to black hero, 2, 55; the
  body and emotions as antagonist in
  Seneca's works, 60–61; Brer Bear,
  144; as counter-hegemonic, 58; in
  Euripides *Hecuba*, 55; "One-eyed" in
  *Juneteenth*, 145, 146–48; protagonist/
  antagonist inversions, 52, 140–41;
  self-definition and, 50, 59; society as,
  2, 55, 133–34
antiheroes, 39, 50, 58, 61. *See also*
  antagonists
Aristotle, 5, 7
Armstrong, Louis, 87
"Art and Protest" (Walling), 152
Aryan model (Bernal), 73–74
Aspasia, 79
assimilation, 30–31, 85, 93, 103
Astell, Ann, 145, 200n23
athletes, 160
audience: for African American
  authors, 27–28, 91–92, 183; alienation
  of, 31, 61, 99–100, 153, 182; black

classicism and, 19, 30–31, 84–85,
  86–87, 93, 197n33; black reception of
  the classics, 67; classicism and, 19,
  153; for classics in antiquity, 51, 52; as
  consuming or cannibalistic, 170–71;
  context and differing receptions of
  Ulysses, 68; Ellison and, 31, 90, 159,
  165, 182; for hip-hop culture, 89;
  Homer and, 38; identity politics and,
  29; literature as speech act or
  contract with, 40; Morrison on, 89,
  104–5, 208n17; for Morrison's works,
  104–5; within the *Odyssey*, 44,
  200n22; reception-theory, 27–28;
  segregation and relationship with,
  28; in Seneca's *Troades*, 63–64;
  spectatorship and, 63–64, 124–25,
  134–35; timeless appeal of the
  classics, 38; in Vergil's *Aeneid*, 70;
  violence as spectator event, 124–25,
  134–35; for Wheatley's works, 85;
  white audience and black artists, 27,
  89, 160, 171; white spectators for
  battle royal, 134–35; written
  literature and interpretation, 58
Auerbach, Erich, 46–47
Aunt Mackie (in "A Coupla Scalped
  Indians"), 167–68
authenticity: black classicism and,
  86–87; cultural, 30–31; hip-hop
  culture and, 89
authority: Homeric verse as, 41;
  *regnum*, 59, 65
autobiography, 4, 8–9, 17; Ellison's use
  of personal experience, 123–24;
  Morrison and reference to personal
  experience, 109–10
Awkward, Michael, 108–9, 112

*Bacchae* (Euripides), 20, 154–58, 178;
  Ellison's allusion to, 154–58; as
  expression of protest or revolution,
  155–56, 158–59, 178

130; fame *(kleos)* and honor *(timē)* of, 43, 47–49, 57; gender and, 52; heroic code, 43–44; Homer on the nature of, 38; Milkman in *Song of Solomon* as heroic, 113–18; as self in struggle with power, 59, 129, 133–34, 140–41, 148

heroic individualism, 92–93, 133–34, 143, 181–83

heroic journey *(katabasis):* archetype of, 16–17; Classical Studies as, 33; in Ellison's works, 19; homecoming or return in, 44, 50–51, 89, 127; race and, 16–19. *See also* abyss; wandering

*Heroism and the Black Intellectual* (Watts), 186

*Hero, The* (Raglan), 122, 125

Hesiod, 10

Heynman, Richard, 109

Hill, Herbert, 83

Hindu epic tradition, 39

hip-hop culture, 29, 89, 159, 163, 170, 171

homecoming: America as homeland in *Invisible Man*, 50–51; black (w)hole trope and, 89; "home" as antagonist, 55; in *Juneteenth*, 148, 149–50; of Ulysses, 44

Homer, 38, 39–43, 113–18, 121, 182; audience and, 41; portrayal of Ulysses by, 44; western literature traditions and, 49. See also *Odyssey* (Homer)

homosexuality, 94, 187

honor *(timē)*, 43, 47–49, 57

Horowitz, Floyd, 123

hospitality *(xenia)*, 49, 50, 51, 52, 114–15, 213n20

hospital scene in Ellison's *Invisible Man*, 138–41

Howe, Irving, 181

Howe, Stephen, 23, 75

*hubris,* 51

Hurston, Zora Neale, 180

Hyman, Stanley Edgar, 128, 130, 132

Hypermestra, 74

idealization of the past (nostalgia), 28–29

identity: *Black Athena* debates and, 8–9; black classicism and cultural identity, 39, 42, 86–87; black esthetics and, 19, 31; collective memory and, 140; concealment of, 133, 136, 142; Cullen's African American identity, 95; diversity and, 12; Ellison and integrity of American identity, 31–33, 89, 152, 165, 188–89; Ellison and racial identity, 78, 103, 127, 153; folklore and, 137; heroic identity, 37; heroic individualism *vs.* group, 92–93; identification with classics, 72, 76–77, 93, 99, 109–10, 138; individual identity in Ellison's works, 139; in *Invisible Man*, 49–50, 87, 89, 137–42, 144, 151; in *Medea*, 61, 95, 100; minstrelsy as identity theft, 130; naming and, 15–16, 133, 134, 142, 146–47, 169–70; as "Nobody," 19, 47–49, 132, 139, 146–47, 150; otherness and opposition in forming, 16–17, 49–50, 90, 108, 113, 160; the past and, 4, 9, 118; politics of, 28–29, 198n43; racial identity, 6, 78, 87, 95, 103, 127, 140–41, 153; ritual approach to myth and, 126, 127; self-definition or autonomy of, 90, 108, 169; in Seneca's works, 61; sexual identity, 167–68; in *Song of Solomon*, 113; Ulysses and, 37, 47–49; Wheatley's poetic identity, 84–85; white identity, 118; "writer" as Ellison's self-identity, 194n19. *See also* black identity; selfhood

imperialism, 51–52, 59–60

incest, 168, 176

ritualistic, 88, 121, 124–25; written epic and, 40
*Rituals of Blood* (Patterson), 154, 159
Rogers, J. A., 27
Romanticism, 71, 72
Rome: Greek influence in, 68–69; imperialism and, 59; interpretive authority in, 58
Ronnick, Michele Valerie, 7–8, 10, 11, 13, 24–25
Rosenmeyer, Thomas, 64
ruptures or breaks in Western narrative, 18, 67–68, 71–72, 73

sacrifice: as aberration or unnatural, 53; of animals, 162; of Astynax, 63–64; in Euripides' *Hecuba*, 56–57; as hubris, 51; of humans, 52–53, 55, 63–65, 162; of Iphigeneia, 62–63; of Polyxena, 52, 53, 55, 63–65, 202n58; social order restored by, 162–63, 202n58; suicide as, 155, 170–71; Ulysses and human sacrifice, 52–53, 63–65
Sappho, 40, 41, 79
Saunders, James, 187
Scarborough, William Sanders, 7–8, 13, 24, 27
"Scottsboro, Too, Is Worth Its Song" (Cullen), 94
Segal, Charles, 53
segregation, 50, 79–80, 123; assimilation and, 32; audience relationships and, 28; "double consciousness" and, 132–33; in *Invisible Man*, 131–32; miscegenation, 29–30, 155, 161–62, 169, 173–78; rituals of, 88, 121, 124–25; "straight white line" in *Invisible Man*, 160–61, 175–76, 177
selfhood: the classics and, 60; collective memory or community and, 117; craft and, 106, 129, 185–86; in Ellison's works, 58, 138–39, 142–44,

169; fragmentation or dis-integration of, 51, 164, 171, 178; integration of the self, 29, 47–48, 51, 138, 149; otherness and self-identification, 49–50, 59, 90–91, 108; self-definition, 90, 108, 139, 169; self-determination as power, 60; in Seneca's works, 58–63, 65; wandering and self-making, 106
Seneca, Lucius Annaeus, 38–39; *Agamemnon*, 60, 62–64; body and embodiment in works of, 61; as counter-hegemonic, 59–62; *Medea*, 61, 102; mercy in works of, 62, 64; power as theme of, 59, 63, 65; self-management as theme of, 58–63, 65; *Troades (The Trojan Women)*, 38–39, 43, 61–66; Ulysses as depicted by, 63–64, 203n64
sex and sexuality: in "A Coupla Scalped Indians," 166–68; Cullen's *Medea* and, 100–101; in Euripides' *Bacchae*, 155–56; gender and sexuality in Classical Studies, 33–34; genital mutilation during lynching, 162–63; homosexuality, 94, 187; initiation rites and, 174; lynching and, 161–62; masculine iconography, 160; miscegenation, 29–30, 155, 156, 161–62, 169, 173–78; objectification in *Invisible Man*, 135–36; rape and race in America, 94, 161, 174; in *Song of Solomon*, 111–12
Shakespeare, William, 102
Shelton, Jo-Ann, 64
sight: sight/blindness and visibility/invisibility dichotomies, 134; "third eye" as symbol, 138–40. *See also* blindness
*Signifying Monkey, The* (Gates), 184–85, 189
Sihler, A. L., 95
Simpson, O. J., 160, 215n15

JOHN H. OAKLEY and REBECCA H. SINOS
*The Wedding in Ancient Athens*

RICHARD DANIEL DE PUMA and JOCELYN PENNY SMALL, editors
*Murlo and the Etruscans: Art and Society in Ancient Etruria*

JUDITH LYNN SEBESTA and LARISSA BONFANTE, editors
*The World of Roman Costume*

JENNIFER LARSON
*Greek Heroine Cults*

WARREN G. MOON, editor
*Polykleitos, the Doryphoros, and Tradition*

PAUL PLASS
*The Game of Death in Ancient Rome: Arena Sport and Political Suicide*

MARGARET S. DROWER
*Flinders Petrie: A Life in Archaeology*

SUSAN B. MATHESON
*Polygnotos and Vase Painting in Classical Athens*

JENIFER NEILS, editor
*Worshipping Athena: Panathenaia and Parthenon*

PAMELA WEBB
*Hellenistic Architectural Sculpture: Figural Motifs in
Western Anatolia and the Aegean Islands*

BRUNILDE SISMONDO RIDGWAY
*Fourth-Century Styles in Greek Sculpture*

LUCY GOODISON and CHRISTINE MORRIS, editors
*Ancient Goddesses: The Myths and the Evidence*

CATHERINE SCHLEGEL
*Satire and the Threat of Speech: Horace's* Satires, *Book 1*

CHRISTOPHER A. FARAONE and LAURA K. MCCLURE, editors
*Prostitutes and Courtesans in the Ancient World*

PLAUTUS
John Henderson, translator and commentator
*Asinaria: The One about the Asses*

PATRICE RANKINE
*Ulysses in Black: Ralph Ellison, Classicism, and
African American Literature*

PAUL REHAK
John G. Younger, editor
*Imperium and Cosmos: Augustus and the Northern Campus Martius*